Instructional Design

for **dummies**®

A Wiley Brand

Instructional Design

by Susan Land

Instructional Design For Dummies®

Published by: **John Wiley & Sons, Inc.**, 111 River Street, Hoboken, NJ 07030-5774, www.wiley.com

Copyright © 2024 by John Wiley & Sons, Inc., Hoboken, New Jersey

Published simultaneously in Canada.

For general information on our other products and services, please contact our Customer Care Department within the U.S. at 877-762-2974, outside the U.S. at 317-572-3993, or fax 317-572-4002. For technical support, please visit https://hub.wiley.com/community/support/dummies.

Wiley publishes in a variety of print and electronic formats and by print-on-demand. Some material included with standard print versions of this book may not be included in e-books or in print-on-demand. If this book refers to media such as a CD or DVD that is not included in the version you purchased, you may download this material at http://booksupport.wiley.com. For more information about Wiley products, visit www.wiley.com.

Library of Congress Control Number is available from the publisher.

ISBN: 978-1-394-21158-6 (pbk); 978-1-394-21160-9 (ebk); 978-1-394-21159-3 (ebk)

SKY10069368_031224

Contents at a Glance

Table of Contents

CHAPTER 10: Show Time! Implementing Your Instruction Successfully

CHAPTER 11: Evaluating Instructional Materials

Introduction

Have you ever been to a class or workshop that was really great or one that was really bad? What made the class great or bad? These are the kinds of questions instructional design is meant to answer by offering a systematic process for creating effective instructional materials, courses, workshops, lessons, or technologies. As such, it offers you a way to develop innovative and effective instructional experiences that can be used to teach others in classrooms, online, or in hybrid (some in person and some online) formats. It can help you design instruction that is meant for learners to use independently on their own time and pace or together with other learners in groups.

Instructional design is also a profession, and you can find instructional designers working in corporations, higher education, museums, the military, and many other settings. It has broad applications to a variety of career paths. Although you can learn all of the skills to be a professional instructional designer by pursuing a college degree, there are some skills you can learn with the help of some practical tips and guidance. This book is designed to do exactly that — provide you with a practical guide to get you up and running quickly on some of the basics of instructional design.

About This Book

This book is written as a practical guide for anyone to discover instructional design and how to apply it in order to design more effective learning experiences. The book is structured systematically according to the different phases and activities of the instructional-design process. It uses examples and tips to help you understand and apply the instructional techniques.

The book is set up to accomplish the following:

>> **It examines the entire instructional design process, from start to finish.** You read how to start a new instructional design project, including the early steps of analyzing what needs to be learned to the end of the process of evaluating if the instruction was successful.

>> **It explains the five-phase instructional design process referred to as the ADDIE model.** ADDIE is an acronym that stands for:

- **A**nalyze
- **D**esign
- **D**evelop
- **I**mplement
- **E**valuate

>> **It gives you practical steps for identifying and breaking down the knowledge and skills you want your learners to know.**

>> **It provides tips on how to deliver your instruction, such as deciding whether the instruction should be taught synchronously (at the same time) or asynchronously (at different times) and how to use technology to support learning.**

>> **It curates best practices and instructional design models that a new designer can pick up to apply quickly.** You can choose from a variety of examples to best suit your situation.

The book is designed with many examples, tips, checklists, and tables to help you ascertain what you want quickly. It is my hope that the book is easy to read and gives you a balance of explaining the principles underlying the practices as well as keeping it practical.

Foolish Assumptions

This book is not only for people who want to be instructional designers. Whether you are a professional in another field or a student thinking about pursuing an instructional design career, you can benefit from reading about instructional design.

I make the following assumptions about the kinds of people who may be interested in this book:

>> You may work as a professional outside of the field of education (for example, maybe you are an accountant or a construction worker) but have responsibilities or interests in teaching others about important skills in your job or field. Your job title is probably not instructional designer, but you are in the right place!

» You may be brand new to learning about instructional design. Maybe you have heard of it but want to read more about what instructional designers do.

» You may not be a professional instructional designer, but you have a passion for teaching others about the subjects that excite you. Maybe you create content on social media, podcasts, YouTube, or perhaps you give workshops for the public at a local library or botanical garden. You want to level up the strategies that you can use to create educational content and programming.

» You may be a student studying instructional design and want another reference manual to help you simplify the detailed, complex material you are studying.

» You may actually be an instructional designer practicing in the field but are interested in refreshing some of the basics or exploring new models you haven't tried.

In sum, this book assumes that you may not have any background or experience in instructional design, but you are curious and passionate about education!

How This Book Is Organized

This book is structured similarly to most books on instructional design. It proceeds through the five phases of the ADDIE process, along with some cross-referencing across chapters where topics overlap. The cross references within the chapters help you jump quickly between chapters. Likewise, the table of contents details the main content of each chapter to quickly direct you to the information you need.

This book is arranged in five different parts:

» **Part 1: Getting Started with Instructional Design.** This part of the book gives you an overview of the ADDIE instructional design model as well as telling you more about what instructional designers do. It also introduces some foundational principles about how people learn and the key factors to consider when designing instruction.

» **Part 2: The Analysis Phase.** Analysis is the first activity of the instructional-design process and involves looking closely at the setting for instruction, your learners, the problem or need for the instruction, as well as the tasks that need to be learned. You read how to classify a task in terms of what needs to be learned and break down a task into subskills.

>> **Part 3: Designing Engaging and Effective Instruction.** Design is the heart of the instructional design process. This phase involves equal parts art and science as you specify the learning objectives (what is to be learned) and how to evaluate what has been learned. You also read about different instructional models to help you design and organize your activities to meet your learning goals.

>> **Part 4: Developing, Implementing, and Evaluating Instruction and Technology.** The fourth part covers how to make decisions about the actual creation and implementation of your instruction. It covers different types of technologies (print, video, audio, website, video conferencing, and so on) and their characteristics to determine the best choice for your instruction. It also presents important factors in developing your instructional materials as well as tips for a successful implementation and evaluation of your instruction.

>> **Part 5: The Part of Tens.** A distinguishing feature of the *For Dummies* series is the Part of Tens chapters. In this part, you read about ten best practices for creating engaging instruction, ten questions to ask about selecting technologies for your instruction, and ten ways to put your instructional design knowledge to work.

>> **Appendix: Example Questions, Checklists, and Worksheets.** The Appendix gives you examples and structured worksheets to guide you in applying the concepts to your own setting.

Icons Used in This Book

Throughout the book, icons in the margins draw your attention to important information. Here are the icons you encounter in this book:

The Example icon highlights where practical examples are provided. The examples give you a concrete illustration of how the process is applied.

The Tip icon points to tips for applying the ideas in a step-by-step or guided process.

The Warning icon helps you avoid these pitfalls to ensure success when it comes to your instructional design projects.

REMEMBER

The Remember icon makes you aware of content that is important to remember. It sometimes is used as a summary of the most important points.

Beyond the Book

In addition to the chapters in this book, you get access to freely accessible content at www.dummies.com. For example, to access this book's online cheat sheet, just go to the Dummies.com website and type "Instructional Design for Dummies Cheat Sheet" into the site's Search box.

Where to Go from Here

Ready to get the show on the road? I recommend you start by finding individual chapters you want to discover more about. I've written each chapter with cross references to other chapters in case you need to look up more background information. I also wrote each chapter to be as understandable as possible independently of the other chapters. Maybe you are curious about one or two chapters only, so you can use the Table of Contents or the Index to jump to the information you need.

1

Getting Started with Instructional Design

Get to know the ADDIE (Analysis, Design, Development, Implementation, Evaluation) instructional design model.

Uncover more about where you find instructional designers at work and what they do.

Discover the five essential foundations for designing effective learning experiences.

Determine how to align the different foundations of your instruction to select best practices.

Discover how different methods and models of instructional design help us to make sound instructional-design decisions.

IN THIS CHAPTER

» Getting to know the instructional
design process

» Discovering what instructional
designers do

» Introducing the ADDIE model of
instructional design

» Recognizing different types of
instructional design models

Chapter **1**

Introducing Instructional Design

D o you want to create educational materials, lessons, or workshops? Instructional design offers you a process for developing instruction that is rooted in principles of how people learn. Chances are, you have experienced both successful and unsuccessful instruction at some point in your lifetime. Although there are likely a number of reasons for your unsuccessful experiences, poor instructional design is likely part of the cause. The benefit of instructional design is that it gives us a process to follow to create educational experiences that lead to more successful outcomes for learners.

This chapter gives you an overview of the instructional-design process and profession. You find out how to proceed with a design process that takes you through the early steps of analyzing the need for the instruction, designing goals and activities, creating and trying out the instructional materials, and evaluating whether the instruction was successful.

What is Instructional Design?

Instructional design is situated within the field of education because its primary focus is to help people learn. At its most basic level, instructional design is both a profession and a process for creating effective instructional experiences.

The field of instructional design is described as both an art and a science. Design itself is a creative act that draws on the imagination of a designer, teacher, and/or content expert. It is also a science because it is rooted in research and scholarship from several overlapping fields, such as the educational sciences, information sciences, and communications.

Instructional design is defined simply as a systematic process of planning and creating instructional materials, activities, and technologies that support learning. Professionals in instructional design work in a variety of settings such as corporate organizations, higher education, or other educational spaces such as museums or libraries.

Instructional design as a field is also commonly referred to using different labels that reflect slight differences in focus:

>> Instructional design

>> Instructional technology

>> Educational technology

>> Learning design

>> Learning technology

>> Learning experience design

>> Training design

>> Curriculum development

Although the previous labels are slightly different from each other, each of them has a common focus on both education and design.

This book uses the term "instructional design" as it has the broadest application and is a longstanding term used to describe the field. Due to advances in technologies that make them easier to use, create content, and connect learners virtually, instructional technology has become more of a central focus to the work of instructional designers.

Here are a few examples of instructional design:

>> Designing training programs for new employees to introduce company policies, regulations, compliance, or job practices

>> Professional development workshops for employees to learn new skills

>> Educational workshops for families visiting a library or museum

>> Patient education about disease management

>> Military training for equipment operation

>> Video instruction on how to use new technology

>> Online instruction for students taking college classes from a distance

>> Exercise videos with demonstrations

These are just a small number of examples that illustrates the range of use of instruction for learning across multiple settings. In the next few sections, I explore what it is like to be an instructional designer as well as the benefits of using instructional design.

Knowing what is involved in the instructional design process

Instructional design uses a systematic process for designing instruction, which means that it uses research and theory on how people learn to help you plan effective instructional materials, activities, and assessments. As a systematic process, it translates principles of teaching and learning into structured, organized procedures that an instructional designer follows to determine the purpose of the instruction, what should be taught, how it should be taught, and if learning has occurred. Each step involves a series of planned actions that an instructional designer follows to achieve a particular instructional goal.

What are some of the different elements of the instructional design process?

>> **The instructional setting.** A key part of the instructional design process is analyzing the context and need for the instruction. This typically involves figuring out what problems exist and clarifying if instruction is the best solution. For instance, a company can have a performance problem, such as excessive error rates from technicians, or an organization is introducing a new technology that requires employees to be trained to use it. Instruction is a good solution for problems that involve a need for new knowledge, skills,

attitudes, or practices. Having a clear understanding of the organizational context, resources, and constraints is essential for all phases of the design process.

>> **The learners.** The instructional design process hinges on understanding who the learners are, their motivations, what knowledge and skills they already have, as well as any accessibility considerations. Instruction is more likely to be effective when you seek information about your learners and tie your instructional goals and activities to your analyses of both the learners and the instructional context.

>> **The type of instructional goal.** Instructional goals are classified into different types, ranging from remembering facts to creating new ideas and innovations. The instructional goal drives decisions about what types of activities and content to use in the instruction. It should also be aligned with the organizational context and need for the instruction.

>> **Technologies and materials for delivering the instruction.** Instruction is delivered to learners using a specific approach — such as an instructor leading a training session in a classroom or as part of an online webinar, or learners working with videos and/or print-based materials. Our selection of materials and technologies is tied to our learning goals, characteristics of the technology, and the logistical resources and constraints of the instructional setting. Making decisions about using a specific technology needs to be considered in concert with all other instructional elements.

>> **Instructors and subject-matter experts (SMEs).** Another critical part of the instructional design process is the instructor or subject-matter expert. *Instructors* are the experts who are responsible for teaching the instruction, either in the classroom or online. They have direct interaction with the learners during the instruction. Subject-matter experts (or SMEs) have expertise in the content of the instruction, but they may or may not be instructors of the course. SMEs work with an instructional designer to determine what ideal performance looks like and to develop the content of the instruction.

Recognizing the benefits of instructional design

Instructional design offers a variety of benefits to both learners and stakeholders who are involved in the instructional process. You can see the importance of instructional design in the following outcomes:

>> **Learning effectiveness.** One of the most important benefits of instructional design is that it provides a structure for you to develop instruction that helps

your learners accomplish what they need to learn. The instructional design process focuses at the outset on what the learner will be able to do after the instruction ends. By first aligning goals and outcomes and then designing instruction to line up with these goals and outcomes, you can determine if the instruction's objectives were achieved. The instructional design process provides a framework to help you choose the most effective strategies and technologies to meet your goals.

» **Potential cost savings.** Although instructional design can have upfront costs in personnel and technology to design, develop, and deliver instruction, its potential payoff lies in the benefits of having effectively trained learners. This payoff can result in an increase in productivity, a decrease in errors, or an increase in customer satisfaction. Having well-designed instruction may also produce intangible benefits such as employee satisfaction due to an organization's commitment to high quality professional development and career advancement. It can also spark new interests as well as a commitment to lifelong learning.

» **Consistency and reliability.** Instructional design is based on a systematic process that leads to the development of instruction tied to specific goals and objectives. After the instruction is designed, it can be used again on multiple occasions with different learners, with the reassurance that learners will experience a consistent instructional product. For instance, an instructional video created to teach learners how to use a new software program can be deployed over and over with multiple learners using the same well-designed instructional materials.

» **Team oriented.** Whereas instructional designers do sometimes work on their own as the sole content expert and instructional designer on a project, instructional design is often a team effort. The steps involved in the design process usually direct instructional designers to collaborate with multiple individuals such as a design team, learners, clients, or stakeholders. This process is beneficial because it helps ensure that the instruction being designed is aligned with the overall goals and needs of the organization and learners. (As an added benefit, it draws on multiple areas of expertise, ensuring that multiple perspectives are incorporated into the final design.)

» **Continuous improvement.** Another advantage of the instructional design process is that it helps a designer assess whether learning has occurred and if the objectives of the instruction have been met. By measuring the learning outcomes at the end of the instruction, a designer can revise the instruction and continue improving upon it by focusing on those areas where it is not working as well as anticipated. In this way, the instructional design process is cyclical and leads to continual improvement of the instruction after each implementation.

>> **Expertise in learning and design.** The instructional design process moves a designer beyond content presentation to the creation of activities and strategies that support deeper learner engagement. In the age of AI, anyone can produce content and put it into a slide deck, a document, or a website. However, instructional designers have expertise in how people learn as well as how to design instructional activities that lead to learning. Knowing how to design effective and motivating activities that support active (versus passive) learning is a needed skillset in today's instructional settings.

Looking at the Life of an Instructional Designer

Instructional design is both a process for creating effective learning experiences as well as a rapidly growing profession. Instructional designers work in a variety of settings such as designing training for corporations to designing eLearning (online) courses for college students in higher education. These are just a few examples of the kinds of work that instructional designers do.

The following sections describe the life of an instructional designer, including where they typically work, what type of work they do, and how you can get started in a career in instructional design.

Where you find instructional designers

You find instructional designers at work in many different types of settings, and in fact, instructional designers don't follow one specific career path. Some may think about a career in education as only happening in schools, but there are many professional opportunities for instructional designers in educational settings outside of school settings. You can find these opportunities in any setting where the focus is on education, teaching, or learning!

Table 1-1 provides a summary of different settings where you may find instructional designers at work, along with a description of the type of work they do. Because the field of instructional design is very broad, the roles of an instructional designer also vary by career setting. (See Chapter 14 for more information.) The description in the table provides a few insights into some typical tasks undertaken by instructional designers in those settings.

TABLE 1-1   # Types of Settings Where Instructional Designers Work

Setting	Description
Business and Industry	The private sector is one of the largest employers of instructional designers.
	Industries that hire instructional designers include banking, insurance, hospitality, automobile manufacturing, among many others.
	Instructional designers often work on teams with subject-matter experts, technology specialists, or project managers to design instruction for employees of the company. Examples include onboarding instruction, on-the-job training programs, or compliance training.
Private Consulting	You find instructional designers in private consulting companies or within a firm of other consultants.
	Unlike instructional designers employed by a specific business to design instruction for the company in-house, consultants are hired externally by a company to design instruction for them. The work instructional design consultants perform is similar to those who work in business and industry. (See the previous description.)
Higher Education	A growing sector for instructional design careers is higher education, specifically colleges and universities.
	With the growth in online distance learning, universities are offering degree programs and courses that are fully online to students who do not attend the university campus. Instructional designers often work with faculty to translate their classroom instruction into an online class. Typical tasks include creating online content, activities, and media for delivery via a learning management system (LMS).
	Instructional designers in higher education also work with units and faculty to design innovative classroom-based instruction for students on campus, including educational technologies, simulations, or games. They also work to support the training and professional development needs of all employees across the broader university system.
Informal Education or Non-profits	You find instructional designers in organizations that provide public educational programming. Examples include museums, libraries, historical sites, or nature centers.
	Instructional design in these settings includes exhibit design, self-guided tours (audio or text), or workshops.
Military	Instructional designers have careers in government and military organizations to design training for military personnel.
	Training in the military often uses advanced and emerging technologies such as virtual reality and simulations.
Medical and Health	Instructional designers work in the medical and health care sector to design medical education for health care workers, medical students, and/or patients. This work also includes related health care organizations such as pharmaceutical companies or nonprofit organizations focused on public health education.

The job of an instructional designer

As shown in the previous section, the job of an instructional designer varies some-what based on career setting (business versus higher education, for example) and size of an organization. However, most instructional designers share a common skillset of design practices — practices I describe in more detail over the course of this book. Table 1-2 provides an overview of common skills and tasks that are conducted by instructional designers.

TABLE 1-2   ## Job Skills of an Instructional Designer

Category	Description
Communication and Collaboration	Instructional designers must be good communicators and collaborators. The job of an instructional designer often involves working collaboratively on a design team with others to create the instruction. Designers use written and oral communication skills to convey the need for instruction as well as to document the knowledge, skills, and content that need to be learned.
	Instructional designers communicate with subject-matter experts (SMEs) around complex material that is often outside of their own area of expertise. Designers work with SMEs to identify key aspects of learners' performance that may be lacking as well as content and skills that need to be learned.
	In some settings, instructional designers may need to collaborate with technical experts or creative artists such as programmers, multimedia specialists, or graphic artists. Together, they develop the technical assets for the instruction such as websites, videos, graphical images, games, simulations, and so on.
Analysis and Design	An instructional designer has strong analytical and design skills. They analyze a performance problem to determine root causes and identify possible instructional solutions. They work with SMEs to analyze the tasks needed for successful performance, and to translate those into goals and objectives.
	Instructional designers use their design skills to create effective and appealing instructional activities and assessments based on the objectives.
	They also use analysis and design skills to select an appropriate technology to deliver the instruction or use their design skills to convert classroom-based instruction into online instruction.
Technology Production Skills	Do instructional designers need to have strong technology skills? The answer may depend on the work setting and if you have a team that includes technology specialists. However, many instructional designers have at least some experience in technology production such as: • Designing online courses for delivery through a Learning Management System (LMS) such as Blackboard, Moodle, or Canvas. • Using authoring tools such as Adobe Captivate or Articulate 360 (Rise and Storyline) to develop instruction that is delivered online or via a mobile device. • Graphics and audio/video production and editing skills.

Category	Description
Project Management	Instructional designers typically manage multiple instructional design projects at different phases. This requires strong project management skills, especially when multiple design teams are involved. Sometimes a designer is starting a new design project at the analysis stage and at the same time working on revisions to another course. Designers need to effectively manage the demands of different instructional projects at different phases of design.

Considering a career as an instructional designer

At the time of this book's publication, the employment website *Indeed* (www.indeed.com) listed over 9,000 jobs after entering "Instructional Design" as a keyword. This search suggests that instructional design is an active and growing profession. In fact, according to the Bureau of Labor Statistics, jobs in Instructional Design are expected to increase 11 percent during the 10-year period between 2016 and 2026. Data from 2017 shows that the median salary of instructional designers was $63,750.

TIP

Here are a few tips to get started in the instructional design field. One path is to opt for an education program offered by a college or university. Several universities offer bachelor's degrees, master's degrees, certificates, or minors in instructional design. In fact, many graduate programs focusing on instructional design are offered online from some of the top accredited universities. Following a formal educational path, you can pursue a degree in instructional design and receive training and experience (possibly an internship) while you pursue the degree. Sometimes the name of the degree may be called "instructional technology" or "learning, design, and technology" or "learning sciences and technology." The advantage of taking this path to a career in instructional design is that you get to take advantage of the networking, alumni, and partnerships set up through the academic program.

Another path to a career in instructional design is more indirect but is quite common. A lot of instructional designers enter the field through a career change. Although they may have started out as a professional in one field outside of education, they eventually pursue an opportunity to teach or train others, often within their existing company. Others may stumble into the job without any formal educational training in instructional design but a passion for the field or for teaching. Regardless of the specific pathway, instructional designers following a more indirect path are often responsible for their own professional development in the instructional design field.

I teach many graduate students in my faculty job at Penn State who fall into this category — that is, they have been doing instructional design work in their jobs but were not trained as instructional designers. They have a lot of instructional design experience and enthusiasm, and they come to our program to learn more about learning design and technology skills. I find they quickly grasp new ideas to apply to their work.

TIP

Being an instructional designer requires continual development and refinement of skills as the field advances. Fortunately, there are well-designed short-courses available online or through universities to update your skillset. Also, you can find professional associations and online networks of instructional designers who can help connect you with professional development opportunities. A few organizations and their websites are listed below:

>> Association for Educational Communications and Technology (AECT): https://aect.org

>> Association for Talent Development (ATD): https://www.td.org

Overview of the Instructional Design Process: The ADDIE Model

The first step to understanding instructional design is to become familiar with some of the basics. In the planning stages for this book, I decided that the best way to help you get familiar with the basics is to structure the major parts of this book around one well-known, 5-phase design process known as the ADDIE model. Using the first letter of each phase, ADDIE is an acronym that stands for **Analyze, Design, Develop, Implement,** and **Evaluate.**

REMEMBER

ADDIE is an overarching design framework that provides a common process for designing instruction for any instructional design goal. Although the parts of this book proceed sequentially, starting with "Analysis" and ending with "Evaluation," the five phases in practice are highly interconnected, flexible, and iterative.

As shown in Figure 1-1, design activities and decisions from one phase of the design process influence the activities and decisions at the other phases. The five phases follow a general sequence that starts with analysis, then design, development, implementation, and evaluation. But, during the analysis phase, for instance, a designer also begins to think about considerations for the development, implementation, and evaluation of the instruction. Likewise, during the implementation phase, designers revisit the assumptions and constraints identified during the analysis phase. All phases of ADDIE work together to achieve the instructional objectives. By continually going back and forth between the different phases of the model at different points in the design process, your instruction continually improves as it becomes more informed by the other phases of ADDIE.

FIGURE 1-1:
The ADDIE
Instructional
Design Process.

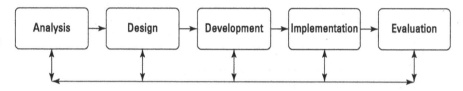

REMEMBER

What's most important to remember about the ADDIE model is that it is iterative and that you make design decisions that are in *alignment* across each of the five phases of the process.

In the following sections, I provide an overview of activities that are performed at each phase of the ADDIE model. Each of these phases is broken out in more detail in the other chapters of this book.

The Analysis phase: Deciding what the needs are for instruction

In the first phase of the ADDIE process (Analysis), you analyze the setting, learners, and need for the instruction. When analyzing your context for the instruction, you typically work with subject-matter experts (SMEs) and other stakeholders to clarify the problem that is creating the need for the instruction and outline possible solutions. Designing instruction is a good solution if your learners need to learn new knowledge, skills, or attitudes.

This type of analysis is often called a "needs analysis" or "gap analysis," where you clarify the problem and potential solutions. After you have identified that instruction is a viable solution to the problem, your next step is to examine the tasks, knowledge, and skills that are to be learned during the instruction, also referred to as a "task analysis." Typically a subject-matter expert (SME) breaks down the tasks, knowledge, and skills needed for effective performance, but the process is facilitated by an instructional designer.

All phases of ADDIE build upon the work of the Analysis phase. During the Analysis phase, you may be conducting the following types of activities:

>> Identifying organizational needs and values (sales targets, strategic plans, quarterly reports, number of patrons) that inform the need for the instruction.

>> Learning about the context where the instruction is to be implemented, such as resources, infrastructures, policies, support systems, or logistics.

>> Conducting a needs analysis by identifying optimal performance, actual performance, possible causes, and initial solutions.

>> Conducting a learner analysis to understand their characteristics, motivations, accessibility needs, or barriers to access.

>> Collecting data to inform your analyses by using interviews, focus groups, or surveys.

>> Classifying the type of learning goals that the instruction entails by using a framework such as Bloom's Taxonomy. (For more on Bloom's Taxonomy, see Chapter 4.)

>> Performing a task analysis to break down the overall goal into the major tasks that need to be learned as well as any subtasks, knowledge, or skills needed to perform the major tasks.

TIP

The output of the Analysis phase are reports that document the most essential information related to the learner analysis, needs analysis, context analysis, and task analyses. You then share these with the stakeholders involved in the project to make sure everyone is on the same page before moving to the design phase.

The Design phase: Figuring out what the learners need to know and how to learn it

The Analysis phase of the ADDIE model is followed by the Design phase. This part of the instructional-design process is where you use the results of your analyses to begin outlining the content, activities, and any assessments that are to be included the instruction.

Here are a few key tasks that take place during the Design phase:

>> Based on your task analyses, write clear statements of learning objectives for each task and subtask. Use action verbs from Bloom's Taxonomy for each objective that aligns with the level of learning that you need to support (remembering versus evaluating, for example). Objectives guide the design of

your instructional content and activities as well as the criteria for evaluating if it was successful.

>> Create assessment items that match your instructional objectives. In practice, you develop your objectives and assessments at the same time to make sure they are aligned.

>> Choose what type of instructional design model or methods you want to use to create the activities for your instruction. Design models guide us to determine how the objectives are learned. Some design models focus on how to effectively present information and practice on specific skills to be learned. Other types of models are more open-ended.

TIP

Be sure to share your objectives, assessments, and plans for instructional activities with all stakeholders. These documents are useful for all members of the design team as well as anyone who is helping with the technical production or development of the instruction (programmers, graphic artists, and so on). This time is good to get more feedback before investing in development.

The Development phase: Hammering out the details

The third phase of the ADDIE model is the Development phase. This phase is a very exciting part of the instructional-design process because your instruction soon comes to life! The Development phase uses the information from Analysis and Design phases to make decisions about the actual creation of the instructional materials. You may be the person who is both designing and developing the instruction, or you may be part of a development team of programmers, graphic artists, or video production specialists. The result of the development phase is an instructional product (an instructional website, a video, a print manual, or presentation slides, for example) that is ready to be delivered by an instructor or on its own to learners.

Here are some common tasks that you may need to do during the development phase:

>> Analyze different options and formats for delivering the instruction to learners. Should the instruction take place synchronously (at the same time) or asynchronously (at the learners' own time and pace) or as a hybrid? Will it take place in a classroom or virtually (online)? These decisions impact the technologies you select for the instruction.

>> Examine different types of technologies (print, video, audio, website, video conferencing, and so on) and their characteristics to determine how they may

enhance the learning of your instructional objectives. Some technologies, for instance, support collaboration better than others. If collaboration is important to your design goals, then you want to narrow down the focus on technologies that promote collaboration.

>> Create instructor manuals, learner guides, media, or other digital materials (presentation slides, for example).

>> Ensure that multimedia instructional materials are accessible for diverse learners and reflect effective multimedia design principles.

>> Develop scripts, storyboards, or flowcharts to communicate the flow of the instruction for programmers or other development team members.

EXAMPLE

This section finishes with some examples of a few instructional development activities:

>> Creating a lesson plan for a corporate training session, including handouts, printed case studies, and presentation slides.

>> Creating a hybrid or flipped classroom, where some instructional activities take place in a classroom at the same time and some parts asynchronously online. For the online instructional elements, you create video lectures, content pages, or discussion boards with a Learning Management System (LMS).

>> Developing a printed manual for learners with step-by-step instructions for them to follow on the job.

>> Recording an audio tour for visitors to a museum.

The Implementation phase: Rolling out the instruction

After the Development phase, it is time to try out the instruction with your learners. Because the ADDIE model is iterative and flexible, we usually begin thinking about implementation during the analysis phase. Early in the instructional design process, it is important to consider the factors that can lead to successful implementation, such as having an accurate assessment of your financial resources, support, policies, facilities, and logistical constraints. Planning for implementation of your instruction looks different for different types of instruction.

EXAMPLE

Examples of implementation activities that you may do as an instructional designer include:

>> Try out the materials with some learners in advance of the full rollout of the instruction and make revisions.

>> Train instructors how to teach by using the instructional materials and any technologies that they need to use.

>> Communicate to learners and instructors in advance about all hardware and software requirements for the instruction.

>> Create introductory lessons for learners on how to use the technology that is used for the instruction (video conferencing software or LMS, for example).

The Evaluation phase: Did the instruction work?

Although positioned at the end of the ADDIE process, evaluation doesn't just occur at the end of the instruction! Evaluation is important at every phase, and an instructional designer continually seeks feedback during each phase of the process so they can adjust the instruction while it is being designed and developed.

At the end of the instruction, however, an instructional designer evaluates if the instruction is successful. Based on the evaluation, you and other decision makers can determine if the instruction needs further revision and whether it met the objectives it was designed to achieve.

There are many ways to evaluate whether the instruction was successful. Kirkpatrick's model of four levels of evaluation (developed by University of Wisconsin-Madison Professor Donald K. Kirkpatrick in the late 1950s) is one of the best ways to analyze different dimensions of effectiveness. The four levels of evaluation are:

>> **Level 1: Reaction.** Level 1 evaluates learners' satisfaction with the instruction. Did they like it and find it useful? Level 1 is commonly evaluated using surveys given to learners at the end of the instruction.

>> **Level 2: Learning.** Level 2 evaluates if learning occurred. It most readily assesses if the learning objectives were achieved. You can use quizzes to assess learning or compare what learners knew about the topic both before and after the instruction.

>> **Level 3: Behavior.** Level 3 asks if learners are applying what they learned on the job or in their everyday lives. You can observe on-the-job performance or ask learners after the instruction ends if they are using what they learned.

>> **Level 4: Results.** The fourth level of evaluation determines if the learning that resulted from the instruction had an impact on organizational results such as costs, goals, job satisfaction, customer satisfaction, employee retention, and so on.

REMEMBER

Not every instructional project requires evaluation at all four levels. Generally, the higher the level of evaluation, the more costly and complicated it is to evaluate.

Understanding Different Methods and Design Models

The ADDIE model is one of the most well-known models in the instructional design field. ADDIE describes the various processes and activities conducted by an instructional designer that are applicable to almost any instructional situation. ADDIE illustrates the essential, interacting elements of the instructional design process, highlighting the systematic nature of instructional design.

However, the ADDIE model does not prescribe specific guidelines on how to design activities, strategies, and methods to achieve your learning goals. Instructional designers use other types of instructional models to help guide them in the development of activities, strategies, and sequences of the instruction. This section briefly describes a few different methods and models to illustrate a range of approaches.

Looking at rapid design approaches

One criticism of the ADDIE approach is that it is time consuming and requires an extremely detailed approach that does not always align with the needs for some designers to design and develop their instruction rapidly and efficiently.

In response to these limitations, some instructional designers advocate for rapid design approaches such as the Successive Approximation Model (SAM). The SAM model is referred to as an "agile" model that allows for more flexibility by developing prototype experiences early in the process and then progressively iterating them through feedback. In this way, it is a less daunting design process that works in those settings where detailed instructional analyses and design practices are not practical.

The SAM process in a nutshell works in two main phases. First is the preparation phase, which reviews background information, assumptions, and needs for the instruction. It then moves quickly into the iterative design and development phase which entails creating design ideas and prototypes of small chunks of the instruction that show what the instruction and interactions will look like. The prototype is then shared across stakeholders, reviewed, and revised in a successive and iterative feedback loop.

Working with direct-instructional designs

I'd be the first to admit that there are far too many different types of instructional design models to cover in one book. Nevertheless, there are common approaches to teaching and instruction that can be categorized into broad approaches. Here I give an overview of one type of instructional design method I refer to as direct instruction.

Direct instruction is instruction that is focused on learning specific knowledge or skills that are well defined. For well-defined instructional goals, such as performing a sequence of steps or learning specific information to apply to well-known problems or situations, the best choice for your instruction is to use a direct instructional-design model such as Gagne's Nine Events of Instruction (a concept I discuss in much greater detail in Chapter 6).

Direct instructional models share several common patterns for organizing your instruction, based on how people learn and remember information. Chapter 6 presents three different models in detail along with tips for design.

A summary of instructional tactics commonly used in direct instructional design models include:

>> Gain learners' attention, show why the instruction is relevant, and establish what learners should expect.

>> Present content information broken down into smaller chunks of information that do not overwhelm learners' memory.

>> Guide learners to process and learn the content with strategies such as examples, non-examples, demonstrations, questions, or summaries.

>> Design practice opportunities as well as feedback on performance.

Opting for open-ended designs

Some instructional design models focus on how to support less defined learning goals such as problem solving. (For an overview of two different models for designing open-ended instruction, see Chapter 7.)

Here, I provide a summary of instructional methods commonly used in open-ended design models:

TIP

>> Start the instruction with an open-ended problem, case, or question. The problem should be complex and have more than one answer. Open-ended instruction is often collaborative.

>> Ask learners for preliminary ideas and solutions to the problem. It is expected that they will not yet have very refined solutions, but the goal is for them to start with what they already think or know.

>> Present content, resources, collaborations, or technologies to help learners solve the problem and progressively build on their initial ideas.

>> Provide guiding questions and ongoing checks of understanding.

>> Ask learners to share what they have learned with others.

In practice, instructional designers often draw upon different strategies and activities to create engaging instruction. You discover more about how to choose different strategies and activities based on your goals in the chapters ahead!

Chapter **2**

Looking at Learning and Design Foundations

Most of us have likely encountered different types of instructional experiences. Our prior experiences often shape how you approach design, based on what worked for us and what did not. Our prior experience often leads us to design the same type of instruction because you are familiar with it.

Many of us are also quite familiar with the instructional model of a teacher in a classroom delivering new information, giving worksheets to practice the knowledge and skills, and providing assessments. However, there are many different types of instructional models. If you think about it, you may have experienced other types of instructional approaches that did not look like "instruction" in a traditional sense:

» Learning how to knit through apprenticeship with more experienced knitters in a knitting club

» Learning strength-training technique through one-on-one coaching

» Performing CPR through practice on a simulator

» Learning to code a programming language by using a web forum to get advice from expert programmers

>> Learning how to troubleshoot a washing machine problem by using videos created on *YouTube*.

All of these represent different types of instructional experiences that draw upon different learning and instructional foundations. In this chapter, I summarize five core foundations for design by introducing a framework to use alongside the ADDIE model I describe in Chapter 1. (ADDIE stands for *A*nalyze, *D*esign, *D*evelop, *I*mplement, and *E*valuate.)

Alignment: A Key Principle of Instructional Design

I spend a lot of time talking about the five phases of the ADDIE model in Chapter 1. While each phase of the ADDIE model can be understood independently, the most important principle of the framework is the following key idea: *The importance of alignment.*

Alignment in instructional design serves the essential function of ensuring that all elements of an instructional design function coherently as a whole. Early phases of the design process should be directly tied to later phases and vice versa. You can see the importance of alignment within and across the various phases of ADDIE in the following examples:

>> The *analysis* phase ensures alignment between the needs of the organization, potential learners, and the instructional goals and objectives of the design phase; it also considers potential future issues that may occur during implementation and evaluation phases.

>> The *design* phase establishes that goals, objectives, learning outcomes, and assessments are all aligned with each other and are tied to the identified needs from the analysis phase; it also considers needs for development and delivery systems, implementation, and evaluation and assessment of learning.

>> The *development* phase ensures that the content, activities, and technology delivery system are aligned with the goals and objectives from the analysis and design phases; it also checks that the expected delivery system can be successfully implemented given available budget, facilities, and so on. During evaluation, assessments may directly be tied to learner experiences with the instructional materials.

>> The *implementation* phase examines whether the broader organization context, such as management, policies, resources, and learner support, are

available and harmonize with the developed instruction and prior analysis and design phases; it also focuses on the logistical support needed to successfully implement the instruction.

>> The *evaluation* phase assesses the success of the instruction and its results on the organization by evaluating if the instruction addressed the problems and needs that were initially identified in the analysis phase; it also evaluates if what was learned was tied directly to the instructional objectives and if the design was developed and implemented effectively to support the learning goals.

REMEMBER

The key point across all phases of the ADDIE model is the concept of alignment! It is less important to focus on the separate phases of ADDIE. They are presented separately for simplicity and for understanding the key activities of each phase but in practice it is more important to focus on alignment across them.

Examining the Five Essential Foundations for Instructional Design

Instructional design is based upon different theories and practices about 1) how people learn, 2) what instructional activities are effective for certain types of learning goals, 3) how technology can be used to create new possibilities for delivering instruction, 4) how the instructional design project is situated within an overarching culture and set of values, and 5) how each project comes to terms with its own set of unique pragmatic constraints. How one answers these questions ultimately shapes what your instruction will become. Together, the answers you come up with will inform your analysis, design, development, implementation, and evaluation decisions.

REMEMBER

Various theories of instructional design are going to influence how you draw upon different activities, strategies, technologies, and practices in your designs. Such theories determine which questions to ask and also how they get answered. These theories can be boiled down and organized together as the five foundations of any instructional design project:

>> *Learning*: Learning foundations reflect beliefs about how people learn and understand concepts, including how they gain knowledge and skills.

>> *Teaching*: Teaching foundations shape the methods and strategies used during the instruction.

>> *Technology*: Technology foundations establish the possibilities for how you can use technology to design and deliver instruction in effective or new ways.

>> *Cultural*: Cultural foundations reflect the prevailing beliefs and values within an organization and/or society (including values about education) that influence what is most important.

>> *Pragmatics*: Pragmatic foundations are the practical constraints that influence instructional design decisions, such as facilities or space constraints, time limitations, technology availability, and financial or budget constraints.

The next section describes each of the five foundations in more detail and explains their role in influencing the design decisions that show up within your instructional program.

Learning: How exactly do people learn?

Learning foundations are rooted in psychological theories about how learning occurs — psychological theories as learning theories, in other words. Because no one theory of learning has managed to gain universal acceptance, it is important that one gain an understanding of the different viewpoints on learning. Such an understanding can help us make informed choices in our designs.

Why is understanding learning foundations important to instructional designers? Clearly one major reason is that our instructional strategies and practices are designed to support *learning*, which can best be defined as a process that results in a change in a person's knowledge, skills, practices, or beliefs. Understanding how learning occurs helps you to create instructional designs that are more likely to result in such changes in knowledge, understanding, or performance.

REMEMBER

Learning foundations are based on assumptions about how people will learn in our specific design context. Your beliefs about learning guide how you frame your learning objectives and design your activities. The instructional design strategies you select reveal the instructional designers' views about how people learn, organize, retrieve, and use information.

Three historical theories about learning have guided different types of instructional designs. The next sections examine each theory in greater detail.

Learning as a change in behavior

An early theory about learning that has been applied to instructional design is known as *behaviorism*. Behaviorism views learning as a change in behavior, focusing on observable and measurable behaviors rather than on thinking or memory processes which cannot be seen.

Behaviorism's central idea is that when learners connect an external trigger with their response and then receive a reward, their behavior changes. Anyone who has tried to train a dog may be familiar with behaviorist principles: Training is achieved by pairing a stimulus (a clicker and the word "sit," for example) and a reinforcement (a treat) with the desired behavior (sitting). Behaviorism uses repetition and reinforcement to shape desired performance, as behavior that is positively reinforced will typically be repeated.

Behaviorism's focus on changes in behavior alone, without considering how people process, retrieve, or create new understanding, has limited application in modern instructional design approaches. Although the instructional design field relies on other theories of learning that consider knowledge construction processes, as is made clear in the next sections, some concepts of behaviorism can still be relevant for some types of design activities. Consider the following examples:

>> Reinforcing desired behaviors in an instructional game via token systems or reward structures (instructional games that use points, badges, leveling up, or unlocking new content, for example)

>> Shaping behavior or factual knowledge over time with repeated practice and feedback opportunities (a math drill and practice program that continually presents new problems and feedback until mastered, for example)

>> Offering feedback that is immediate or very close in time to a desired behavior or performance (a tutorial on how to identify different types of trees gives corrective feedback immediately after an answer is given versus waiting until the instruction ends, for example)

A key idea of behaviorism is that learning involves a change in behavior that is supported by repeatedly reinforcing desired behaviors or skills.

Learning as acquiring knowledge

Over time, learning theory expanded from a behaviorist view of learning towards a theory of how people think and acquire knowledge, called cognitive psychology. According to the theory, learners actively process new information through internal mental processes such as paying attention to important information, organizing information by making new connections, integrating new information with prior knowledge, and retrieving and applying knowledge from memory.

Cognitive theory emphasizes how you organize knowledge and acquire new information. *Schema theory* is a concept within cognitive theory that explains how you categorize and structure new knowledge with existing knowledge. Schemas are like mental models that represent what you know based on past experiences. If you think about a filing cabinet, schemas are like the various folders set up to hold different concepts, procedures, or ideas. Schemas help us interpret new information using the various mental "folders" based on what you have learned in the past. When you encounter new experiences, your brain tries to fit the new experience into an existing schema (or folder). These schemas are flexible, however, and over time, we constantly update and reorganize them based on new experiences and information.

Cognitive learning theory recognizes that there are limits to the amount of information that can be processed at one time due to memory limitations. It also emphasizes that the complexity of the material influences how hard it can be for learners to learn the new information. Material that is less complex or that is more familiar to learners is easier to process. Instruction that is complex needs to employ instructional strategies to help learners manage the cognitive effort of their learning.

REMEMBER

Cognitive learning theory sees learning as an active process of linking new information to prior knowledge. A learner who already has a lot of background knowledge on a topic can use that knowledge to help them more easily learn new information. On the other hand, a learner with limited prior knowledge has fewer connections that they can make between new and prior knowledge.

Theories about the nature of cognition have greatly influenced instructional design practices, leading to the development of principles that inform designers as they come up with learning-appropriate methods to help learners organize and interpret new information. With a basic understandings of cognitive learning theory, instructional designers can use different guidelines and strategies to facilitate information processing.

EXAMPLE

Some examples of the kinds of design guidelines using cognitive learning theory include the following:

>> Channel learners' attention to important information by using visual cues such as bolding, highlighting, arrows, or animations.

>> Segment information into smaller chunks to help learners manage the processing demands that come with the learning of new information.

>> Encourage meaningful organization of knowledge by showing conceptual connections by using graphical diagrams, and/or sequencing material from simple to complex.

>> Reduce complexity of learning and remembering by using mnemonics, memory aids, or the chunking of information.

>> Help learners make meaningful connections between new and prior knowledge by using strategies such as metaphors, real-world examples, explanations, and links to what has been learned before.

>> Encourage active learning strategies such as reflecting, elaborating, and practice.

A key idea of cognitive learning theory is that learners *actively* acquire, process, and store information.

Learning as constructing meaning

Another view of learning (called *constructivism*) underscores the key belief that learners actively construct new understanding from their prior knowledge and experiences. Whereas cognitive views of learning emphasize the acquisition, storage, integration, and retrieval of knowledge from external sources (such as instructional content), constructivism goes beyond the processing of information to explain how learners create new knowledge from their experiences.

Constructivist theories explain why learning does not always occur when information is simply "told." Learning is presented as a dynamic and active process of making sense of experiences, not a process of absorbing information. Constructivism assumes that learners bring a perspective, a point of view, and/or a set of beliefs to any learning experience. The argument here is that actively engaging what learners know and think about an idea — even before they have been taught about it — helps them build upon and refine what they know in meaningful ways.

Some instructional designs reflect a view of learning as memorizing and acquiring knowledge, rather than understanding and using it. Constructivism focuses on broad, complex learning goals and the use of realistic problems, so concepts can be applied, not just memorized.

Learning is seen as more meaningful when it's situated within real-world contexts, often while collaborating with others. Instructional materials should be designed to reflect authentic scenarios and challenges, enabling learners to connect concepts to practical applications to broader contexts.

Applying constructivist learning theory to instructional design involves creating learning experiences that align with its core principles. Here are some sample strategies:

>> Provide active, hands-on experiences that give learners the chance to construct meaning and create new ideas or solutions.

>> Design activities or problems that encourage learners to analyze and solve problems similar to realistic contexts. This method can include case studies or problems that may be experienced in a real-world context. Provide support as they are solving the problem.

>> Provide opportunities for learners to collaborate, discuss, and share perspectives with others. This tactic can include collaborative problem-solving tasks that foster negotiation of diverse viewpoints, which can lead to richer discussions and a deeper understanding of complex topics.

>> Intentionally draw out learners' prior knowledge at the start of the instruction and give opportunities to build upon it. This can be fostered by starting the instruction with questions or prompts for learners to give their initial ideas about a problem or situation.

>> Encourage learners to reflect on their learning, such as when they need more information or when they do not understand.

REMEMBER

A key idea of constructivism is that people construct new knowledge and understandings based on what they already know.

Teaching: What educational strategies are possible?

Teaching foundations reflect the activities and methods used in the instructional experience. Although referred to here as teaching foundations for the sake of simplicity, this foundation is broader than teaching alone. It also includes instruction more generally — even stand-alone instructional designs that do not involve a teacher at all, such as a self-paced online tutorial.

Teaching foundations inform how instruction is designed according to varied design models. Different teaching foundations yield different instructional strategies and approaches. Taken together, learning and teaching foundations work to link together the instructional activities you use and your assumptions about learning. Different learning theory foundations usually dictate different teaching and design strategies. The sections that follow illustrate different types of teaching foundations and strategies.

Direct instructional strategies

Traditional instructional design strategies reflect common instructional methods such as breaking down information into smaller chunks, presenting information, and providing activities that support memory, elaboration, and practice. I refer to such instructional design practices as *direct instructional strategies.* Direct instructional methods are commonly used in workshops, classrooms, or seminars where an instructor lectures on a topic, provides activities on the concepts presented in the lecture, and allows for practice and feedback. The instructional process involves breaking down the content into manageable steps, generating instructional activities related to the objectives, providing feedback, and assessing progress towards mastery. Instructional strategies and activities are closely aligned with predefined knowledge and performance standards (goals and objectives in other words).

Direct instruction is commonly presented in a structured way, with a focus on defined objectives and a "basics first" approach to learning. Simpler content is presented first, with ever more complicated material systematically brought into play as the schedule advances. Concepts are introduced based on clear objectives and strategies are implemented to achieve these objectives. Learning outcomes are evaluated based on the objectives that have been established and adjustments are made if necessary (reviewing material or providing more practice, for example).

TIP

Direct instruction is often referred to as a "tutorial" approach and follows a general instructional pattern of:

>> Presenting objectives for the planned instruction

>> Introducing instructional content

>> Providing different types of examples

>> Giving opportunities to practice knowledge and skills

>> Providing feedback on results of practice

Open-ended instructional strategies

In contrast to direct instruction, open-ended learning strategies feature activities that give learners the opportunity to develop their own ideas and solutions, often through problem-based scenarios, cases, or motivating questions. They typically reflect real-world situations as well as problem- or project-based scenarios and are deliberately open-ended, implying that there isn't usually a single correct answer or way to solve the problem.

REMEMBER

Open-ended instructional strategies may include some direct instruction but are driven foremost by an engaging or complex problem, dilemma, or question. They often integrate technology tools, information resources, or cases and provide guidance for learners as they collaborate on the complex task or problem.

Open-ended learning strategies engage a learners' own experiences, ideas, or beliefs; their initial understanding is therefore the basis for building more refined understanding over time. Open-ended learning strategies support learners to engage in reflection, monitoring, and self-assessment of what they already know and what they need to know.

EXAMPLE

Look at an example of how open-ended learning strategies may look in practice. Take, for instance, an activity where learners are asked to investigate and analyze environmental sustainability issues in their community. They can be provided with a scenario of a polluted local waterway in their community, along with factual information related to nearby farming, vegetation, or manufacturing plants.

Working together, learners may apply their understanding of environmental science to generate an explanation and a possible solution that considers environmental, social, economic, and ethical impacts. Learners may be asked to use Internet resources to gather statistics and environmental information related the problem. To foster a sense of authenticity, learners may work in groups to create a multimedia presentation that communicates the group's findings and proposals; members from the local community governance can be invited to listen to the presentations.

This activity aligns with constructivist principles by encouraging learners to actively engage in collaboration, critical thinking, and problem-solving. It also integrates real-world problems and encourages learners to apply their knowledge to complex, meaningful situations.

TIP

Open-ended learning strategies often follow a particular pattern. The steps are as follows:

>> Present an open-ended problem, case, or question that can have more than one answer.

>> Invite learners to provide their initial ideas or solutions.

>> Provide access to information, expert opinions, data, or resources to help learners explore the problem and build on their initial thinking.

>> Provide guiding questions or coaching to give feedback.

>> Ask learners to create a product (a presentation or poster, for example) that shows their ideas in a format that can be shared with others.

Individual versus collaborative learning

Individual and collaborative learning are two distinct approaches for how learners engage and participate with others in the instructional design. Each has its own benefits and limitations. The choice between individual and collaborative learning often depends on the learning objectives and the delivery mode of the instruction.

REMEMBER

For most instructional designs, it is not an "either-or" choice. It is common to integrate both individual and collaborative learning experiences to address the different goals of the instruction.

Individual learning involves a learner working independently to acquire knowledge and skills. This method is typically used in situations where learners need to show individual competence. It may also be useful when a learner needs to focus on personalized goals that they have chosen or to grasp foundational concepts. Individual learning can be useful when learners need to progress at their own speed and on their own timeline, such as during self-paced training that they are fitting in on their own time schedule.

EXAMPLE

The most common types of instructional designs in which individual learning occurs are:

>> Self-paced, stand-alone instruction that is taken at the learner's own time-frame and pace

>> Tutorials that requires demonstration and verification of individual competence, such as compliance training for a safety procedure

Collaborative learning involves groups of learners working together during an activity or several activities of the instruction. It emphasizes social interaction, peer-to-peer teaching, and/or the exchange of different perspectives. Collaborative learning is often used to support skills such as critical thinking, communication skills, and working effectively in teams, as well as activities such as brainstorming or problem-solving. One key benefit of collaborative learning is the opportunity to learn from different perspectives or points of view.

Collaborative learning does not reflect a single approach; rather, you are free to use different types of collaborative learning strategies, as shown in Table 2-1.

Technological: Expanding the designer's toolkit

Technological foundations represent how the capabilities and limitations of available technologies can be used to support an instructional designer's learning and instructional goals. Technology influences the design of instruction by establishing the toolkit available to both the designer and the learner. For instance, technology can monitor learner responses, provide feedback about choices, and maintain records of performance.

TABLE 2-1   Types of collaborative learning strategies

Type of collaborative strategy	Description
Group discussions	Learners engage in discussion questions as a group, with each person sharing perspectives, ideas, and insights.
	Discussions are a useful strategy when the instructional activity encourages sharing of diverse viewpoints.
Jigsaw method	Learners within a small group specialize in a specific topic or area of expertise related to a problem being addressed. Then, learners from different groups come together and share their specialized knowledge with each other.
	This method can lead to deeper understanding of many different perspectives about a problem or its potential solutions.
Peer teaching	Learners are asked to learn a topic or skill and teach it to other learners.
	This strategy assumes that teaching others leads to a deeper level of comprehension, investment, and engagement in learning.
Peer review	Learners provide feedback or constructive critique of others' work.
	Peer review expands access to more ideas or solutions and helps learners evaluate their own ideas.
Think-Pair-Share	Learners are asked to think about a question individually, then pair up with a partner to discuss their thoughts, and then the pairs share their ideas with the larger group.
	This strategy is often used in large groups to give learners a chance to work through some initial ideas individually and with another before participating in the larger group discussion.
Collaborative problem solving or projects	Learners collaborate in teams to solve complex problems or challenges such as real-world problems or case studies that require analysis, research, and proposing solutions.
Role plays or debates	Learners take on different roles or perspectives to explore scenarios or issues from different points of view.
Online discussions or collaboration	Learners engage in collaborative discussions online either asynchronously or synchronously.
	Asynchronous discussions typically use online discussion boards; synchronous discussions typically use break-out rooms (videoconferencing) chats, or virtual whiteboards.

However, the instruction's goals and objectives determine how, or if, technology should be used. Technological foundations suggest what is possible through advances in technology to support instruction, not necessarily what is required or desired.

Technology possibilities for learning

Technologies support different operations and functions, as they have specific attributes that make them better suited for certain types of instructional goals or strategies than others. Some technologies, for instance, employ graphics, sound, video, and animation, which might be important to use for instruction to visualize ideas, concepts, or procedures that are hard to see otherwise.

The possibilities opened up by advances in technology (also known as *technology affordances*) describe what a specific technology has to offer instructional designers to support their instructional goals and objectives. (See Chapter 8 for a more detailed treatment of technology affordances.) Ideally, you align your views about learning (learning foundations), instructional strategies (teaching foundations), and technology choices (technological foundations) in complementary ways to support our learning goals.

Technology as a delivery tool

During the instructional design process, you conduct instructional analyses and create instructional goals, objectives, and strategies. Given the outputs of those instructional design activities, you have key information to help you determine how you need to develop and deliver the instruction and what your best options for using technology are.

Chapter 8 discusses different delivery modes for your instruction, and technology is central for many of them. A *delivery mode* is the format that the instruction is be delivered in. For instance, this mode can include printed manuals, electronic PDFs, videos, or a *learning management system (LMS)* — a technology platform for delivering online instruction.

TIP

It's best to think of delivery modes in terms of dimensions of time and place. *Time* defines whether the instruction is being offered at the same time for all the learners (synchronously) or at different times (asynchronously). *Place* defines the general location of the instruction — is it in the same place for everyone (a classroom, for example) or are learners in different locations?

Taken together, different delivery mode configurations are possible, such as same time and same place (such as classroom instruction), same time and different place (such as video conferencing), different time and different place (asynchronous LMS), and so on.

REMEMBER

Technological foundations and delivery modes constrain or enhance the types of learning goals that are possible. For instance, some instructional designs need the instruction to be delivered in a way that can be accessed anytime and anywhere. Given this goal, an LMS that supports asynchronous learning has technology characteristics that serve the particular needs of these learners and this instruction.

Cultural: An important element of the learning context

Cultural foundations reflect the beliefs and values of an organization, educational institution, or community and, not surprisingly, these values are often reflected in our instructional designs. The following sections explain how the culture and values of an organization play a role in shaping instructional-design decisions.

Values and mission of the organization

Organizational or other cultural values shape our educational efforts because our instructional designs need to align with the guiding values of its overarching organization.

EXAMPLE

Take for instance the following examples:

>> A corporation's core value may be focused on innovation, as shown in their ability to quickly adapt to new situations and perform and create new solutions for different contexts. Instructional design efforts that align with such values may use methods such as interdisciplinary teams, real-world challenges, and problem solving.

>> A university's strategic plan presents core values around diversity, equity, inclusion, and belongingness. Instruction aligned with this core value considers during its analysis who the instruction benefits and who it excludes as well as cultural competence, potential implicit biases, equitable treatment, and community building.

REMEMBER

These are just a few examples of how organizational values can be reflected in our instructional-design decision making. Aligning instructional designs with individual, organizational, or cultural values strengthens the likelihood of the instruction being implemented successfully and in ways that align with the overall mission and values of the organization.

Rote learning versus 21st century skills

If you want to see the role cultural foundations play in our instructional designs, start by tracing how the values and culture can be reflected by an organization's educational priorities. For instance, educational values of the early 20th century primarily focused on basic literacy skills such as reading, writing, and arithmetic. Classrooms reflected these values in the kinds of activities in which students engaged as well as what and how they were taught.

In contrast, recent cultural values of education have shifted towards fostering critical thinking, innovation, problem solving, and information and digital literacy. These values are driven by evolving requirements of the modern workforce. Often referred to as 21st-century skills or "future-ready skills," these values focus on fostering knowledge and skills that are considered essential for individuals to thrive and succeed in the rapidly changing and complex modern world.

Informal versus formal learning

Prevailing cultural values also show up in different types of educational settings that have different educational missions or goals. For instance, some educational institutions such as museums, botanical gardens, or libraries have a strong educational mission, but they value free-choice and interest-based learning of\on the part of their visitors. They honor the importance of sparking interest more so than in teaching specific skills.

Instructional designs for informal learning settings may encourage concrete experiences with exhibits, play spaces, and learner choice of what they want to learn based on their own curiosity or interests. This type of instructional design would look very different from instruction used in a college classroom that is guided by content coverage, standards, assignments, grading, and assessment.

Pragmatics: You can't have everything

Each setting has unique situational constraints that affect the design of instruction. Pragmatic constraints involve the practical reasons that a particular instructional-design strategy or approach can or cannot be used in a particular setting. Analyzing the pragmatic constraints early in the analysis phase of the instructional design process is important, as these constraints impact how the instruction can be implemented.

People and context constraints

In a very real sense, pragmatics shape the design of instruction through both resource constraints and situational factors. Pragmatics determine the feasible elements that can be implemented in the instructional design, taking into consideration the people, resources, and organizational constraints of a setting. One of the most commonly encountered pragmatic constraints in instructional design center around limited resources.

EXAMPLE

Examples of pragmatic constraints include the following:

>> **Financial:** What is the budget for the instruction and what are the financial costs needed to pay for the instructional analysis, design, development, implementation, and evaluation?

> » **Time:** When do the learners have time for the instruction? Will it have to be squeezed into their current schedule or will they be given time off from their work to participate?

> » **Facilities or travel:** Are there travel costs for learners to take the instruction or instructors to teach it? Are facilities needed for delivering the instruction, and are they available and affordable within the budget?

> » **Personnel expertise:** What expertise is available to help design, develop, and implement the instruction? For instance, expertise is needed from subject-matter experts (SMEs) to define the performance requirements and instructional content. Instructional design or technology production expertise may also be needed.

Technology constraints

Technology plays a central role in many instructional design efforts. As technology has advanced and become more widely available, it is often used to deliver instruction. Take for example digital video-based instruction, video conferencing (Zoom, for example), LMSs, or even printed workbooks. Like people and context constraints, technology constraints can also limit the options available to you to deliver your instruction.

EXAMPLE

Examples of possible technology constraints include:

> » **Hardware/software requirements and availability:** Do the learners have the technology or Internet bandwidth they need to participate in the instruction?

> » **Technology costs:** What are the costs of the technology needed? Are these one-time costs or are they ongoing for maintenance, upgrades, or annual fees?

> » **Technology expertise:** Is the expertise available to develop the technology needs of the instruction as well as maintain and update them? Do instructors need to be trained in how to use the technology for instruction?

Aligning the Five Foundations to Select Best Practices

Although presented separately, the five foundations I cover in this chapter are integrated in instructional-design practice. They show up at different times during the analysis, design, development, implementation, and evaluation phases. The five foundations echo the ADDIE model's emphasis on alignment.

REMEMBER

The five foundations provide a broad framework for aligning instructional design decisions with different views on learning, instructional strategies, and uses of technology. The important point is that they reflect alignment across each other.

As shown in Figure 2-1, each foundation should intersect to some extent with the others. The more aligned the different foundations are, the better integrated the instructional-design decisions are. The better integrated the foundations, the greater the likelihood of success in the setting for which the instruction is designed. In practice, the larger the intersection among foundations, the better aligned are the five foundations.

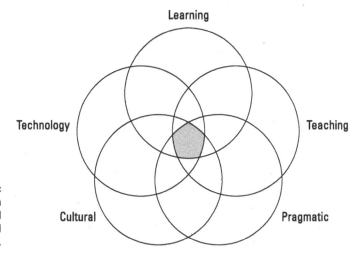

FIGURE 2-1:
An illustration of an aligned instructional design.

EXAMPLE

The following example shows how the five foundations may be selected in an integrated way for a training program for employees that focuses on design thinking:

>> **Learning:** The instructional designer draws upon constructivist views of learning, emphasizing authentic practices, and learner-centeredness.

>> **Teaching:** Teaching or instructional strategies are aligned with learning foundations, as the instructional activities center on problem-based scenarios where learners are given the opportunity to develop their own ideas and solutions collaboratively.

>> **Technology:** Because many employees are remote workers, the instruction may use video conferencing with break-out rooms for group work and presentation software to present ideas and solutions to the problem.

>> **Cultural:** The organization's cultural values prioritize idea sharing and collaboration across diverse units in order to support innovation and continuous improvement.

>> **Pragmatics:** A detailed analysis is conducted to ensure that the financial, personnel, time, and technology resources are available to complete the design thinking training design. The organization has software licenses and support personnel for the video conferencing and presentation software.

Perfect alignment is relatively rare. You make trade-offs as you proceed through the ADDIE process. Do the best you can with the resources, expertise, and constraints you are given, but sometimes the best-laid plans fall short.

Figure 2-2 illustrates how a disconnect across the five foundations may look in practice. Here, the instructional design foundations for a training program are clearly less aligned.

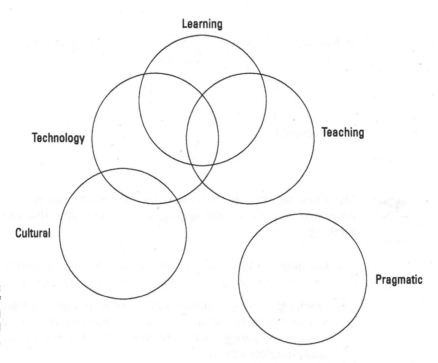

FIGURE 2-2:
An illustration of
a partially aligned
instructional
design.

In this example, the instructional design begins with a situation where a specific technology drives the instructional design process. The organization expressed a desire to use the latest virtual reality software for training on the topic of workplace safety.

In this instance, the five foundations are only partially aligned:

>> **Learning:** The instructional design is based on constructivist views of learning, emphasizing the application of knowledge to authentic work situations.

>> **Teaching:** Teaching and learning foundations are aligned, as the instruction uses narrative scenarios and role playing with realistic scenarios.

>> **Technology:** The organization decided to use virtual reality, as its affordances can support immersive visualizations of workplace safety situations. The instructional design is mostly well-aligned in learning, teaching, and technology foundations.

>> **Cultural values:** The organization values being on the forefront of adopting new technologies, and in this sense, is aligned with technological foundations, but is not tightly connected to other foundations.

>> **Pragmatics:** Group training time is not possible due to their workload demands, so learners need to schedule when they take the training on their own. Some employees work remotely, so having access to the specialized equipment needed for VR is not possible for them without travel to the company's physical location. Financial resources have been exhausted purchasing the VR technology and are insufficient to train personnel how to design and develop instruction with it or to provide technical support for learners.

This scenario is a common example of an instructional design that relies too heavily on one foundation (a technology) that is disconnected from other foundations. An innovative instructional idea was developed, but it simply did not fit the pragmatics of the setting for which it was implemented.

REMEMBER

The ADDIE process can help you to begin your design process with a thorough analysis of the instructional context, problem, and possible solutions as a way of avoiding such misalignments. Each successive phase revisits and reinforces what was decided in previous phases, helping to ensure greater integration and alignment.

2

The Analysis Phase

Analyze important aspects of the organizational context to understand the resources, constraints, mission, and values of the setting that impacts the success of the instruction.

Clarify performance problems by analyzing gaps between optimal and actual performance, identifying possible causes, and generating potential solutions to determine if an instructional solution is warranted.

Get to know your learners by analyzing their characteristics and instructional needs, with an eye towards equity, access, and inclusion.

Classify different types of learning outcomes and goals by using Bloom's Taxonomy.

Find out how to conduct task analyses by breaking down instructional tasks into subskills, sub steps, and required knowledge.

Discover how to use data collection methods for your analyses such as interviews, focus groups, questionnaires, surveys, or observations.

Chapter **3**

Analyzing Learners, Contexts, and Instructional Needs

n the ADDIE model I introduce in Chapter 1, the first "A" stands for "analysis." It stands to reason, then, that the analysis phase occurs at the very beginning of the instructional design process and is the first important task of an instructional designer. During the analysis phase, the instructional designer analyzes the situation, learners, and problem to clarify the best course of action. All later instructional design decisions build upon the outcomes of the analysis phase.

Not all performance problems have an instructional solution, so understanding the problem, the situation, and the learners help you in confirming the need for, and scope of, the instruction. The questions asked during this phase will, among other things, help you decide if instruction is even the best way to address the problem.

Instructional solutions are in response to an identified need, goal, or situation that can show up as:

>> A performance problem on the job (high rates of customer complaints)

>> An organizational challenge (decreasing sales)

>> A new opportunity (a new technology being implemented)

>> A mandate (compliance training)

In this chapter, I give you the guidance you need for conducting the different types of analyses necessary for laying a solid foundation for your future instructional design, development, implementation, and evaluation decisions.

Looking at Planning Considerations

Before beginning any instructional design project, you need to spend some time analyzing the situation, the potential learners, and the need for the instruction. Conducting an instructional analysis also includes analyzing the tasks, goals, and outcomes of the instruction, but I cover that part of the process in Chapter 4, because it assumes the instructional need has already been determined through a performance or needs analysis. In this chapter, I want to focus on the earlier analyses needed to understand the problem and propose initial solutions.

An important goal of the analysis phase is to determine the anticipated scope of the project. This determination is one reason why it is important to spend time early on in the design process to gather information so you can a) increase the likelihood that the instructional intervention will work to solve the problem, and b) plan how much time and resources need to be dedicated to design, develop, implement, and evaluate the instruction.

Yet, the analysis phase is often overlooked, or at least streamlined, in many instructional-design projects. The reasons for this are usually related to one of three factors:

>> You have limited time, schedule, and resources to spend on analysis.

>> The need for the instructional design has already been identified for you.

>> Your job description is not an instructional designer; rather, you are an expert in the area for which the instruction is needed and you will also be designing (and possibly developing) the instruction. In this instance, you have directly experienced the problems, needs, or goals for the instruction firsthand, or have been assigned the solution from a supervisor.

For these reasons, there is not one standard method for conducting an instructional analysis.

EXAMPLE

To illustrate through examples, some instructional designers are asked to engage in a detailed analysis of the problem and offer potential instructional solutions. Others are told by a client or the organizational leadership what the instructional need is, the resources that can be allocated, and even the delivery mode of the instruction.

In this type of scenario, say you are an instructional designer for a tech company that is experiencing rapid growth and you have been tasked to develop new onboarding training for employees on the company's culture, policies, and technical skills required for specific roles. You are also told that the instruction needs to be delivered through video conferencing to reach multiple offices and remote employees.

Given this framework, your analyses takes less time because the problem and solution have already been decided. Likewise, if your core job is not "instructional designer" (say, you're a financial analyst instead), you may already be well aware of the problems and have already determined the best instructional solution.

The sections that follow introduce various types of instructional analyses that can be performed by an instructional designer, depending on your role and whether the instructional need and/or solution has already been confirmed for you.

Determining organizational mission and core values

For instructional designers who work for organizations, such as a company or educational institution, a good first place to start your analysis is with an investigation of what the organization needs and values. Having a clear idea of the organizational needs helps you clarify if, or what kind of, instruction may be valued. Table 3-1 presents some tips for identifying different types of organizational information that may be useful for your analyses.

REMEMBER

Collecting data about organizational needs — which are not necessarily the same as instructional needs — help you focus on the larger set of values that are most important to the organization. These data can help you to keep in mind an organization's priorities as you analyze problems or develop possible solutions.

TABLE 3-1   **Tips for Finding Organizational Information for Analyses**

Type of Information	Examples
Document analyses	Does the organization have existing documents or reports such as sales figures, quarterly reports, customer satisfaction data, enrollment data, strategic plans, or mission statements that you have access to? If so, those data may be useful to clarify what is most important to the organization.
	Document analyses may reveal trends in performance, sales, and so on that suggest a need for change or improvement. These data give you a starting point for asking questions and seeking more specific information.
Stated goals or opportunities	Has the organization identified specific goals or opportunities it wants to pursue, such as increasing sales by 10 percent or increasing customer satisfaction ratings?
	Are there plans for new programs, products, or changes in the future?
	Identifying the goals or opportunities the organization is striving towards can point to potential learning needs, performance problems, and/or instructional solutions that align with the new direction.
Interviews with management or supervisors	Interviewing management is useful for gathering their priorities for the organizational needs and opportunities for growth.
	Interview questions to ask may include:
	• What are the most pressing needs or problems the organization is facing right now?
	• What are the most important opportunities or goals that you want to pursue?
	• What customer needs or feedback are being targeted for improvement?
	Conducting interviews with multiple individuals can inform you whether there is general agreement around the most important problems, needs, or opportunities for change in the organization.

Conducting a context analysis

Context analysis examines the setting where the new change, performance improvement, or solution takes place. A context analysis is particularly useful if you don't actually work in the performance context for which you are designing instruction; it is less important if you work in it day-to-day. For instance, if you have been hired as a consultant who does not work at the organization or if you work at a different location from the setting, conducting a thorough context analysis can help you understand both the learning and performance context.

This section on context analysis is broken into two different categories of analysis:

>> Analysis of the organizational context, which focuses on gathering information about the organizational infrastructure, setting, resources, and constraints

>> Analysis of the implementation context, which focuses on factors that are relevant to implementing an instructional solution

Organizational context

Analyzing the organizational context focuses on the performance setting in which a change or solution takes place. It also includes an analysis of general aspects of the organization that are relevant to understanding the problem.

Table 3-2 summarizes a list of tips for analyzing the organizational and performance context.

TABLE 3-2   **Tips for Analyzing the Organizational Context**

Task	Description
Clarify who is asking for the new change or instructional solution	This information gives you clues about the range of possible interventions. Is the problem or solution being raised by the employees or is it being mandated by a manager? This knowledge helps you figure out where to ask more questions about the problem.
Analyze the location for the performance or solution	Where will the change or new performance occur? Will it occur during interactions onsite with customers? Will it happen while working together on teams? In a factory setting while operating dangerous machinery? Or working individually on a new software being introduced? Answering these types of questions can help you identify constraints, opportunities, or logistical considerations to the solution.
Observe or analyze the workplace climate and culture	Observe the location to pick up environmental cues and overall climate or atmosphere.
Communication systems	How do employees communicate with each other, supervisors, or clients? How does information flow down, up, and across the unit? This information helps you identify opportunities and constraints for communicating with stakeholders as well as potential instructional delivery modes.

Implementation context

At times, you can jump right into planning for the context in which the instruction will take place. One important planning activity for the analysis phase is to begin with the end in mind! That is, what kinds of information do you need to collect now in order to successfully design, develop, implement, and evaluate the instruction later?

REMEMBER

Although I discuss the implementation stage of the ADDIE model in more detail in Chapter 10, the analysis phase is the first place where you begin to analyze the contextual factors that may impact the success of your instructional implementation later (assuming your analysis of the problem points to an instructional solution).

TIP

Even though you learn about the ADDIE model as a series of steps in this book, experienced instructional designers know the process is not rigid or linear. You often go back to revisit earlier steps and look ahead to upcoming steps in the model.

Chapter 10 discusses the RIPPLES framework for implementation, developed by Dr. Dan Surry. Presented briefly here, you can use this framework as a general guide for what type of data to collect *now* to ensure a more successful instructional implementation further down the road.

Table 3-3 presents a summary of the seven components of the framework, each of which starts with the first letter of the acronym RIPPLES. Not all seven areas may be relevant for each instructional design project, but they do provide a good starting point for planning.

TABLE 3-3 **Summary of the RIPPLES Framework for Analyzing Factors for Implementing Instruction**

Planning Category	Questions to Ask During the Analysis Phase
Resources	What are the financial resources available to pay for this instructional design project, including elements such as personnel expenses, materials or technology costs, and travel or facilities costs?
Infrastructure	Does the instructional solution work within our current system, including communication requirements, facilities and technology constraints, support for learners and/or instructors?
People	Who can work on the project, and what are their key roles and responsibilities? Possible roles include subject-matter experts (SMEs), graphic artists or multimedia designers, programmers, or instructional designers.
Policies	What policies may need to be considered? Policies may include security, technology, or other HR or compliance-related policies.
Learning	What types of instructional solutions may lead to learning and/or addressing the performance problem?
Evaluation	How do we know if the instruction can be effective and address performance problems?
Support	What types of logistical support may be needed to support an instructional implementation, such as instructor, learner, or technology support?

REMEMBER

Analyzing the implementation context helps you identify any existing constraints or resources that may impact the possible scope and effectiveness of your instructional design and implementation effort.

Needs Analysis: Digging Deeper into the Need for the Instruction

Instructional design has one primary purpose: To support change. The types of change that instructional designers support best are those that involve a need for changes in knowledge, skills, performance, or attitudes. Some changes, on the other hand, may be better supported by actions other than instruction, or in combination with instructional solutions.

Take for instance the following example:

EXAMPLE

Say you are a faculty member at a university that is experiencing a decline in student enrollments in their online programs. The college administration is concerned about meeting enrollment targets and maintaining the quality of education. They approach you with the idea of conducting mandatory workshops to help faculty use more creative and engaging instructional strategies in their online classes, with the idea that this will lead to increased enrollments and better quality of instruction for students.

Although engaging in professional development with faculty about best practices seems like a good idea, you also share that it may not directly address the root cause of the enrollment decline. You point out that competition from other, less expensive universities that offer the same type of academic programs are increasing, and the college lacks cohesive marketing efforts and recruitment of prospective students.

In addition, the program websites are hard to navigate, do not provide clear instructions on who to contact for more information and are not up to date. An instructional solution to train faculty may address part of the problem, but other non-instructional factors also may be playing a significant role in the enrollment decline.

Given this, you suggest a more thorough needs analysis to better pinpoint the problem and clarify those that can be addressed through instructional solutions. Then, the administration can consider a more comprehensive approach that includes, but is not limited to, the design of new instructional workshops.

This example points to an important goal of the analysis process: to clarify the problem, possible causes, and possible solutions. This type of analysis is commonly referred to as a *needs assessment* or *needs analysis*. The end goal of a needs analysis is to help the instructional designer clarify the problem and determine if an instructional solution can help to address it successfully.

Four steps to conducting a needs analysis

The goal of a needs analysis is to gather data that an instructional designer can use to develop the most effective solution for solving a performance problem or creating change. A needs analysis leads to a more thorough understanding of the problem and an initial set of possible solutions.

REMEMBER

A needs analysis investigates the gap between actual and desired performance and gathers specific information to help generate potential solutions to solve the problem.

Although there are different types of needs analyses models in the instructional design field, the following four steps are commonly followed:

>> **Step 1:** Identify optimal performance

>> **Step 2:** Identify actual performance

>> **Step 3:** Identify possible causes

>> **Step 4:** Identify initial solutions

According to Dr. Allison Rosset, an expert in needs analysis, a needs analysis drives the instructional design process because it shapes all the early decisions that eventually impact those made in the future. The sections that follow elaborate on the four steps to take for a needs analysis.

REMEMBER

Sometimes instructional designers are assigned the job of developing specific instructional solutions or training programs — they are not asked to do a needs analysis of the problem. This often happens in response to a new initiative (such as a new software solution being unveiled), where the learning of new knowledge and skills is a part of a broader solution. In these cases, the problem (and/or the solution) has already been decided by others in the organization.

In such situations, your needs analysis may focus more on understanding the context, learners, and optimal performance goals rather than a deeper analysis of the problem and potential solutions; it is not a good use of time and resources to invest in full-scale problem analyses. However, it is always beneficial to continue revisiting your instructional decisions in light of the organizational needs that are expressed and for which the instruction is being designed.

Identifying optimal performance

Often referred to as a *performance gap analysis*, one of the first steps of a needs analysis is to collect data that helps you identify the differences between the desired performance and the actual performance. Identifying what the performance *should be* (optimal) versus what it is now (actual) is the focus of this step of the needs analysis process. Figure 3-1 illustrates how identifying optimal performances fits into the performance gap analysis.

FIGURE 3-1: Identifying optimal performances in a gap analysis.

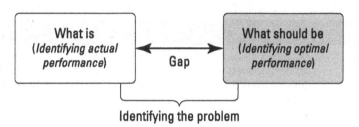

Identifying optimal performance in a needs analysis means figuring out the highest standard of achievement that people, teams, or organizations can perform in a specific area. You want to discover what "optimal" performance looks like when someone is doing an excellent, high-quality job, and getting desired results. Identifying optimal performance is about aiming for the stars!

Here are some examples of optimal performance in different contexts:

>> **Sales team:** Consistently exceeding sales targets, maintaining strong customer relationships, and securing new clients regularly

>> **Manufacturing process:** Producing products at maximum efficiency while minimizing defects, errors, and waste, leading to high-quality output

>> **Customer service:** Responding promptly to customer inquiries, resolving issues on the first contact, having regular repeat customers, and receiving consistently positive feedback from customers

>> **Health and fitness:** Consistently helping clients achieve their fitness goals by creating customized fitness programs, motivating, and encouraging perseverance, prioritizing safety, building positive and lasting relationships, and attracting new clients through a strong social media presence

>> **Project management:** Completing projects on time, within budget, and meeting or exceeding all project goals and quality standards

>> **Product development:** Consistently producing innovative and market-leading products, staying ahead of industry trends, and securing patents for new inventions

How does an instructional designer identify optimal performances? The methods used can look very different depending on each situation, but instructional designers often analyze a variety of sources, such as expert interviews, reports, supervisor recommendations, and so on.

Table 3-4 presents some tips for collecting and analyzing information on optimal performances:

TABLE 3-4   ## Strategies for Identifying *Optimal* Performance

Strategy	Information to Collect
Interview supervisors	Ask supervisors who the top performers are and what makes them a top performer. Questions to consider: Who is the best at this skill or performance? Who are the first people you go to in your unit when you have a problem or need advice?
Interview and/or observe top performers	Find out what the top performers know or do differently that distinguish them from other employees. Interview those people and ask them how they do their job so effectively. This can include knowledge, best practices, working collaboratively, tips, strategies for time management or organization, and so on. You find example interview questions in the Appendix.
Conduct focus groups with experts	Conduct a focus group with a small group of experts to discuss the knowledge, best practices, and strategies that they feel leads to their successful performance. Use flipcharts, whiteboards, or sticky notes to brainstorm and document important, common practices. Follow up later with a copy of the list and ask if anything is missing.
Ask "hindsight is 20-20" questions	Ask experts what they wish they knew or were trained on when they first started the job. Were there pivotal situations where they had to learn a new skill or practice to solve a problem? How did they learn them?
Conduct benchmarking	Benchmarking is an analysis technique that identifies optimal performances by comparing them to an established standard, best practice, or key performance outcome. Benchmarking can be comparing against a similar organization, industry standards, or internal performance metrics. Identify documents that may provide information related to differences in performance or benchmarking data. Example documents can include sales reports, budget documents, customer satisfaction, costs, production timelines, and so on.

Identifying actual performance

As mentioned in the last section, a performance gap analysis is the difference between the desired performance and what it is now. The prior section covered identifying optimal or desired performances. This section explains the process of identifying actual performances. The difference between these two give you a clearer sense of the problem you are addressing. Figure 3-2 illustrates how identifying actual performance fits into the performance gap analysis process.

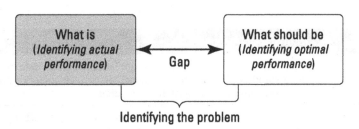

FIGURE 3-2:
Identifying actual
performances in
a gap analysis.

Identifying actual performances during a performance gap analysis involves analyzing how tasks are currently being performed and comparing the results with the desired outcomes. The goals here are to clarify what performance(s) need to change and to gather data on what factors are influencing them. You can analyze actual performance data at the level of individual employees, a department, a job classification, or an entire organization itself, depending on the type of problem or situation.

Data collection methods for identifying actual performances are like those for identifying optimal performances. Table 3-5 presents some tips for collecting and analyzing information on actual performances.

TABLE 3-5 **Strategies for Identifying *Actual* Performances**

Strategy	Information to Collect
Gather information from supervisors	Interview supervisors at varying levels of management and ask them to describe the current situation from their perspective and what tasks they believe are not being performed effectively by employees.
	Possible questions include: Where do you see weaknesses in your unit? What are employees not performing well? What would you like to see changed to improve their performance that they are not doing now? What are competitors doing better?
Gather information from the target population of learners	Gather data from potential learners about the problem from their perspective. You can collect data by using methods such as interviews, surveys, or observing the employees directly. See Chapter 11 for more information on survey design and the Appendix for sample questions you can ask for the needs analysis.
	For example: What are the most common problems you experience while doing your job? What do you need the most to improve your performance? What are the biggest roadblocks or challenges you face? What knowledge or skills would you need in order to perform your job more effectively? What incentives are in place? How motivated are you to perform your job?

(continued)

TABLE 3-5 *(continued)*

Strategy	Information to Collect
Analyze data from customers or clients	If you have access to customer or client feedback, those data may be useful for understanding performance problems. Focus on customer complaints and/or common patterns of suggestions or feedback.
Collect examples	Gather and review examples of completed tasks or products by including reports, completed forms, or other work products.
Find information and documents to analyze	Identify documents that may provide information related to current performances. Example documents include sales reports, budget documents, accident reports, error rates, production timelines, and so on. Analyze the collected data to identify trends, patterns, and areas of concern.

After you have collected data on actual performances, you want to compare them with optimal performances, benchmarks, standards, or expectations. This process involves identifying the gaps where the current performance falls short of what is required or desired. This method may generate a list of many different performance problems or needs, some small and some more significant. With these needs in mind, the next step we cover is to more thoroughly investigate possible causes of the problem.

TIP

After you identify gaps in performance, this is a good time to think about how to best measure actual and optimal performances. This may become important during the evaluation phase (see Chapter 11), when you seek to answer questions about whether your instruction led to learning, better performance, or made an impact.

There are different levels of evaluation of an instructional intervention. (Again, see Chapter 11 for a more detailed look at that topic.) To summarize the points I make there briefly, in addition to evaluating if learners liked the instruction and learned from it, you can also evaluate whether they applied what they learned or if the instruction impacted broader organizational goals such as productivity, cost savings, and so on. The data you are collecting now about actual and optimal performances may be useful for comparing or analyzing changes after the instruction ends.

Identifying possible causes

As you collect data related to optimal and actual performances, you begin to gain insights into possible causes of the problem. Often referred to as a *root cause analysis*, the next step in a needs analysis is to identify and prioritize possible underlying causes of a problem. Sometimes the cause is straightforward, such as when an organization is rolling out a new initiative and training is needed. Other times, problems are complex and may have multiple causes, only some of which can be addressed through instruction.

The "Five Whys" technique

One method that is often used to drill down to the root cause of a problem is the Five Whys technique. This technique, developed by Sakichi Toyoda, the founder of Toyota Industries, involves repeatedly asking "why" questions. For instance, when looking at a performance problem, ask yourself, "Why did this problem occur?" Then, identify the most obvious reason. Then, repeat the process by taking the answer to the first "why" and asking "why" again. Each time, you gain deeper insights into the range of possible causes of a problem.

EXAMPLE

Take for instance a performance problem of employees failing to apply what they learned from a cyber security onboarding training, exposing the organization to various data security risks. Asking the five whys about why this problem is occurring may look like this:

1. **Why?** The employees find the training content difficult to understand.

2. **Why?** The training materials are heavy on technical jargon and complex explanations.

3. **Why?** The training content was created by IT experts who are accustomed to technical terms.

4. **Why?** No instructional design review or instructional strategies are in place to help employees apply what they learned to the job.

5. **Why?** The training development process lacks collaboration between IT experts and instructional designers.

In this example, a possible root cause of low application of the cybersecurity training is the lack of collaboration between IT experts and instructional designers during the instructional development. Given this, one solution could involve restructuring the existing training materials to make them more accessible to a non-technical audience and adding activities that focus learners on how to apply the knowledge and skills gained to workplace situations.

Three common reasons for performance problems

Dr. Allison Rosset has identified several possible reasons for performance problems, three of which are described in Table 3-6.

TABLE 3-6   ## Typical Reasons for Performance Problems

Possible Cause	Example Questions to Ask
Lack of skill or knowledge	Do the learners know how to perform successfully and consistently?
	Are there knowledge or performance deficiencies?
	Is the information needed for the job up to date?
	Do learners understand the performance standards they are expected to meet?
	Do learners get feedback on their performance?
Limiting factors within the environment	Do learners have access to the tools, equipment, or technology they need to perform effectively?
	Do learners have the supplies, resources, or people available to them to help them perform effectively?
	Can learners find or get important information related to the performance?
Lack of incentives or motivation	What are the consequences or incentives for poor performance?
	What are the incentives for effective performance?
	Is compensation tied to merit or performance?
	Do learners want to perform the job well?
	Has there been a change in motivation over time?

Identifying initial solutions

After a range of possible causes to performance problems are identified and prioritized, the next step is to brainstorm and develop potential solutions to address them. These solutions can target many different underlying factors; however, solutions involving instructional design are those that are most concerned with knowledge or skills needs, because they can be potentially resolved through an instructional intervention.

Determining if instruction is the best solution

The *first step* in generating solutions is to confirm what problems or needed changes can be addressed, partially or fully, through instruction. Ask yourself, "is instruction the best way to address the problem?" Instruction is often a potential solution to one of the following problems or needs:

>> Performance problems caused by lack of knowledge, skills, or access to important job information

>> New initiatives that require learning of new knowledge or skills to effectively perform a new technique, procedure, or business purpose

>> New mandates that require documentation that specific knowledge or skills have been achieved by learners in specific units or across an entire organization

REMEMBER

Instruction is the most appropriate solution when the change needed requires new knowledge or skills.

The *second step* is to identify whether instruction is currently being offered related to the problem. If it is, ask yourself, "Why is the current instruction not working to solve the problem?" Do you want to revise the instruction, add new sections to the existing instruction or develop completely new instruction?

EXAMPLE

Your analyses likely uncovered causes of the problem that help you identify possible solutions. For instance:

>> Perhaps the instruction is using an outdated delivery system that no longer is compatible with technology systems. In this case, you may want to revise and refresh the instruction with a new delivery mode.

>> If the instructional content is relevant, but it lacks interactivity, practice opportunities, or applications to the job or real life, then you may be able to revise the instruction to include more interactive practice opportunities.

>> On the other hand, perhaps the instruction has outdated content and lacks relevance to the performance. In this case, you may instead choose to create new instruction, because the content needs an overhaul.

>> If no instruction exists related to the need, then you likely would create new instruction if it is useful in addressing the problem.

You may find other causes to problems you identified that do not require an instructional solution but can be part of a comprehensive solution.

EXAMPLE

Examples of non-instructional solutions may include:

>> Job aids that are displayed where the work is performed (flowcharts, infographics, checklists, and forms, for example)

>> Development of a mentoring system

>> Performance reviews and feedback

>> Incentives, rewards, or recognition systems

>> Reference manuals

Proposing solutions based on the needs analysis

After you narrow down some possible solutions, it is advisable to summarize your findings into a report. The report can be succinct and focused. An example outline of a report may look like the following:

>> Summarize the purpose, problem, and needed change (the task not being performed effectively and the new initiative being proposed, for example).

>> Present how you conducted the analysis (interviews, observations, focus groups, surveys, stakeholders, and/or reports, for example).

>> Summarize performance differences between actual and optimal performances.

>> List the most likely causes of the problem.

>> Present possible solutions to the problems (both instructional and non-instructional, if applicable), along with a statement of goals.

>> Present plans for implementation (delivery system preferences or constraints, budget, personnel needed, and projected timeline, for example).

Leveraging Learner Analyses

A learner analysis focuses specifically on your target learners for the instruction. The purpose of a learner analysis is to gain a better understanding of their characteristics and needs. A learner analysis helps you ensure that you are considering the perspective of the learner from the outset of the design process.

Your goal is to discover more about their background, knowledge, skills, attitudes, and points of view. You may have already started a learner analysis during the gap analysis phase if you were analyzing optimal and actual performances. A learner analysis extends prior analyses by focusing on characteristics of the learners that may influence your instructional design decisions.

Getting to know your learners

Establishing at the outset of a learner analysis that, in most situations, learners are a diverse group, is important. Even if they work in the same unit and have similar levels of prior training, they come to the learning situation with very different background knowledge and experiences. As I discuss in Chapter 2, any new learning is always affected by our prior knowledge and experiences. Although we cannot typically design personalized learning experiences for every learner individually, we can learn about their commonalities and differences in order to design for a broad range of learner needs more effectively.

What kind of information is important for an instructional designer to know about learners? The answer depends on your context and how much you already know about them. Table 3-7 provides some key elements typically considered in a learner analysis.

TABLE 3-7 **Common Elements of a Learner Analysis**

Element	Description or Questions to Ask
General information	Includes information such as job titles, number of years in the unit, demographics, languages spoken, and so on.
Knowledge and performance needs	What do the learners already know or perform well now? Where is there room for improvement? Collecting this information helps you confirm what needs to be learned and figure out what learners need to know as a starting point. (**Note:** This part of learner analysis may have been conducted already as part of a gap analysis).
Reason for participating in the instruction	Identifies learners' motivations for engaging in the instruction and their goals or expectations. Learner motivation is very different for a situation where the instruction is mandated versus when an individual chooses it based on interests or an intention to learn new skills or to work towards a promotion.
Delivery mode or technical experience	Identifies learners' attitudes toward certain types of delivery systems. Are there certain delivery systems they like or don't like? In what ways do they like to learn or be trained? What is their level of proficiency with technology and digital tools, especially if you are considering online learning or technology-based instruction?
Time constraints of learners	Understanding any time limitations or scheduling constraints that learners may have due to their job requirements is important to consider early in the instructional design process. This information may help you think about different delivery modes such as whether the instruction is better delivered asynchronously or synchronously.
Accessibility needs	Identifies the learners' accessibility requirements, such as accommodations for individuals with disabilities or differing language needs. It also identifies access needs as related to virtual or in person instructional delivery methods. This information may help you in developing instructional materials that are accessible and inclusive.

REMEMBER

By conducting learner analyses, instructional designers can create instructional materials and strategies that are more learner-centered and better aligned with the needs and characteristics of the target audience. See the Appendix for a sample learner analysis questionnaire.

Identifying incentives and motivations

When conducting a learner analysis, identifying what's actually motivating your learners to participate in the instruction will help your instructional design, development, and implementation decision making. Learner motivations are the reasons they are participating in the instruction, but the nature of those motivations is quite different if the instruction is mandated or is self-selected based on the learner's own goals and interests.

Interest-driven motivations — in contrast to compliance-oriented — generally lead to more active and engaged learners who recognize a need for the instruction. Analyzing whether learners are on board with the instruction gives you a sense of whether they are willing to invest the time required of them to participate. Are they satisfied with the status quo? Or are they interested to learn more about this topic?

Another related area that may impact learner motivation involves the incentives for participating in the instruction. Are there incentives in place, such as time off from work or a flexible work arrangement to take the instruction on their own time? Having strong support from supervisors to create the time and space for the instruction is important for a successful instructional implementation.

Some questions related to incentives may include:

>> Are employees accountable to HR or managers for completion of the training? Are there consequences for not completing it?

>> Do learners have an allocated budget, travel, and/or leave time to participate?

>> Do learners need to fit in the instruction during or after the workday or do they need time off to participate?

REMEMBER

Understanding learner motivations toward the instruction helps increase the likelihood that they are actually present and engaged for the length of the course.

Ensuring equity, inclusivity, and accessibility

Supporting equity-focused instructional design begins during the analysis phase to ensure the instruction is inclusive and accessible to all learners. A learner analysis considers any factors that can lead to a design where not all learners feel safe, welcome, and represented in the learning experience due to their race, ethnicity, gender or gender identity, sexual orientation, socioeconomic status, language, religious affiliation, disability, and so on.

Prioritizing an equity-centered approach starts with an analysis of potential differences or inequalities that may exist for learners and then recognizing how they may be inadvertently perpetuated by the instructional solution without explicit awareness of them.

Equity-focused perspectives for instructional design recognize the role that power structures and systemic inequities have had on historically marginalized groups of people and are cognizant of the fact that our designs can continue to perpetuate those same inequities without conscious awareness and active dismantling of them. Although equity-focused perspectives on instructional design cannot be reduced to tips and strategies, I nonetheless draw your attention to a few ideas that can be included in our learner analyses. (See Table 3-8.)

TABLE 3-8   Learner Analyses for Inclusivity

Tasks	Purpose/Examples
Analyze learner information with an intention towards inclusivity	Collecting information about your learners helps you anticipate their unique needs and enhance the probability that your design is inclusive and accessible. If you are using a survey, your questions should make all learners feel welcome.
	For instance, asking learners to select their gender as "male" or "female" excludes those with non-binary gender identities. Instead, use gender-inclusive language, preferred pronouns, or ask learners to optionally report information in an open-ended question. Ask if there is any information that they provide that they do not want to be shared with others as part of the instructional design process.
Ask learners about technology availability	If you are considering remote, technology-delivered instruction such as a learning management system (LMS), video conferencing, or other technology, solicit information about learners' access to those technologies at home and at the workplace. Technology access can present challenges for some learners as related to cost, bandwidth speed, and device/computer availability. Equitable decisions about technology recognizes that there may be disparities in access for your learners that need to be addressed at the outset.

(continued)

TABLE 3-8 *(continued)*

Tasks	Purpose/Examples
Identify barriers to accessibility	An equitable approach to instructional design actively seeks to identify and remove barriers to accessibility of the instruction. The instruction being designed should be accessible to, and inclusive of, a wide range of learners, including those with disabilities or diverse language needs. Be aware of any existing policies of your organization related to disability accommodations and seek to make the instruction accessible to as many different learners as possible. Ask learners to provide information related to accessibility needs and preferences.
	The Universal Design for Learning (UDL) framework helps an instructional designer to remove barriers to creating inclusive instruction where all learners can succeed. The core principle of UDL (discussed in more detail in Chapter 9) is to provide multiple means of representation, expression, and engagement for learners. Applying an equity lens to universal design may include:
	• Making instructional materials available in multiple formats, including multimedia elements captioned and described for those with diverse language, sight, or hearing needs and/or accessibility features for text, PDFs, videos/audio, LMS pages, and alternative formats.
	• Using images, language, or photos that reflect a broad range of potential learners as related to race, ethnicity, gender, disability, age, and so on. Learners should be able to see themselves represented in the instructional materials.
	Find out from the target learners if there are any accessibility needs before designing the instruction.

Methods for Collecting Data

Thankfully, you can use a variety of data collection methods during the analysis phase, to gather information. These data collection methods may be employed during any of the different types of analyses covered so far, including context, implementation, needs, or learner analyses. Sometimes, due to time constraints, you may want to use the same data collection method (interviews with experts, for example) to collect different types of information that inform a variety of analyses.

Your choice of data collection method can vary depending on the project, the information needed, and the available resources. Each method has pros and cons and your selection is based on your project's needs and constraints. Also, some methods may be better suited for different types of analyses. For example, interviews or focus groups with a select number of expert performers may be the most useful method for identifying optimal performances in a gap analysis.

Four of the most common data collection methods include interviews, focus groups, questionnaires or surveys, and observations. The next few sections look at each method in greater detail.

Interviews

Interviews are useful early on in a project to collect in-depth information to inform you about the problem. Interviews can be conducted with subject matter experts (SMEs), potential learners, and key stakeholders to gain insights into their perspectives, experiences, and expectations related to the problem or need at hand.

TIP

Some practical tips for conducting interviews during the analysis phase include:

>> Conducting interviews either in person, by video conferencing, or by telephone, depending on your budget, access, and time constraints. Conducting interviews by phone or video conferencing may cut down on expenses if travel would be necessary for an in-person interview. The downside of phone or video conferencing for interviews is that you lose a sense of the actual work environment.

>> Using some pre-determined questions as part of the interview but also allowing for open-ended discussions. Send the questions to the individual(s) in advance, so they have a chance to prepare. Ask if there are any questions that you did not ask that are important for understanding the situation, job, problem, and so on.

>> Recognizing political and power structures with interviews. Organizations often have hierarchical structures that potentially impact the power dynamics of interviews. Individuals may feel uncomfortable sharing perspectives that may possibly be shown to supervisors and that could identify them. Fears related to power and political dynamics can influences interviewees' willingness to be open with you in their interviews.

>> Conducting interviews either with one person at a time or including others. (The latter option may save you some time.)

REMEMBER

The advantages to using interviews are that they are easy to conduct, can be used for many different types of analysis, and can help you understand the people and situation from their point of view. Disadvantages are that interviews can be labor and time intensive.

Focus groups

Focus groups involve small, structured group discussions. Focus groups can include experts in a position to identify optimal performances and important tasks for the job or the target audience or learners. Focus groups provide a collaborative forum for open-ended discussions. By holding discussions with multiple participants at the same time, you gain insights into shared concerns, attitudes, and opinions regarding the problems or needs of learners as well as what, for them, counts as an optimal performance.

The first step in setting up a focus group is determining who participates. Will it be a panel of experts? A group of people with varying levels of expertise and time in the job? The target learners? You can also run more than one type of focus group if needed. For instance, you may want a focus group with top performers if you are identifying optimal performances, but supervisors or target learners if identifying actual performances.

As with interviews, be aware of hierarchical structures within your focus groups and encourage multiple viewpoints. Your goals inform how you select focus-group participants. Functional focus groups (individuals with similar roles and responsibilities) or cross-functional focus groups (individuals from different areas in the organization) will give you different types of information. Choosing one will depend on whether you want a broader view of the issues from multiple areas of expertise or want to stay focused on a specific area.

Focus groups have advantages and disadvantages. The main advantages are that they bring a variety of individuals together to share a range of experiences and perspectives relatively efficiently. Focus groups may lead to insightful discussions through collaborative brainstorming and building on each other's ideas. The main disadvantages of focus groups are the potential for power dynamics, limited representation of participants, and dominant voices that restrict the perspectives discussed.

TIP

After you identify the focus group participants, some practical tips for structuring and facilitating a focus group include:

» Getting the conversation started with an open brainstorming session where the participants write down everything that comes to mind that they think is important for the job, performance, or need at hand. Flip charts work well if you are in the same physical location. Otherwise, web-based word processing, chats, or whiteboard software work well in video conferencing situations. Take notes on everything said.

» Asking participants to first look over the lists created during brainstorming sessions and then start categorizing and sorting the topics in ways that are meaningful to them. Facilitate discussion on what topics are duplicates or reflect different concepts, problems, ideas, tasks, and so on. If meeting in person, post-it notes or large post-it charts are useful for facilitating this task. If the group is not in person, web-based software (such as a shared word processing program) enables them to move text around.

>> Preparing your participants in advance with questions you want them to discuss during the focus group.

>> Following up after the focus group with a summarized list of the topics discussed. Ask for confirmation and clarification where needed.

Questionnaires and surveys

Surveys and questionnaires are paper-based or web-based instruments that ask people questions about a topic, problem, or need. They are useful for gathering information and opinions on performance problems, training needs, knowledge gaps, or learner characteristics. You use surveys and questionnaires to collect information from people who are widely dispersed geographically.

Advantages for using surveys or questionnaires include:

>> They can be administered to many stakeholders, learners, or experts (in contrast to 1-on-1 interviews, which are more time consuming).

>> They can be administered and returned anonymously.

>> They are cost- and time-efficient.

>> Web-based survey tools (Qualtrics, for example) compile survey responses, making analysis of large numbers of surveys easier.

Disadvantages of using surveys or questionnaires include:

>> The information collected is narrow in scope. For this reason, surveys are not always the best data collection method to use early in a project when you are focused on figuring out problems, optimal and actual performances, causes, and solutions.

>> Learners can misinterpret questions and aren't easily able to ask clarification or follow-up questions.

>> Return rates of surveys are often low.

For more on the different ways you can evaluate an instruction's effectiveness with the help of surveys and questionnaires, check out Chapter 11.

Examples of different types of question designs for surveys are presented briefly here. See the Appendix for additional examples of survey questions that could be asked during the analysis phase.

An example of an open-ended question:

Please answer the following question about your experiences.

- Are there any performance gaps or deficiencies you observe among employees in this role?

An example of a yes-no question:

Please circle Yes or No to the following questions:

- I feel I have the necessary knowledge and skill to perform my job well. Yes or No.

An example of a rating scale question:

On a scale from 1 to 5, how would you rate your current level of knowledge and skills related to your job responsibilities:

1. Not at all knowledgeable

2. Mostly unknowledgeable

3. Knowledgeable about some skills

4. Knowledgeable about most skills

5. Highly knowledgeable

Observations

Observations involve directly watching individuals or groups perform tasks in their natural work or learning environments. Observations can help identify performance gaps, the general culture and atmosphere of the environment, and areas where performance is effective. You can conduct observations of expert performers as well as of your target audience of learners.

Advantages of observations are:

>> You get a clear idea of the environment and the job performance.

>> Observations can be combined with interview questions before, during, or after the observation.

>> It may point to other problems in addition to performance issues.

Disadvantages of observation are:

>> They are time intensive.

>> If you are unfamiliar with the job requirements, you may not catch all the situations where problems occur.

>> You may not pick up on how the expert performs the job differently without repeated observations of them as well as observations of your target learners.

REMEMBER

Conducting analyses requires careful planning and selection of the most appropriate data collection methods based on the goals and context of your project. Although presented separately for clarity, it is common for instructional designers to combine multiple methods during the analysis phase.

Chapter **4**

Analyzing Tasks, Goals, and Outcomes

I introduce the Analysis phase of the ADDIE model in Chapter 3, focusing specifically on analyses of learners, contexts, and needs. After completing those analyses, the next step in the Analysis phase is to begin examining the tasks, knowledge, and skills to learn during the instruction. This is referred to as a task analysis. (If you're not familiar with the ADDIE model, check out my overview in Chapter 1.)

This chapter is all about conducting a task analysis, an important step for instructional designers because it outlines and identifies the content that will eventually become the basis for the instruction. After you outline the knowledge, skills, and sequences of tasks that need to be learned, you then are ready to start designing the instruction. In this chapter, I walk you through the different skills and methods of performing a task analysis.

TIP

Some important tips to keep in mind about task analyses before diving into the chapter:

>> Task analyses define the essential content needed for the instruction.

>> Unless you are both the instructional designer and subject matter expert, task analyses require working with subject-matter experts (SMEs) to clarify the knowledge and skills to be learned.

>> Task analyses help you organize and sequence the content.

Classifying Types of Learning

If you conducted a thorough needs analysis (see Chapter 3 for more on that topic), you probably already started identifying broad goals for the instruction that are based on an understanding of the problem and need for the instruction. After you know the goals for the instruction, you are ready to classify what type of learning it involves.

REMEMBER

In Chapter 2, I define learning as a change in a person's knowledge, skills, attitudes, or performance. Instructional designers are focused on designing instruction that leads to this kind of learning. So, before you start a task analysis, classifying the type of learning outcome is important. There are significant differences in the way you would go about analyzing tasks and designing instruction for learning how to perform a golf swing versus computing taxes correctly. You categorize different types of learning outcomes because you often use similar types of instructional strategies for a given category of learning.

In this chapter, I cover several ways of categorizing different learning outcomes. First, I talk about what's involved in classifying the overall type of learning that is needed. Learning is traditionally classified according to one of three distinct types of learning outcomes:

>> **Cognitive:** Learning new knowledge, concepts, and cognitive skills

>> **Attitudes or values:** Developing a new intention, belief, motivation, or choice

>> **Physical skills or actions:** Performing physical or psychomotor skills

Although some instructional designs may be complex and involve multiple types of learning, I present them separately here for clarity's sake.

Learning new knowledge, concepts, or cognitive skills

The cognitive category of learning outcomes entails developing new knowledge, skills, or understanding. It is associated with cognitive or thinking processes such as remembering, analyzing, classifying, or solving problems. This category is a very common learning outcome for instructional design solutions. Later in the chapter, I show you how to categorize different cognitive learning outcomes using a well-known model in the instructional design field called Bloom's Taxonomy. For now, look at a variety of examples of the cognitive category of learning.

EXAMPLE

Examples of the cognitive category of learning include:

>> Solving a health problem by troubleshooting its cause

>> Solving a math problem by applying an equation

>> Comprehending a text by analyzing and interpreting its meaning

>> Analyzing and evaluating information, such as critically assessing the credibility of sources when conducting research

>> Distinguishing between works of art from different historical periods (Renaissance, Baroque, Neoclassicism, Impressionism, Modernism, Post-Modernism)

>> Making predictions and drawing conclusions from evidence about the best insulation material for keeping liquids cold or hot

In sum, the cognitive category of learning outcomes involves changes in knowledge, thinking, understanding, or application of knowledge to solve problems.

Developing attitudes and values

The next category of learning is about attitudes, intentions, interests, beliefs, values, and emotions. Development of attitudes typically occurs over time. For instance, an individual participating in an opportunity to explore the performing arts may first attend a ballet performance, pay attention to it, and possibly find it enjoyable. Over time, that same individual, after attending many ballets, learning more about it, or possibly taking ballet classes themselves, may grow to appreciate the art form more deeply, as reflected in values and interests that developed over time and their increased participation.

Examples of the attitude and values category of learning include:

>> Applying mindfulness practices to manage stress, improve self-awareness, and channel attention to the present moment

>> Valuing environmental stewardship, sustainability, conservation, and responsible consumption as a lifestyle choice

>> Learning to appreciate and participate in gratitude practices daily

>> Learning to enjoy and appreciate a new genre of music

>> Prioritizing volunteerism in one's community

>> Valuing diversity, equity, inclusivity, and belongingness

The attitudes and values category of learning outcomes focuses on emotions, attitudes, values, and the development of a person's choice of personal action or emotional state. It encompasses how individuals feel as well as their motivation or intention. In general, attitude formation is difficult to define, develop, and measure, as it is driven by personal choices, interests, and values.

Performing physical actions

Another category of learning is what is referred to as *psychomotor* — learning that involves physical actions and skills related to performing or coordinating movements. This type of learning involves moving one's body to perform certain tasks or activities, such as athletics, fitness, dance, performing arts, or operating machinery or equipment. Physical performance skills can range from simple physical actions to more complex and creative physical actions. These skills often require practice, coordination, and/or muscle memory.

Examples of the physical performance category of learning may include:

>> Riding a bicycle by using balance, pedaling, and steering

>> Weightlifting movements such as performing a deadlift by using a kettle bell with proper form

>> Learning to inject medication to patients

>> Performing different dance styles by using proper form and musicality

>> Cooking skills including measuring, chopping, frying, or baking

>> Carpentry skills such as measuring, sawing, drilling, and sanding with precision

- >> Gardening skills of planting, pruning, weeding, and watering

- >> Driving a vehicle (steering, braking, accelerating, looking for blind spots, parking)

In sum, the physical category of learning involves developing physical skills and abilities.

REMEMBER

Although presented separately, instruction frequently involves more than one type of learning category. For instance, engaging in environmental conservation (attitudes and values) may also entail gaining new knowledge about the types of materials that can be recycled or how to plant trees (physical action). In such cases, you have to outline tasks and objectives for each type of learning and show how they are interconnected.

Classifying Goals and Tasks with Bloom's Taxonomy

Bloom's taxonomy is a framework for classifying learning goals and tasks that was developed by a group of educators with Benjamin Bloom in the 1950s and later revised by Lorin Anderson and David Krathwohl in 2001. This taxonomy is a foundational tool in instructional design that provides a comprehensive framework for classifying different types of instructional tasks within the cognitive category of learning.

The word *taxonomy* in this context simply means classification. A framework such as Bloom's taxonomy is useful for categorizing different types of learning goals and tasks in order to create instructional objectives, strategies, and assessments. (See Chapter 5 for more on that topic.)

By focusing on the cognitive actions that learners actually do, instructional designers can then break down goals and tasks by using action verbs that describe the thinking process. A framework such as Bloom's taxonomy gives us a starting point for translating goals into tasks and learning outcomes. This framework makes it less daunting for an instructional designer to start linking performance goals with specific instructional methods.

The goal of Bloom's taxonomy is to classify cognitive skills into varying levels of complexity. In this way, Bloom's taxonomy is a hierarchical framework comprised of six levels, with each level advancing on a continuum from simple to complex. Higher levels of the framework are assumed to be inclusive of all lower levels of skills in the framework.

Table 4-1 gives a summary at-a-glance of the six levels of Bloom's taxonomy.

TABLE 4-1 **A Brief Summary of the Six Levels of Bloom's Taxonomy**

Level	Description
Remember	Goal is to remember or recall facts or information.
	Learners engage in recognizing and recalling previously learned material.
Understand	Goal is to demonstrate meaning and comprehension by explaining ideas or concepts, summarizing major points, generating examples, or classifying examples.
	Learners grasp the meaning of what they have learned and create connections between the new knowledge and their prior knowledge.
Apply	Leaners apply knowledge and procedures to a situation to solve problems or address real-world challenges.
	Learners execute a sequence of steps or apply procedures to life or work challenges.
Analyze	Learners break down complex information into its components, identifying patterns, relationships, and connections between different ideas.
	Tasks include differentiating between relevant and irrelevant parts and understanding the underlying structure of concepts.
Evaluate	Learners make judgments, assessments, or decisions based on criteria, evidence, or standards.
	Tasks include critically evaluating the relevance, reliability, and soundness of an idea.
Create	Learners generate new ideas or solutions.
	Tasks include synthesizing knowledge to produce ideas, hypotheses, or products that are both new and original.

In the following sections, I present more detail on each of the six levels of classification of Bloom's taxonomy.

Remembering

The Remembering level of Bloom's taxonomy involves recalling facts and information. This first category is about developing a foundation of factual knowledge that you can later use for understanding, applying, analyzing, evaluating, and creating knowledge in the higher-level categories of learning.

The remembering category of learning has two main thinking processes:

>> Recognizing

>> Recalling

EXAMPLE

The Remembering category means that learners can memorize, recognize, or recall something they learned.

Example cognitive tasks associated with the Remembering category include:

>> Recognizing facts, such as recognizing where the emergency exits are located

>> Recognizing salient information, such as recognizing the symptoms of a heart attack

>> Labeling information, such as labeling the sections of a form correctly

>> Stating of a rule or procedure such as stating the steps to performing CPR

>> Recalling specific regulations or policies such as data security policies

>> Recalling information such as the key features, pricing, and specifications of a new product

After you identify that you have a task or objective in the Remembering category, you use strategies and assessments later in the design phase that specifically reinforce the learning of facts and information necessary for that task or objective.

REMEMBER

The Remembering category is about recalling facts and information. It does not mean that learners understand or apply it, but it is a step along the way. Later phases of understanding draw upon a foundation of factual knowledge, as it provides the groundwork for learners to build upon when engaging higher levels of understanding.

Understanding

The Understanding level of Bloom's taxonomy involves more than just memorizing facts (more than just the Remembering level, in other words); it requires learners to comprehend concepts and relationships between ideas. In the Understanding category, learners translate facts into personal meanings through interpreting and explaining ideas, classifying, comparing, and making inferences.

Understanding involves a process of meaning-making and generating connections between what is being learned and prior knowledge. (See Chapter 2 for more on that topic.) At this level, learners demonstrate understanding by explaining ideas or concepts in their own words, summarizing information, or interpreting data. They can grasp the meaning and significance of what they learned.

Examples of the Understanding level of Bloom's taxonomy include:

>> Explaining the physiological processes behind a specific medical condition

>> Classifying different examples of trees as either broad leaf or needle leaf

>> Inferring principles of effective leadership after comparing biographies of successful leaders

>> Giving examples and non-examples of active listening

In contrast to the Remembering category, the focus of the Understanding category is on promoting deeper comprehension of concepts and principles. Understanding sets the stage for higher-order levels of thinking. During your Design phase, you select instructional strategies that align with the tasks of the understanding category.

Applying

In the Applying category of Bloom's taxonomy, learners apply their knowledge and understanding to solve problems or carry out a procedure in real-world situations. That is, learners use their knowledge in practical situations in life or on the job. In this category, learners are not simply remembering and understanding information; they are actively using their knowledge to solve problems or complete tasks in the real world.

The Applying level can be thought of as executing knowledge and/or procedures to address familiar tasks, such as following specific steps in a fixed order. It can also involve implementing conceptual knowledge to situations that are not familiar, such as applying legal theory to analyze a new situation. At the applying level, learners use their knowledge in new situations outside of the instructional environment.

Examples of the Applying level of Bloom's taxonomy include:

>> Applying math and spreadsheet skills to calculate a family budget

>> Applying a previous case law ruling to a current legal case

>> Using financial software skills learned in a training program to run a financial report

>> Applying sales techniques learned with instructional role playing while engaging with potential customers on the job

>> Applying foreign language skills conversationally with others in the real world (at the market or on public transportation, for example)

REMEMBER

The Applying category of Bloom's taxonomy focuses on learners extending their understanding from the instructional context to the real world in new situations.

Analyzing

The Analyzing category of Bloom's taxonomy requires a higher level of abstraction and critical thinking than prior levels. Analyzing involves breaking down concepts, examining them closely, and drawing connections between ideas. It entails taking a complex idea or situation and differentiating its parts and understanding how they relate to one another in a coherent way.

At the Analyzing level, you're not just memorizing or applying information; you're thinking more deeply about it and drawing new connections between ideas. Analyzing involves looking for patterns, connections, or causes and effects. An example is when you're studying a novel and you analyze the characters' motivations, the plot, and the historical time period to gain a deeper understanding of the story.

EXAMPLE

Examples of the Analysis level of Bloom's taxonomy include:

>> Identifying the recurrent themes in a novel and providing evidence from the text to support your claims

>> Analyzing financial reports to identify trends or patterns in the data

>> Comparing the artistic styles and differences of two different choreographers from the same time period

>> Analyzing the strengths and weaknesses of a business's marketing strategy and proposing improvements

REMEMBER

Tasks at the Analysis level involve examining all the pieces to see how they fit together and what they mean. Although it is similar to the Understanding or Applying levels, it goes a step further to explore and uncover new insights and relationships within a topic or problem.

Evaluating

The Evaluating level in Bloom's taxonomy extends beyond understanding, applying, and analyzing ideas to making judgments or critical assessments based on criteria or merit. When evaluating, you consider multiple perspectives, criteria, and evidence to form your opinions or conclusions. You may be making decisions, ranking choices, or critiquing based on established standards or your own set of criteria.

The Evaluating level of thinking involves a high degree of critical thinking and often leads to reasoned or evidence-based judgments. Evaluating may look like detecting inconsistencies or errors in a product, process, or data. It also may involve critiquing or judging the best solution to implement to solve a problem. Learners are expected to weigh multiple factors, consider alternatives, and justify their conclusions or recommendations.

EXAMPLE

Examples of the evaluating level of Bloom's taxonomy include:

>> Evaluating whether a scientific study has met ethical standards

>> Making a recommendation about a software vendor to use after evaluating features, costs, user friendliness, and integration factors of different software

>> Evaluating the bias in historical accounts of a specific period based on power and privilege and proposing an interpretation

>> Comparing and evaluating different investment portfolios and recommending the most suitable one based on investment goals and market analyses

>> Evaluating the effectiveness of your instructional design for improving learning outcomes, solving performance problems, and impacting the mission and results of the organization

REMEMBER

The Evaluating category of Bloom's taxonomy features thinking processes such as making informed judgments about the quality, value, or effectiveness of something based on criteria or standards. It's a step beyond analyzing, as it requires you to weigh evidence, consider alternatives, and arrive at reasoned conclusions. It involves making decisions, critiques, or judgments about the value of an idea or solution.

Creating

The Creating level of Bloom's taxonomy represents the highest level of cognitive skills, where learners go beyond remembering, understanding, analyzing, and evaluating to produce something entirely new. It requires creative thinking to generate original ideas, solutions, or products. Learners are inventing, designing, composing, or constructing new ideas or products. They also may reorganize concepts into new patterns or themes that were not presented previously. At this level, learners draw upon all previous levels of thinking and transcend what has been learned to produce a novel idea.

Examples of the Creating category of Bloom's taxonomy include:

>> Creating a proposal for ensuring everyone has adequate medical coverage

>> Writing an original novel or screenplay

>> Developing a detailed business plan for a new business, including a marketing strategy, financial projection, and operational plan

>> Designing an innovative architectural structure or building that incorporates sustainable and energy-efficient features

>> Creating an urban planning proposal to revitalize a city district and optimize public transportation

>> Creating an educational game

The Creating level of Bloom's taxonomy applies knowledge and skills to create something entirely new, whether it's a work of art, a scientific discovery, a business innovation, a new theory, or other original creation. It's the pinnacle of cognitive achievement, representing the highest level of thinking and problem-solving.

Choosing Action Verbs to Describe the Outcomes

Instructional designers often use action verbs to describe the different cognitive processes or tasks associated with each level of thinking in Bloom's taxonomy. Using action verbs to describe the level of thinking helps you to focus on observable knowledge, skills, and behaviors. (This concept is very helpful when writing learning objectives for your instruction, which I cover more thoroughly in Chapter 5.) Use verbs that best describe the thoughts, behaviors, or skills that a learner must be able to do.

For example, one verb that may be used to describe the Understanding level of the taxonomy is "compare." An example of using the action verb "compare" to describe the understanding level may be: "Compare and contrast nectar and pollen and how they help bees."

Table 4-2 lists some common action verbs associated with each level of Bloom's Taxonomy.

TABLE 4-2 ## Common Action Verbs for Each Level of Bloom's Taxonomy

Level of Bloom's Taxonomy	Description of Example Action Verbs
Remember	Define
	List
	Name
	Recall
	Recognize
	Identify
	Memorize
	Repeat
	State
Understand	Explain
	Describe
	Interpret
	Summarize
	Paraphrase
	Compare
	Contrast
	Classify
	Infer
	Exemplify

Level of Bloom's Taxonomy	Description of Example Action Verbs
Apply	Apply
	Use
	Implement
	Solve
	Demonstrate
	Operate
	Show
Analyze	Analyze
	Examine
	Compare
	Contrast
	Differentiate
	Integrate
	Break down
	Deduce
	Distinguish
	Organize
Evaluate	Evaluate
	Judge
	Assess
	Critique
	Appraise
	Recommend
	Justify
	Defend
	Choose
	Detect

(continued)

TABLE 4-2 *(continued)*

Level of Bloom's Taxonomy	Description of Example Action Verbs
Create	Create
	Generate
	Design
	Invent
	Compose
	Construct
	Hypothesize
	Plan
	Develop
	Produce

Performing Task Analyses

Conducting a task analysis involves breaking down a complex task or job into smaller components to understand the steps, skills, knowledge, or attitudes required to perform them successfully. A task analysis helps you to identify the major tasks that need to be learned, the subtasks needed to perform the major tasks, and how they are organized and related to each other.

A task analysis occurs after you identify your instructional goal and categorize the type of learning that is required. A task analysis helps you to create your instructional objectives. (See Chapter 5 for more on creating instructional objectives.) In fact, conducting task analyses and designing learning objectives often happen side-by-side.

REMEMBER

You may have also already identified many of the tasks needed for your instruction during other phases of the analysis process (for instance, during a gap or needs analysis; see Chapter 3). This section provides strategies and procedures for performing task analyses.

Working with SMEs to identify essential job tasks and content

The role of the subject-matter expert (SME) in performing a task analysis is critical. In your instructional situation, you may be both the designer and the

SME. Otherwise, you are likely a designer who is working with a SME to figure out the performance needs and identify all the knowledge, skills, and tasks required to perform them effectively.

Your first task is to identify the individuals who are experts or experienced in performing the task. Chapter 3 and this book's Appendix detail some questions and tips for conducting interviews with experts to better understand the performance problem.

One strategy for identifying the essential tasks is to observe the SME performing the task while documenting each step and action taken. This tactic is a useful technique to perform if the instruction is procedural, such as demonstrating the proper operation of equipment.

TIP

Video recording or notetaking is essential for documenting the initial list of tasks identified by the SME.

Many designers get the information they need for task analyses through interviews or focus groups with SMEs to gain a deeper understanding of the task. (See Chapter 3 for more on that topic.) Ask SMEs to talk aloud about the rationale behind each task and what variations are possible. The SME plays a core role in helping the instructional designer analyze the job requirements and instructional goals, and their ability to clarify the tasks, subtasks, and sequences-to-follow (what needs to be learned first and in what order, in other words) can also be a great help. You then use the list of tasks you jointly come up with to create the content that will comprise the instruction.

TIP

The following tips for working with SMEs on task analyses should come in handy:

>> Keep focused on the essential tasks versus nice-to-know tasks. Ask SMEs which tasks are most essential to prioritize.

>> When interviewing SMEs, document all the tasks as well as any equipment or resources that are needed to support performing the task.

>> Experts have a rich knowledge base that is often tacit or implicit. Given this, helping them make their hidden knowledge more explicit is important. Use questions such as the following to draw out their expertise:

- What rules of thumb do you use for specific situations or problems?

- What is your mindset or your general approach for working with people or customers?

- How do you organize your time and work tasks?

- What are you thinking about as you perform this task?
- What would a positive or negative outcome for this task look like?
- What tricks have you learned to perform this task better or faster?

REMEMBER

When you are not also serving as the SME, remember that the SME is a key person during several phases of the instructional design process. Sometimes, they are being asked to take time away from their jobs to work with you on the instruction, and they also may be responsible for developing the content or teaching it later. Working around their schedules and being prepared for all meetings with them is important. Clarifying the expectations of them early in the instructional design process is also useful; making sure everyone is on the same page is simply a must.

Breaking down the tasks, subtasks, and content

Developing the content for your instruction requires detailed identification of the tasks, knowledge, and skills required to solve the performance problem or meet the needs for the instruction. Although there are many different techniques and names for conducting task analyses, they all serve similar goals of detailing the scope and sequence of the instructional content by breaking down the essential tasks into smaller steps and chunks of content. A task analysis will break down the knowledge, skills, and practices in ways that will help you see the relationships between the different elements of the instruction.

A task analysis starts with the instructional goal or need that was identified earlier in your analyses. (See Chapter 3 for more on that topic.) If you're not an expert yourself when it comes to the content, you have to involve a SME in the task analysis — someone who can provide the detailed information needed to solve the performance problem. During observations or interviews with SMEs, you record all the tasks they identify along with the subskills, knowledge, steps, equipment, or resources needed to successfully achieve the identified tasks. It is a process of progressively breaking down what a learner needs to be able to do for each task effectively.

The end result of a task analysis is a detailed list of all of the tasks, knowledge, and skills that are required. It is possible that some of the tasks listed are not included in your instruction, but by knowing what they are in advance, you can make an informed decision about the necessary scope of the instruction.

Performing a task analysis includes three main steps:

1. Describe the main tasks.
2. List the subskills and knowledge needed to perform the main tasks.
3. Differentiate between tasks assumed to be known versus need to be taught.

The next sections examine each step in greater detail.

Describing the main tasks

The first step in a task analysis is to describe the main tasks, including visible tasks that can be directly observed as well as thinking or cognitive skills that are less easy to observe. Using Bloom's taxonomy can help you identify what type of knowledge is required for each task.

Make a sequential list of all the main tasks needed for successful performance. After you have completed an initial list, ask the SME to check it over and add or delete tasks. You can record the tasks in either a flowchart or outline form. (See the next section for examples.) The depth of your task analysis depends on how much time you have and whether you or the SME is primarily responsible for developing the content for the instruction.

Listing the subskills and knowledge needed to perform the key tasks

The second step in a task analysis is to list the subskills and knowledge needed to perform the key tasks effectively. This step of a task analysis helps ensure that you clarify any prior knowledge that is needed for the instruction to be effective. For instance, a task of identifying a tree as either broadleaf or needleleaf first requires knowing how to recognize different types of leaf structures.

Start with the highest-level tasks and then further divide them into subtasks. This part of the task analysis is more in-depth; the idea is to keep asking questions such as, "What does an individual need to know in order to do that task?" or "What information is needed to perform that action?" until all tasks and subtasks are identified and you reach a point where you can safely assume the learner has that prior knowledge.

Differentiating between tasks assumed to be known versus need-to-be-taught

The last step in a task analysis is to differentiate between the tasks, knowledge, and skills assumed to be already known and what needs to be taught in the instruction. In the previous example of distinguishing between needleleaf and broadleaf trees, you may assume that the task of "recognize a leaf on a tree" is already known by all learners in the target audience, so it does not need to be taught.

To figure out what tasks do not need to be included in the instruction, look at your list of subtasks with your SME and decide:

>> Which tasks you believe that *none* of the learners already know how to do

>> Which tasks *some* of the learners already know how to do

>> Which tasks you believe *all* learners already know how to do

Cross out those tasks that do not need to be covered in the instruction and highlight those that are the most critical.

TIP

Determining which tasks to include or exclude from the instruction because learners either already know them or do not know them is a simpler solution than situations where some learners may already know and others not. In those instances, you will need to decide how to best meet the needs of learners in both categories. If your learners present themselves with differing levels of prior knowledge, then perhaps consider a pretest or self-assessment to direct them to the appropriate starting point in the instruction.

Methods for documenting task analyses

A task analysis typically results in a document that visually displays the hierarchical relationships among the tasks, knowledge, skills, or procedures. Two of the most common techniques for representing tasks are:

>> An outline method that lists the main tasks and the subtopics or subtasks that comprise them

>> A flowchart method that illustrates the tasks and subtasks with boxes and arrows showing relationships

Working with an outline format

The outline technique is typically faster to create and works well for listing out the content or topics associated with each task. The outline format is likely already familiar to many people, as it entails creating an outline of the main tasks with subheadings and indented text to illustrate the supporting tasks or details:

I. Task 1

    a. Subtask 1a

        i. Prerequisite knowledge 1a (already presumed before instruction)

    b. Subtask 1b

        i. Factual knowledge 1b

        ii. Factual knowledge 2b

    c. Subtask 1c

        i. Step 1

        ii. Step 2

        iii. Step 3

EXAMPLE

The following example shows a simple outline format for a task analysis with the goal of baking a cake:

1. **Preheat Oven**

    Set the oven temperature to 350°F (180°C).

2. **Prepare Ingredients**

    - Gather flour, sugar, eggs, butter, and baking powder.

    - Measure required quantities of each ingredient.

3. **Mix Batter**

    - Combine dry ingredients (flour, sugar, baking powder) in a mixing bowl.

    - In a separate bowl, whisk eggs and melt butter.

    - Gradually add wet ingredients to the dry mixture while stirring.

4. **Prepare Baking Pan**

    - Grease the cake pan with butter or cooking spray.

    - Dust with flour to prevent sticking.

5. **Pour Batter**

    - Pour the cake batter into the prepared pan.

6. Bake

- Place the pan in the preheated oven.

- Bake for 30-35 minutes until a toothpick comes out clean when inserted into the cake.

7. Cool and Serve

- Remove the cake from the oven and let it cool for 10 minutes.

- Transfer the cake to a serving plate and allow it to cool completely before serving.

Using a flowchart format

Flowcharts are another method for displaying your task analyses and are effective for illustrating procedures and tasks that have a hierarchy of tasks and subtasks. Figure 4-1 illustrates an example of a flowchart format for a task analysis for the tasks associated with applying time management techniques to improve learners' productivity — an illustration of the Application level of Bloom's taxonomy.

The instructional goal for this example task analysis is:

Apply time management techniques to improve performance and productivity on making deadlines, prioritizing tasks, and allocating the right amount of time to a given assignment.

EXAMPLE

After you complete your task analysis and identify all the relevant tasks and sub-tasks, you want to share them with SMEs to ensure accuracy and completeness. Include any additional notes or requests for clarification or elaboration.

TIP

Another way to review task analyses is to consider asking another SME who was not part of the initial task identification process to look over the task analysis documents and provide feedback on accuracy and thoroughness. It is worth the time to revise and refine the task analysis based on feedback and additional clarifications!

No matter which format you choose, after you complete your task analysis, the next step in the instructional design process is to begin the Design phase of the ADDIE model.

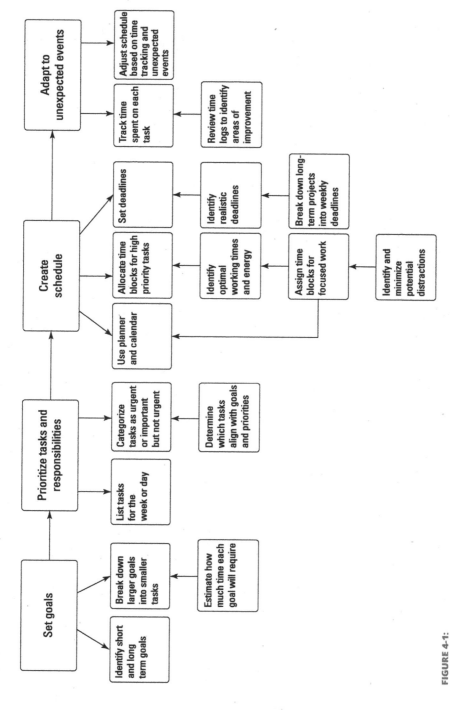

FIGURE 4-1:
Flowchart format of a task analysis on time management techniques.

3

Designing Engaging and Effective Instruction

Write effective instructional objectives based on your task analyses by including the four parts of a well-written objective.

Create assessment items that match your instructional objectives to ensure that your instructional goals and outcomes are aligned.

Choose when to use different instructional-design frameworks to create instructional activities and strategies.

Discover how to use design guidelines for sequencing, structuring, and ordering instructional events and activities for different types of instructional goals.

Distinguish between direct instructional design and open-ended instructional design frameworks and design strategies.

Chapter **5**

Creating Instructional Goals and Objectives

One common practice in teaching and instructional design is providing lesson objectives. In fact, many of you have probably heard about objectives before picking up this book. Using objectives during instructional design is like planning out a roadmap for your trip. Successful teaching (and instruction) starts with knowing where you are going. Otherwise, how will you know you have arrived at your destination?

We have all been students at some point in our lives. Chances are, if you have had some unsuccessful teaching or learning experiences, they may have been partially due to a lack of clarity between the goals of the course, the instructional content that is taught, and how learning is assessed. Have you ever had an experience where an instructor lectured on one topic but then covered something entirely different on an exam? This reflects a lack of alignment between the goals, instructional material, and the assessment. Instructional objectives can help us bridge these different design elements and help make for a successful learning experience. Objectives are a key part of this alignment in the instructional design process.

In this chapter, you find out how to create instructional objectives from your task analyses and instructional goals. This process becomes the basis for writing the instructional objectives, so I provide you with step-by-step procedures for writing effective objectives. Last, I give some recommendations on how to plan assessment items that are aligned with your objectives.

Starting with the End in Mind

Creating instructional objectives is the first main task of the *design* phase of the ADDIE model. (For more on the ADDIE model, see Chapter 1.) In the *analysis* phase, you spent time analyzing the problem to make sure that instruction was a good solution for it. You also conducted task analyses and classified goals that you wanted learners to be able to successfully perform at the end of the instruction. Designing instructional objectives is an extension of that process.

Instructional objectives clarify in more detail what those identified tasks entail and how the instruction can be designed to support the intended outcomes. Objectives are useful for elaborating your outcomes in ways that guide the future development of content, instructional strategies and assessments. In essence, objectives describe the *ends*, or stated differently, the intended results, outcomes, or changes in learning and performance that are expected.

REMEMBER

Instructional objectives can be written in different ways and are often called a variety of terms, such as behavioral objectives, performance objectives, competencies, or standards. All these terms, while having slightly different uses and practices, share a similar goal of identifying what learners will be able to do when the instruction ends.

EXAMPLE

This section brings us to a point of clarification about what objectives are not. Objectives are not statements about what the instructional activities will be, such as reading text information, engaging in a role play, or viewing a video. Objectives are statements that are focused on ends or outcomes. The activities that are designed reflect the means through which the ends can be achieved. Take a look at Table 5-1, which lists the ways a statement written with a focus on outcomes differs from a statement written with a focus on activities.

Although the activities identified in the second example may be effective strategies for achieving the intended learning outcomes, the statements are not written as an instructional objective. After instructional objectives are created, then the instructional designer begins to explore different sequences and instructional strategies for achieving those learning outcomes. Although there are varying levels of specificity that designers may choose in their statements of instructional objectives, they should serve to clarify the outcome.

TABLE 5-1 **Example Statements Written as a Learning Outcome (Left Column) and as a Learning Activity (Right Column)**

Example of a Statement Focused on Learner Outcomes after the Instruction Ends	Example of a Statement Focused on Activities Learners Perform during the Instruction
At the end of the field trip, groups of learners will be able to identify five trees in the forest at different phases of the tree life cycle and label them with correct criteria for their claim. They will identify the tree life cycles with 100 percent accuracy.	Learners will be asked to participate in a scavenger hunt and take photographs of trees they see. They will work together on a labeling activity at the end.

REMEMBER Instructional objectives are written from the perspective of the intended learning outcomes for the learners, not a list of the intended instructional activities. Although objectives can sometimes specify activities, they always point to the expected learning outcome.

Recognizing the benefits of a well-written objective

Well-written instructional objectives offer a variety of benefits, in addition to defining more clearly the learning outcomes. As you saw in the last section, objectives guide the instructional designer to clarify what attainment of the learning outcomes looks like at the end of the instruction. However, instructional objectives are also valuable for many other reasons:

>> **Objectives guide the development of instructional strategies.** Objectives outline the learning outcomes at the end of the instruction. After you have instructional objectives, you can break down the lessons and align your instructional strategies in ways that support those learning outcomes. For instance, if the objectives are to apply knowledge learned to the job or everyday life, they guide the designer to use activities that maximize the likelihood that learners can apply knowledge in the way intended.

>> **Objectives give the learners a clear understanding of what to expect from the instruction.** Objectives point to the content to be covered as well as the priorities for learners to focus on during learning. When learners know what to expect (and what is expected from them), they are more likely to focus their energies on learning this information. They can also determine if the instruction can be beneficial to them. Oftentimes, instructional designers slightly revise the objectives when communicating them to learners so that they are clearer and simpler to understand.

- >> **Objectives focus the instructional designer on essential information.** Instructional objectives help keep the instructional designer on track with the most important outcomes for learners. After objectives are defined, instructional designers can more readily see if areas of redundancy or non-essential content are there.

- >> **Objectives help communicate what's most important to all members of the instructional design team.** Objectives are valuable to the design and development team, include subject-matter experts (SMEs), graphic designers, or programmers. They keep everyone on the same page and working together. They are also useful for communicating to stakeholders such as supervisors, clients, instructors, and management, so that any mismatches in needs or goals can be identified.

- >> **Objectives define how to assess learners' achievement.** A well-written objective helps a designer determine how to best assess whether learning has occurred. Objectives point to the kinds of questions or performances that would indicate if learning has occurred. Objectives also define the criteria for successful performance and attainment of the objectives.

- >> **Objectives guide the evaluation of whether the instruction was successful.** The success of an instructional design is driven by whether it has met the needs of the organization outlined during the analysis phase. If the intent of the instruction is to solve a performance problem on the job, the objectives and lesson activities should all work together towards that end. Objectives help guide the creation of assessments that are aligned with evaluating the overall success of the instructional solution.

Conceding the limitations of instructional objectives (in some circumstances)

Despite the many clear benefits of instructional objectives, they also have limitations. Although countless instructional designers accept that writing clear, measurable objectives is important, others have found them limiting. A few of these potential shortcomings of objectives are described in this list:

- >> **Time consuming.** Some instructional designers believe that the process of creating detailed objectives is too time consuming and often unnecessary, claiming that the results of the analysis process (task analysis, learner analysis, context analysis) yield sufficient detail for guiding the development of the instruction. When time is limited, this may be a tradeoff that some designers make. Striking a balance is important, as objectives that are too general may not offer enough guidance for designers and instructors to facilitate learning.

>> **One size may not fit all.** Instructional outcomes are often complex and difficult to define in observable ways. Indeed, a "one size fits all" approach may not work well for all instructional projects. Some designers believe that detailed objectives are too narrow and limit creativity or learner-centeredness, especially in instruction that is longer-term and complex.

>> **Importance of personalized learning.** Some designers believe that, although creating the same objectives for all learners will likely lead to the learning of those objectives, they also may limit learners' interests and abilities to personalize their learning experience. Some instructional goals require more openness and expressiveness, enabling learners to move outside the boundaries of designed outcomes to make them personally meaningful. Designing instruction to influence learners' appreciation of art, for instance, requires uniquely personal learning outcomes.

>> **Dealing with complex learning outcomes.** Some designers note that the more specific a learning objective is written, the easier it is to assess. When tasks and learning outcomes are more complex, assessments also need to be more complex. Designing highly specific and observable instructional objectives may not capture the complexity of a learning outcome.

TIP

Despite these limitations, most instructional designers recognize the importance of defining learning outcomes through instructional objectives. My advice is to not get too focused on the wording; just write them in a way that is useful for your needs, then move on to developing your instructional strategies. I provide step-by-step tips for writing instructional objectives in the sections that follow.

REMEMBER

The ADDIE process is cyclical, so it is quite common to come back to the objectives at different times and refine them. Keep in mind that the work you put in to defining your instructional objectives early in the design process will likely pay off later.

How to Create Instructional Objectives

Learning how to write detailed instructional objectives is a valuable and relatively simple skill for instructional designers. Objectives guide the development of your instruction as well as the criteria for determining whether the instruction was effective. By following the step-by-step procedure presented in the following sections, you can develop instructional objectives that detail your lesson outcomes, even if you have little to no experience with instructional design. Well-written objectives help to focus and guide all the latter phases of the ADDIE process.

Table 5-2 provides a high-level summary of the process for writing effective instructional objectives (which is then discussed in more detail in the following sections).

TABLE 5-2
Summary of the Process of Creating Instructional Objectives

Steps in Creating an Instructional Objective	Description
Review the task analysis that classified tasks, goals, and action verbs. (See Chapter 4.)	During a task analysis (introduced in detail in Chapter 4), you break down the essential knowledge, skills, and practices into smaller chunks of content. The organization of the tasks is often displayed in outline or flowchart format to visually see how they relate to one another.
	Classify the type of task or goal for the instruction by using Bloom's Taxonomy. (See Chapter 4.) Choose action verbs that represent one of the six levels of instructional goals: remember, understand, apply, analyze, evaluate, create.
Use the ABCD method to create an instructional objective for the tasks, knowledge, or skills identified.	Use the action verbs identified during your task analysis to help you to focus on observable knowledge, skills, and behaviors. This focus is useful when writing your instructional objectives later.
	Use the ABCD method to refine the objective:
	A: Identify the **audience** for the instruction.
	B: Describe the observable **behavior** that learners must be able to do. This usually includes the action verb you identified.
	C: State the **conditions** under which the behavior (verb) the learner needs to demonstrate.
	D: Indicate the standard or **degree** of proficiency.

Classifying tasks and objectives

In Chapter 4, I cover the procedures you use in a task analysis to categorize and identify the tasks and subtasks that lead to the achievement of the instructional goal. A task analysis helps you to identify the major tasks that need to be learned or performed by learners as well as the subtasks needed to perform the primary tasks. For this reason, task analyses are usually portrayed visually, such as in outline or flowchart form meant to show how the tasks are organized and related to each other.

A task analysis occurs after you have identified the overall instructional goal and categorized the type of learning or thinking that is required. I introduce Bloom's Taxonomy in Chapter 4 as a tool for categorizing different types of goals and tasks that are within the cognitive or "learning new knowledge" category of learning. After you have categorized the goal and identified all the tasks and subtasks associated with it, you are ready to create your instructional objectives from the results of this task analysis.

REMEMBER

Bloom's Taxonomy is comprised of six different levels of thinking that are ordered hierarchically. (Again, see Chapter 4.) This means that higher levels on the hierarchy are more complex and usually entail the levels beneath them. When you are analyzing the goals and learning needs for your instruction, you first identify what type of learning the goal or performance represents. Bloom's Taxonomy then suggests corresponding action verbs that make the learning activities more concrete and observable.

Table 5-3 provides a summary of the six levels of Bloom's Taxonomy, along with a list of possible action verbs that can be selected to describe the type of learning that the instruction is designed to support. These action verbs can be useful when creating your instructional objectives.

TABLE 5-3 A Quick Review of Bloom's Taxonomy

Level	Description and Example	Action Verbs	
Remember	Remember or recall facts or information. *Recall the key features, pricing, and specifications of a new product.*	Define List Name Recall	Recognize Identify Memorize Repeat State
Understand	Demonstrate meaning and comprehension by explaining, summarizing, or generating examples. *Explain the key events that led to the Spanish Civil War.*	Explain Describe Interpret Summarize Paraphrase	Compare Contrast Classify Infer Exemplify

(continued)

TABLE 5-3 *(continued)*

Level	Description and Example	Action Verbs	
Apply	Apply knowledge and procedures to a real-world situation. *Apply math and spreadsheet skills to calculate a family budget.*	Apply Use Implement Solve	Demonstrate Operate Show
Analyze	Break down concepts and draw connections in new ways between ideas. *Analyze financial reports to identify trends.*	Analyze Examine Compare Contrast Differentiate	Integrate Break down Deduce Distinguish Organize
Evaluate	Make judgments, assessments, or decisions based on criteria, evidence, or standards. *Evaluate whether a scientific study has met ethical standards.*	Evaluate Judge Assess Critique Appraise	Recommend Justify Defend Choose Detect
Create	Generate original ideas, solutions, or products. *Create a detailed business plan for a new business.*	Create Generate Design Invent Compose	Construct Hypothesize Plan Develop Produce

The ABCDs of creating instructional objectives

As I mention earlier in this chapter, task analysis is the technique used by an instructional designer to identify the knowledge, skills, or performances that need to be learned during the instruction. After the task analyses are complete, you can create your instructional objectives. In this section, you learn how to translate those tasks into written instructional objectives that guide the rest of the design, development, and evaluation phases.

An *instructional objective* is a detailed description of what learners will be able to do after they complete the instruction. Objectives are derived directly from our task analyses. Typically, at least one objective is written for each skill or task identified in the task analysis. The objective should be aligned with the category identified in the task analysis or Bloom's Taxonomy. (See Chapter 4 for more on Bloom's Taxonomy.) For instance, if a learning goal involves "remembering," then the objective should focus on recall and remembering. Likewise, for a goal focused on "applying," the objective should focus on applying knowledge to new situations.

In the sections that follow, you learn the ABCD method of writing detailed objectives. The ABCD method is an acronym to help you remember the following four elements to include in your instructional objectives: audience, behavior, condition, and degree.

A: Identifying the <u>audience</u>

The first element of a well-written objective is to identify the learners. In many instructional contexts, the instruction is being designed for one primary target audience with similar learner characteristics — all sales associates at an automobile manufacturing company, for instance. In these situations, you may only need to identify the audience of learners once.

Sometimes, the audience of learners for the instruction may represent multiple groups with different characteristics. For instance, sometimes learners may be comprised of small groups, rather than learners learning independently. In other situations, such as instruction at an art museum, the audience may be varied — families, children on field trips, or individuals. In these situations, the audience for the objective may be different, and if it is, you want to clarify which audience the objective is referencing.

To illustrate, audiences of learners can include:

>> High school students

>> Employees

>> Families

>> Nurses

>> Sales representatives

It is also acceptable to refer to the audience of learners in less specific terms such as "learners" or "students." When learners are the same target audience for all objectives, instructional designers often state it one time, instead of repeating it for each objective. Another method is to abbreviate the audience when it is used repeatedly. For instance, "The learner will be able to. . ." is often abbreviated to "The LWBAT."

EXAMPLE

Example instructional objectives that clarify the **audience** (in italics) are:

>> *High school biology students* will be able to explain the process of photosynthesis on a written test with 90 percent accuracy.

>> *Summer camp youth* will be able to distinguish between seedling and sapling trees while walking on a trail, correctly providing at least two reasons for their choice.

>> *Finance Department employees* will be able (given an example scenario) to demonstrate adherence to the company's ethical and legal compliance standards for expense reporting, with no errors.

B: Describing the <u>behavior</u> the learner must demonstrate

The second element of a well-written instructional objective involves identifying the behavior, action, or performance that learners need to demonstrate to show what they have learned. The "B" or behavior element of the objective is best written in specific, observable terms, such as:

>> To state

>> To compute

>> To demonstrate

>> To compare and contrast

>> To operate

This part of the instructional objective is directly tied to the action verbs that you identified during your task analysis. Specifically, the verb you use describes the skill, knowledge, or behavior that you identified for each task in your analysis. Using this method keeps you focused on what the learner should be able to do versus what activity you plan to use.

TIP

Keep the list of action verbs aligned with Bloom's Taxonomy (see Chapter 4) handy while you create your objectives! See Table 5-3 for a list of sample verbs.

What do you do in cases where the task or skill to be learned is not easily observable as a behavior, such as when learners are engaging in problem solving or creating new ideas? In these cases, try to specify actions or performances that learners can display as evidence that they have learned. In fact, one reason Bloom's Taxonomy originated was to serve as a tool to help instructional designers design instruction that supports cognitive or more creative (and less behavioral) goals.

Some instructional designers advocate that you should not use action verbs such as "know," "understand," or "appreciate" because they do not reflect observable behaviors and are thus difficult to assess. Other designers suggest that these verbs reflect higher level thinking goals that cannot always be defined by observable behaviors, but that can be described in terms of a series of performances that reflect this understanding. (See Chapter 7 for more on that topic.) As a general rule, especially if creating objectives is new for you, I advise choosing a verb that is as specific and observable as possible.

Example instructional objectives that clarify the **behavior** (in italics) are:

>> High school biology students will be able to *explain the process of photosynthesis* on a written test with 90 percent accuracy.

>> Summer camp youth will be able to *distinguish between seedling and sapling trees* while walking on a trail, correctly providing at least two reasons for their choice.

>> Given an example scenario, Finance Department employees will be able to *demonstrate adherence to the company's ethical and legal compliance standards* for expense reporting, with no errors.

C: Stating the conditions under which the behavior is performed

The third element of a well-written instructional objective is to specify the conditions under which the behavior, task, or performance occurs. *Conditions* specify the environment, resources, circumstances, or "givens" that exist when a learner carries out the behavior specified in the objective. Conditions can specify use of resources, such as "without use of notes or books," "with a calculator," "given 25 flashcards," and so on. They clarify when, where, and how the behavior is demonstrated.

Conditions can be stated anywhere within the instructional objective, but they are commonly stated at the beginning, as illustrated (in italics) in these examples:

EXAMPLE

>> *Without access to books or notes,* the learner will be able to list the five phases of a tree life cycle.

>> *Given a calculator, a scenario, and a formula,* the students will be able to calculate the compound interest rate of a loan.

>> *Given 25 flashcards of words in English,* the learner will be able to correctly translate the word to Spanish.

>> *Given an example scenario,* Finance Department employees will be able to demonstrate adherence to the company's ethical and legal compliance standards for expense reporting, with no errors.

Conditions located in other sections of the sentence may look like these:

>> High school biology students will be able to explain the process of photosynthesis *on a written test* with 100 percent accuracy.

>> Summer camp youth will be able to distinguish between seedling and sapling trees *while walking on a trail,* correctly providing at least two reasons for their choice.

D: Specifying the degree of accuracy expected

The last element of a well-written instructional objective is to indicate the criteria that will be used to evaluate the degree to which learner performance of the objective is considered successful. The degree gives the instructional designer (and learners) an idea of the standards on which performance will be evaluated. For instance, is 100 percent accurate performance or correct answers expected? Or is there a range of acceptable performance, such as 80 percent accuracy?

Some situations may demand 100 percent perfect performance, such as those where the instruction has a safety consequence (safe operation of equipment or a medical procedure, for example). Other situations may not demand the same degree of mastery to be considered successful.

The **degree** is often stated in terms of the range of responses that will be acceptable, as shown in these examples:

EXAMPLE

>> Total number of responses identified

>> Time limits or constraints

>> Accuracy rate or percentage (9 times out of 10 or 90 percent)

>> The number of attempts (the first time, for example)

>> Frequency (providing three pieces of evidence, for example)

Other examples of **degree** are presented in these objectives (in italics):

>> High school biology students will be able to explain the process of photosynthesis on a written test *with 90 percent accuracy.*

>> Summer camp youth will be able to distinguish between seedling and sapling trees while walking on a trail, *correctly providing at least two reasons for their choice.*

>> Given an example scenario, Finance Department employees will be able to demonstrate adherence to the company's ethical and legal compliance standards for expense reporting, *with no errors.*

REMEMBER

The degree is often listed at the end of an objective as shown previously, but it can be placed anywhere that it makes sense. It is also important to note that objectives do not need to be constrained to only one sentence. As the ABCD's of the objective are clarified, you may notice that the objective adds more information and details that may read more clearly if separated into a second sentence. In those situations, it is not uncommon for an instructional designer to write a second sentence that specifies the "degree."

Another detail to note about the degree — not all instructional situations may call for specificity of a degree or criteria for success. Some instructional contexts do not strive for mastery in the same way that formal educational systems do. Informal learning or professional development, for example, may not require specifying what is considered successful or accurate, because the outcomes are driven by learners' needs or interests. Specifying degree may not be necessary in those situations.

Linking Objectives and Assessments

I began this chapter with a statement about "beginning with the end in mind." Developing an effective instructional objective leads to a clear statement about what learners can do for each major task of the instruction, including the behaviors, conditions and degree to which learners can demonstrate success on the objectives. After your objectives are identified, you then develop your assessments. In practice, the development of objectives and the development of assessment of those objectives usually go hand in hand.

As you may have gathered, the process of identifying the ABCD's of your objectives gives you a pretty good idea of the types of assessment items that make sense to assess your objective. Typically, you want to create at least one assessment item for each instructional objective. When assessment items match your instructional objectives, success on the assessment item means that the learner has achieved success on that objective.

After the instruction has been completed by learners, you may need to show clients or stakeholders that the instruction was effective in solving the performance problem. Although there are many ways to evaluate the success of the instruction (see Chapter 11 for more on that topic), one way is to show that learning of the objectives has taken place.

EXAMPLE

One tip for aligning your objectives and assessment items is to use a table, so you can see them side-by-side. Table 5-4 lists a few examples of how this may look in practice:

TABLE 5-4 ### Aligning Objectives and Assessments

Objective	Assessment Question
Given a blank diagram of the human respiratory system, learners will be able to recall and label the key components of the human respiratory system. The learners need to correctly identify and label each part within 80 percent accuracy. [remembering level]	On the following diagram, label the main components of the human respiratory systems, specifically the trachea, lungs, bronchi, and diaphragm.
On a written quiz, learners will be able to list at least two characteristics that distinguish seedling and sapling trees [remembering level]	List at least two characteristics that distinguish seedling and sapling trees.
Summer camp youth will be able to distinguish between seedling and sapling trees while walking on a trail, correctly providing at least two reasons for their choice. [applying level]	While walking on the trail, take photographs of at least one seedling tree and one sapling tree. List at least two characteristics as evidence for each type of tree identified.
Given an example scenario, Finance Department employees will be able to evaluate their adherence to the company's ethical and legal compliance standards for expense reporting, by justifying their decisions with company policies, and with no errors. [evaluation level].	Scenario: You have been provided with an expense report from an employee that contains several errors and possible unjustifiable expenses. Instructions: Given this expense report provided, generate a plan of action for ensuring that ethical compliance standards are met. Justify your plan using company policy standards for correctly and ethically submitting expense reports.

Tips for Sequencing Your Instructional Objectives

One important reason to align your objectives and assessments is that they will guide the next step of the design process — selecting and sequencing your instructional strategies. Your instructional objectives (what learners will learn), assessments (how you will determine if objectives were achieved), and instructional strategies (activities designed to facilitate achievement of objectives and assessments) work together to create an effective instructional product.

In this section, I provide some tips on some common ways of sequencing your instructional objectives.

Procedural order

One tip for organizing and sequencing instructional objectives is to follow a procedural order. This method of sequencing works well for instruction that teaches a step-by-step approach, a physical activity, or how to perform a procedure in a specific order.

EXAMPLE

An example of procedural ordering of objectives is on the topic of how to complete a bodyweight squat. Successfully performing the activity requires following a specific, step-by-step order of tasks such as:

1. Stand with feet should width apart, toes slightly pointing out.
2. Hinge at the hips, as if sitting in a chair.
3. Bend knees, keeping in line with feet.
4. Lower body into the squat position.
5. Push through your heels to raise to the starting position.

In this example, you would want to sequence your objectives in procedural order of the steps required. It would not make sense to teach Step 4 before teaching Step 1! Each step may have additional tasks associated with it, and those also follow their procedural order. These steps are outlined in your task analyses.

Other types of instruction may also use procedural sequencing:

>> Physical skills such as operating a piece of machinery

>> Software operation skills

>> Calculating a solution using an equation

>> Following procedures such as filling out a tax form

Simple to complex

Another common strategy for sequencing how objectives are organized is to present simpler tasks first before tackling more complex ones. Your task analyses (see

Chapter 4) outlined all the tasks, subskills, and knowledge needed to perform the key tasks effectively. These skills often have a hierarchical relationship, meaning that a subskill needs to be learned before completing one of the more complex skills.

EXAMPLE

For instance, in the task analysis diagram for time management instruction initially presented in Chapter 4 (Figure 4-1), the instruction has the following goal: *Apply time management techniques to improve performance and productivity on making deadlines, prioritizing tasks, and allocating the right amount of time to a given assignment.*

This goal has four main tasks:

» Set goals

» Prioritize tasks and responsibilities

» Create schedule

» Adapt to unexpected events

In Figure 5-1, you can see that the first-level task of "prioritize tasks and responsibilities" has two subtasks that need to be learned first (see the shaded section of Figure 5-1):

» List tasks for the week or day.

» Categorize tasks as a) urgent or b) important, but not urgent.

   Note: This subtask has another subtask that needs to be learned first: "Determine which goals align with goals and priorities."

Best practices suggest that these objectives be clustered together and that you sequence your objectives to align with the order of the skills and subskills that need to be learned first. In this case, you teach the subskill of "determine which goals align with goals and priorities" before teaching learners to "categorize tasks as a) urgent or b) important, but not urgent," both of which are taught before the task of "prioritize tasks and responsibilities."

Instructional designers also draw upon instructional-design models to prescribes different ways to structure or sequence your instructional strategies, depending on your goals, audience, and needs. Chapters 6 and 7 go into more detail about different design models you can use to guide the development of your instructional strategies and activities. After your instructional strategies and activities are designed, you are then able to approximate time estimates needed for the instruction.

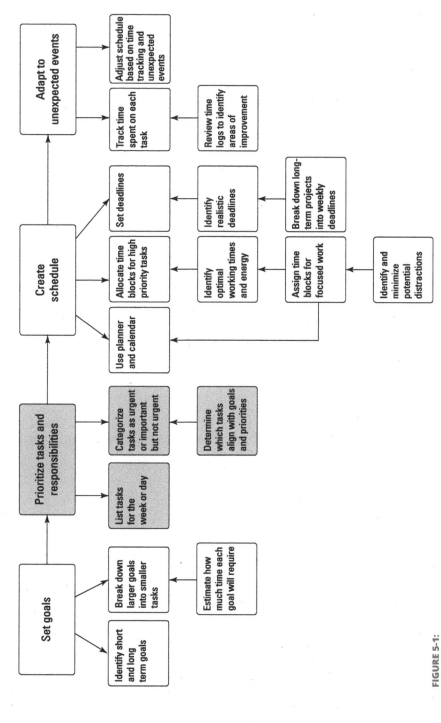

FIGURE 5-1:
Flowchart format of a task analysis on time management techniques.

Chapter **6**

Introducing Instructional Design Frameworks

When the instructional design process has gone smoothly, you identify the particular instructional or performance problem you're facing, analyze the tasks needed for effective performance, and then develop objectives and assessments for the instruction. (For more on those topics, see Chapters 3, 4, and 5.) You may also analyze your options for the best instructional delivery system to use (synchronous classroom or online asynchronous delivery, for example; see Chapters 3 and 8 for details on those concepts). These details are essential elements of defining the scope and sequence of the instruction.

In addition to all these tasks, however, you also have to develop the instructional strategies you'll use to meet your objectives. Instructional strategies are best thought of as the activities you use to organize and present the instruction — the methods you use to communicate content to the learners and generate activities for them, in other words. We can use instructional models as frameworks for how to design and sequence our instructional strategies.

You can find hundreds of books and resources on different instructional-design models. In this chapter, I introduce you to three commonly used instructional design frameworks to help you get started on designing and sequencing your instructional strategies:

>> Gagné's nine events of instruction

>> Mayer's framework for active learning

>> Keller's ARCS model of motivation

Choosing When to Use an Instructional-Design Framework

You can use different instructional strategies and models to guide how to go about designing instruction. I introduce the idea of how different types of instructional design models are based on different goals, assumptions, and learner needs in Chapter 2, but this chapter expands on that introduction by providing guidelines for how to design your instructional strategies for particular types of learning outcomes. The strategies in this chapter focus on how to support learners to learn new content information and connect it to prior knowledge.

When planning your instructional design project, deciding which instructional design frameworks works best for you begins with analyzing your learning goals and your instructional and organization context. The sections that follow introduce guidelines for designing instructional strategies using three common instructional-design frameworks. I focus on presenting key strategies of these frameworks that get you up and running quickly.

REMEMBER

Before choosing any instructional design strategy, ensuring that your prior analysis and design phases are aligned with the strategies you want to use is important. This tactic means that your instructional strategies are aligned with the following:

>> Your analyses of the organization, instructional need, tasks, and potential learners

>> The learning outcomes, objectives, assessments, and evaluation strategies for your instructional program

>> Your delivery system constraints and opportunities (remote versus face-to-face instruction, for example)

>> The pragmatic constraints, budget, and expertise needed for implementing the instruction

The main rule of thumb for applying the ADDIE model is that our design decisions across various phases of the model are **aligned**.

Determining the assumptions behind direct instructional-design frameworks

In Chapter 2, I briefly introduce direct instructional-design frameworks that focus on learning content to acquire new knowledge. Such frameworks assume that learning involves acquiring knowledge by relating it to prior knowledge. It focuses on systematic presentation of information, such as breaking down content into smaller steps. Other frameworks focus on providing guidelines for supporting other types of goals, such as understanding and problem solving. (See Chapter 7 for more on those frameworks.)

REMEMBER

Although our choice of instructional strategies do not fall neatly into only two types of categories (direct instruction and open-ended instruction), the distinction I use in this book provides a starting point for choosing the best approach for your goals. Instructional-design frameworks typically follow core assumptions about learning as well as assumptions about the best methods and instructional strategies to support learning.

Table 6-1 provides a summary of three key assumptions and example strategies that are commonly followed in direct instructional-design frameworks:

TABLE 6-1 Assumptions and Strategies of Direct Instructional Design Frameworks

Assumptions	Example Instructional Strategies
Learning involves changes in knowledge by building on prior knowledge.	Support learners to make connections between new and prior knowledge with strategies such as metaphors, real-world examples, explanations, organizing, and integrating new information with prior knowledge, and retrieving knowledge from memory.
Instructional strategies can be designed to trigger internal cognitive processes of learners, such as focusing attention, retrieving from memory, and elaborating new information with prior knowledge.	Use instructional strategies that align with the type of cognitive processes that learners need to learn effectively, such as using questioning strategies to direct learner attention or remember information.
Information is learned more effectively when taught using a structured, hierarchical approach.	Present basic information or subskills first and segment it into smaller chunks to help learners manage the processing demands of learning new information.

As summarized in Table 6-1, the first assumption of direct instructional design frameworks is that learning is a process of paying attention to relevant information, organizing and integrating it with prior knowledge, and retrieving and applying what was learned from memory. For this reason, these instructional-design frameworks use strategies to help learners pay attention to relevant information and elaborate new information with prior knowledge to make new connections.

A second assumption is that the instructional strategies are designed to explicitly trigger or support internal thinking processes. For instance, by using visual cues such as highlighting or animation, we support learners in the cognitive process of focusing attention on relevant information. Likewise, a designer may use graphical diagrams or mind maps to support learners to organize their thinking and to make new connections among ideas. There is a tight connection between the instructional strategies we choose and the learning processes we want learners to activate.

A third assumption recognizes that learning is best supported when we sequence the presentation of content from simple to complex. The task analysis process is a key method for organizing content and tasks in ways that support this assumption. (See Chapter 4 for more on that topic.) Direct instructional design models recommend teaching prerequisite skills first.

Examining common approaches to ordering your instructional activities

In Chapter 2, I outline a general sequence of instructional activities that are commonly used with direct instructional-design models. Often referred to as a tutorial approach, the activities follow a general sequence. You can notice this pattern — broken down in more detail — in the three instructional models presented in this chapter.

Instructional activities aligned with a direct instructional approach follow a similar sequence: Activating learners' attention, presenting the content information, providing activities and practice opportunities to make the material more meaningful, and then providing feedback and assessment.

TIP

General tips for ordering instructional activities in a direct instruction approach include the following:

>> Start with introductory instructional material, such as gaining attention, presenting objectives for the instruction, then clarifying how and why the instruction is relevant to learners.

- >> Present the content information and focus learners' attention on the essential information.
- >> Provide guidance for learners to process and learn the material, such as with examples or demonstrations.
- >> Give opportunities to practice knowledge and skills.
- >> Provide feedback or assessment on the practice activities.

Choosing based on your goals

Different instructional frameworks call for different planning processes and instructional strategies. The key is to find and use guidelines that help you identify strategies to foster the type of learning outcomes you identified. The instructional-design models I present in this chapter are particularly well-suited for instructional goals that involve remembering and comprehending concepts. They also are well-suited for learning tasks that require following a specific procedure or series of steps that need to be learned.

EXAMPLE

Direct instructional-design frameworks are a good choice when your instruction involves the following types of goals:

- >> **Content knowledge:** Learning facts and concepts through information presentation and practice
- >> **Procedural skills:** Learning tasks that involve a specific sequence, steps, or procedures, such as safety protocols or software operation
- >> **Training:** Demonstrating awareness of rules or regulations, such as onboarding information, product training, or compliance training
- >> **Skill development:** Practicing tasks that involve repeated opportunities for practice, such as multiplication skills, foreign language vocabulary, or test preparation

REMEMBER

It's important to note that while direct instructional-design approaches are effective for achieving specific learning goals, they may not be the most appropriate approach for every educational context. The choice of instructional design models should consider the nature of the content, the characteristics of the learners, and the desired learning outcomes. In some cases, more experiential, problem-based, or constructivist approaches may be more suitable (see Chapter 7 for such types of design frameworks).

Gagne's Nine Events of Instruction

In the 1960s, Robert Gagné developed the "Nine Events of Instruction," which is a guide for developing effective instruction. Gagné's Nine Events of Instruction outlines a series of nine events (or structured activities) that are followed in a specific sequence to facilitate learning. This method is still widely used today by instructional designers. The instruction is easy to apply for many different types of instructional situations, even for designers with limited experience in education.

Gagné's Nine Events of Instruction are aligned with cognitive theories of learning (see Chapter 2), which means that it focuses on thinking processes such as directing attention, connecting to prior knowledge, and retrieving knowledge. Each of Gagné's nine events is designed to support a specific cognitive process that is a needed during that part of the learning process.

The sections that follow introduce the steps of the Nine Events of Instruction in more detail, along with examples.

Nine Steps to Designing Effective Instruction

Gagné's Nine Events of Instruction gives you a structured framework to designing instruction. As to why Gagne's theory uses the word "events" instead of "steps," it's because it focuses on the correspondence between a specific instructional event, such as an instructional strategy and the internal thinking process that it activates. In this book, I refer to the events as "steps" for simplicity and clarity. By following these nine steps in order, your instruction covers the main foundations needed to help your learners effectively process the instructional material.

Table 6-2 provides a summary of Gagné's Nine Events of Instruction.

Each step of Gagné's nine events of instruction is presented in more detail in the following sections:

Gain Learners' Attention

The first step is to gain learners' attention and interest in the instructional material. You can gain learners' attention at the start of the instruction through a variety of methods, including those detailed here.

TABLE 6-2   Gagné's Nine Events of Instruction

Order of Gagné's Nine Events	Description
1. Gain attention	Focus learner's attention on the instruction.
2. Inform learners of the objectives	Support learners to realize what to expect and what is important.
3. Stimulate recall of prior knowledge	Remind learners of what they learned in the past and how it is related to what will be learned in the instruction.
4. Present the content	Present or show the content material for the objective(s).
5. Provide learning guidance	Create guided learning activities to help learners process and learn the content.
6. Elicit performance or practice	Prompt learners to try out or practice what they are learning.
7. Provide feedback to learners	Give learners formative feedback on their performance or activity.
8. Assess performance	Assess whether learners have learned the objectives.
9. Enhance retention and transfer of what was learned	Help learners remember the content and apply it to new problems or situations.

EXAMPLE

Example strategies to gain learners' attention:

- ≫ Present a compelling or thought-provoking question to pique learners' interests.
- ≫ Refer learners to current events that may be related to the instructional topic.
- ≫ Present an interesting story or scenario that may be surprising.
- ≫ Use icebreakers related to the topic that require group participation.
- ≫ Present a short, interesting visual or video clip.

Inform Learners of the Objectives

For the second step of Gagne's Nine Events of Instruction, you should clearly communicate the learning objectives and expected outcomes of the instruction to help learners understand what they are expected to do. The objectives can be more general statements of goals, rather than listing every objective that you designed for the instruction. This step is about helping learners to understand what they can do or know after completing the instruction.

Example strategies to inform learners of the objectives include the following:

>> Present written objectives within the instruction itself, a course syllabus, or on one of the first presentation slides of a lecture.

>> For online courses that use a learning management system (LMS) or a website, create a page that covers the instructional objectives for that lesson.

>> Describe what is required of learners, what is assessed, and/or what is expected for successful performance.

Stimulate Recall of Prior Knowledge

The third step of Gagné's Nine Events of Instruction is to encourage learners to recall their existing knowledge and experiences related to the instructional topic. This event will help learners to make sense of what they are going to learn by relating it to something they already know or experienced. The goal of this step is for your learners to build on what they already know.

Example strategies to stimulate recall of prior knowledge include the following:

>> Provide a summary of prior topics or content learned previously that is relevant to the instruction.

>> Ask questions about prior knowledge or related experiences.

>> Create an activity that requires learners to think about their prior knowledge and represent it in some way, such as through a concept map or a whiteboard summary.

>> Create short, ungraded games or quizzes of the expected prerequisite knowledge. Explain why answers are correct or incorrect and how they are important to the present instructional content.

Present the Content

During this step of Gagné's Nine Events of Instruction, you present the instructional information or content. The content should be organized and delivered in a way that aligns with the instructional objectives. The content should be clear, well-structured, and focused on essential information identified from the objectives.

Example strategies to present the content material include the following:

>> Give a lecture on the topic with presentation slides.

>> Present the content as text for either print-based instruction, instructional websites, or an LMS.

>> Present audio or video as multimedia instruction for mobile devices, websites, or LMSes.

>> Present instructional content as a self-paced tutorial where learners decide when to learn the material at their own pace.

>> Use a variety of presentation methods and media such as text, audio, lecture, graphics, or visuals to communicate the instructional content.

>> Present small, organized chunks of information in ways that are accessible to learners.

Chapters 3 and 9 introduce the concept of learner accessibility and Universal Design for Learning. The framework presents three main guidelines for presenting instructional content that is accessible for a variety of learners.

The guidelines focus on three main recommendations:

>> Provide multiple means of engagement

>> Provide multiple means of representation

>> Provide multiple means of action and expression

Provide Learning Guidance

During this step of Gagné's Nine Events of Instruction, you provide guidance to learners to help them understand and make sense of the new content information. This guidance may include explanations, examples, demonstrations, or guidance on how to process the information effectively.

Example strategies to provide learning guidance include the following:

>> Present plenty of examples to support recognizing instances of a concept or idea.

>> Model or demonstrate a process, procedure, or performance.

>> Create activities that help learners use learning strategies such as mnemonics (memorization support), concept maps (to show relationships), elaborations, metaphors, or analogies.

>> Use case studies or stories to show how the concepts or ideas look in action.

>> Use peer collaboration to share ideas and best practices for learning.

Elicit Performance or Practice

Step 6 of Gagné's Nine Events of Instruction involves supporting learners to actively engage with the instruction. Often referred to as active learning strategies, this step may involve activities such as practice exercises, discussions, or assignments. The goal is for learners to practice or apply what they are learning.

EXAMPLE

Example strategies to elicit performance or practice include the following:

>> Create activities that help learners try out what they are learning, such as answering questions, summarizing and organizing, or trying out a procedure or skill on their own.

>> Provide formative assessment opportunities, such as writing assignments, presentations, or quizzes.

>> Use role plays, problem scenarios, simulations, or games to practice applying the instructional concepts.

>> Support collaboration with peers to work together to solve problems and check each other's understanding.

Provide Feedback to Learners

During this step of Gagné's Nine Events of Instruction, you provide feedback to learners to let them know how well they have performed. Feedback can be formative, meaning that the purpose is to improve performance. It can also be informal, such as from peer feedback from other learners or instructors. Feedback can focus on reinforcing correct responses, correcting errors, or providing other points of view to improve understanding.

EXAMPLE

Example strategies for providing feedback to learners include the following:

>> Confirm that learners' performance is on track, such as with a quiz that informs learners what they answered correctly or incorrectly.

>> Use peer evaluations where learners give feedback to each other on a common assignment or activity.

>> Promote self-evaluation to identify shortcomings in understanding or performance.

>> Give constructive feedback on a performance to help learners identify where they need improvement along with additional resources or opportunities for practice.

Assess Learner Performance

During this step of Gagné's Nine Events of Instruction, you assess how well learners have mastered the content and met the instructional objectives. Assessments can include quizzes or performance demonstrations. Chapter 11 introduces different forms of assessing learner performance.

REMEMBER

You have many different ways to assess learning of instructional objectives. The important detail to remember is that the assessment is aligned with the objectives and the requirements of the performance environment. So, if successful performance involves parallel parking a vehicle, you should require demonstration of the parking skill, versus only answering questions about how to perform the skill.

EXAMPLE

Example strategies of assessing learner performance include the following:

>> Give pre- and post-tests to show learning improvements after the instruction.

>> Use quizzes or tests to assess learning.

>> Use rubrics or criteria that learners see in advance to evaluate demonstrations, performances, presentations, or created products.

>> Make sure learners have the opportunity for formative feedback before final assessments.

Enhance Retention and Transfer of What Was Learned

The last step in Gagné's Nine Events of Instruction is focused on helping learners retain what they have learned and apply their knowledge to new, real-life situations. This activity may involve reviewing key points, providing additional resources or job aids to have easy access to content on the job, or encouraging learners to apply their knowledge beyond the instruction.

EXAMPLE

Example strategies to enhance retention and transfer include the following:

>> Provide a review of the most important content to be remembered.

>> Create activities that support learners to apply or integrate what they are learning with real-world problems or tasks.

>> Use multiple analogies, examples, or contrasting cases to promote more flexible understanding of how knowledge can be applied across different types of situations.

>> Ask learners "What if?" questions to consider how to apply what was learned in new situations.

In sum, Gagné's Nine Events of Instruction outlines nine steps to help you design and sequence your instruction.

Gagne's Nine Events of Instruction: Putting it all together

This section presents a brief example of how your instruction may unfold using Gagné's Nine Events of Instruction. The overall instructional goal for this example is the following: Learners are able to identify and demonstrate effective conflict resolution techniques during customer service interactions, as measured by improving customer satisfaction ratings.

Table 6-3 provides a brief example lesson outline:

TABLE 6-3 **Example Lesson Outline Using Gagné's Nine Events of Instruction**

Gagné's Nine Events	Example Strategies
1. Gain attention	*Focus learner's attention on the instruction.* Begin the instruction with a brief role-play scenario demonstrating a challenging customer interaction. Ask learners to reflect on their own experiences and feelings in similar situations and to share them in small groups. Have small groups report out to the larger group.
2. Inform learners of the objectives	*Support learners to realize what to expect and where to focus their attention.* Clearly state the instructional objective: "By the end of this instruction, you will be able to effectively resolve customer conflicts and improve customer satisfaction ratings."
3. Stimulate recall of prior knowledge	*Remind learners of what they learned in the past and how it is related to what will be learned in the instruction.* Encourage learners to share their existing knowledge of conflict resolution techniques and any previous training or tips they may have received. This provides a starting point for building on existing understanding.

Gagné's Nine Events	Example Strategies
4. Present the content	*Present or show the content material for the objective(s).* Present a framework for conflict resolution (for example, active listening, empathy, problem-solving), and describe communication techniques.
5. Provide learning guidance	*Create guided learning activities to help learners process and learn the content.* Break down each aspect of the conflict resolution framework, providing detailed explanations and strategies for applying each element. Offer guidelines and best practices. Use real-life examples and case studies.
6. Elicit performance or practice	*Prompt learners to try out or practice what they are learning.* Conduct role-play exercises where learners can practice conflict resolution techniques in pairs or small groups. Provide scenarios of common customer complaints. Ask learners to present best practices they have experienced and share them with each other.
7. Provide feedback to learners	*Give learners formative feedback on their performance or assignment.* After each role-play, provide constructive feedback on learners' performance. Highlight what they did well and suggest improvements. Encourage peer feedback through a rubric of key strategies of effective resolution.
8. Assess performance	*Assess whether learners have learned the objectives.* Administer interactive quizzes or polls that assess learners' identification and application of conflict resolution strategies. Include scenario-based questions to evaluate their ability to apply the techniques learned.
9. Enhance retention and transfer of what was learned	*Help learners remember the content and apply it to new problems or real-world situations.* Conclude the instruction by asking learners to generate an action plan of strategies they can draw upon in their day-to-day work in the future. Provide additional resources, such as job aids or reference materials, to support ongoing learning and application in the workplace.

Mayer's Framework for Active Learning: The Selecting-Organizing-Integrating (SOI) Model

The instructional-design frameworks presented in this chapter support learners to process instructional content and information in a way that activates cognitive processes that are helpful for their learning. This section covers another instructional-design approach, developed by Richard Mayer, that entails using instructional strategies that activate three learning processes: Selecting, Organizing, and Integrating (abbreviated as SOI):

>> **Selecting** relevant information

>> **Organizing** information in a meaningful way

>> **Integrating** information with prior knowledge

An instructional designer can use this model to design instructional strategies that support these learning processes. The sections that follow explain how to apply Mayer's SOI model to your instruction.

Helping the learner process instructional information

The SOI model is designed to support an *active learning* process. This means that both the instruction (or the instructor) and the learner work together to achieve active learning, versus passive engagement, with the material. It is not enough to simply present information and assume that learners will use active learning strategies to comprehend the material more deeply. Mayer's framework provides a series of steps to help you better support learners in an active approach to learning.

EXAMPLE

Suppose you view a YouTube video on learning about artificial intelligence (AI). Although you may understand the words and follow the images, after you finish the video, you can't explain AI to others or why it may be relevant to you. What can an instructional designer do to better support learners to understand the content?

Mayer's SOI model gives us a framework for designing instructional strategies that align with the types of learning processes needed to engage in deeper learning of the material. These strategies are intended to prime learners to engage in active learning, such as attending to important information, organizing what they are learning, and relating it to prior knowledge. By following the framework, you can help learners to activate and use these learning processes.

The next section explains the process as tips or steps that you can follow to better support the active learning processes of selecting, organizing, and integrating.

Three tips to support active learning

The goal of the SOI framework is to help you develop activities that support the active processing of instructional materials: Paying attention to relevant content information (named "selecting"), organizing it in ways that you're your learners can make sense of it (named "organizing"), and integrating it with their prior knowledge or experiences (named "integrating").

Table 6-4 provides a high-level summary Mayer's SOI model. The sections that follow give tips for supporting each of the three processes in more detail.

TABLE 6-4   ## The SOI Model for Designing Active Learning Strategies

Learning Process	Description
Selecting	• Use instructional strategies to help learners focus their attention on relevant information they are reading, hearing, or seeing. • Highlight important information visually in the instruction (for example, highlighting, bolding). • Support summarizing of key points.
Organizing	• Support learners to organize the details of the instructional concepts. • Visualize or elaborate concepts with images and text.
Integrating	• Help learners connect prior knowledge with new information • Generate explanations for yourself or others. • Apply what is learned.

Prompt Learners to Select Relevant Information.

The first tip for creating instruction that supports active learning strategies is to present information and activities in ways that focus learners' attention on the key ideas that are important. Example strategies that you may use to guide learners to select relevant information include the following:

EXAMPLE

>> Help learners distinguish between important and unimportant information by highlighting information visually. This may include strategies such as the using the following:

- Headings

- Bullet points

- Arrows and color highlighting of terms

- Repetition of key concepts

- Margin notes
- Bold text for important terms

>> Use summarizing strategies to help learners summarize the key concepts. You can present written or oral summaries as part of the instruction or, if practical, ask learners to summarize the key points themselves. Asking learners to create short summaries supports active processing.

>> Ask questions that highlight important details you want to reinforce (for example, fill-in-the-blank questions, short quizzes).

>> Present instructional objectives at the beginning of the instruction so that learners can identify the most important goals to focus on.

Support Learners to Organize Information.

After learners select relevant information to pay attention to, the next active learning process is organizing the details of the information into memory. Supporting learners to organize information involves helping them to make sense of the ideas being presented.

Strategies that instructional designers can use to support learners to organize instructional information include the following:

EXAMPLE

>> Ask learners to elaborate the information using strategies such as comparing and contrasting, classifying, outlining, or explaining causes and effects.

>> Support learners to visualize connections among the information they are learning, such as through a concept map, matrix, flowchart, graphic organizer, or drawings that represent relationships among key ideas.

>> Generate guiding questions for learners to self-assess what they are learning.

>> Encourage discussion and sharing of understanding with other learners to elaborate and create new connections.

>> If using multimedia, use both text and graphics together to illustrate and organize complex concepts.

Encourage Learners to Integrate New and Prior Knowledge.

After you help learners to attend to relevant information and then teach them how to organize and elaborate their thinking about the instruction, it is time to support them to integrate their new learning with prior knowledge. During this process, learners activate relevant prior knowledge and apply it to create new meaning.

Example strategies that instructional designers can use to support learners to integrate instructional information include the following:

EXAMPLE

>> Use questions, analogies, or stories to help activate learners' prior knowledge.

>> Provide examples that learners recognize as familiar or relevant to their jobs or daily lives.

>> Ask learners to engage in explanation, including self-explanations (explaining information to themselves in their own words) or explaining information to others in ways that are personally relevant.

>> Ask learners to apply what they are learning to an example they have experienced or may experience in the future.

>> Practice applying skills in a realistic context.

>> Ask learners to teach others what they have learned.

Putting it all together

Putting the three parts of the SOI model together in an example instructional lesson may look like the following:

EXAMPLE

Assume that the instructional goal is to use a learning management system (LMS) to teach learners how to apply principles of effective multimedia instruction by designing a multimedia lesson. Learners may first be supported to **select** relevant information by being presented with content information on principles and best practices, along with visual examples of both effective and ineffective uses of graphics, audio, and video. Learners may then be asked to focus their attention to specific areas on the screen through use of arrows and audio explanations of what they are seeing. Then, they may be asked to complete an assignment where they summarize the key points and principles in their own words.

To support **organization** of the material, learners may be asked to create a matrix of effective principles along with images that illustrate the concept. They may then be asked to analyze three different examples of multimedia instruction and evaluate what principles are present or missing. These activities may take place via a discussion board, where learners present their thoughts to their classmates and learn from each other's analyses.

To support **integration**, learners may be asked to generate their own examples of a multimedia lesson and to explain how it represents best practices and principles of multimedia design as well as any trade-offs they made in the design process.

The SOI model helps you to generate instructional strategies that guide learners to use cognitive processes of selecting, organizing, and integrating.

Keller's guide to creating motivating instructional strategies

John M. Keller is a researcher from Florida State University who developed a framework for designing instructional strategies called the ARCS model, which focuses on motivation. ARCS is an acronym that stands for **A**ttention, **R**elevance, **C**onfidence, and **S**atisfaction, which are the four major components that Keller identified as important for motivating learners. The model is intended to guide the design of instructional materials and strategies to enhance motivation and engagement.

Instructional designers often assume that if our instruction is well designed with respect to our learning objectives, learners will be automatically motivated. This scenario is not always the case. Learner motivation is particularly important for self-paced instruction, as motivation affects persistence and completion of instruction. Given this, it is important to consider learners' motivation when designing instructional strategies.

The ARCS model offers guidance for how to incorporate strategies and information to increase motivation, rather than it being a comprehensive instructional design model that guides the entire design process. This means that ARCS is ideally used in conjunction with other instructional design frameworks. The focus of ARCS is on designing instruction that considers learners' motivation.

Four elements for designing for motivation: Attention (A), Relevance (R), Confidence (C), and Satisfaction (S)

The ARCS model presents four categories of motivating conditions that can help you design instruction that is interesting, rewarding, and appropriately challenging for learners. The four categories, which are described in more detail in the sections that follow are:

» Attention (A)

» Relevance (R)

» Confidence (C)

» Satisfaction (S)

Attention

The "A" component of the ARCS model focuses on capturing the learners' interest and directing their attention to the instructional material. It involves stimulating their curiosity and maintaining their interest throughout the learning process. A learner must first choose to direct their attention to the learning experience. Maintaining attention over time is best accomplished when learners engage in activities that trigger their curiosity or allow them to act upon their curiosity.

TIP

Tips for engaging learners' attention to increase their curiosity include:

» Use the element of surprise to pique learners' interest in the instruction. This method may include presenting a surprising story.

» Give examples or personal anecdotes that are concrete and realistic to maintain interest.

» Present a puzzling situation or an attention-grabbing problem that learners are asked to resolve during the instruction.

» Use a variety of instructional strategies and media (for example, videos, discussions, games, and such) to sustain interest.

EXAMPLE

In an instructional module about environmental conservation, the designer can start with a captivating video showing the impact of pollution on wildlife. The purpose of the video is to capture the learners' interest and attention to get them curious about the subject matter.

Relevance

The "R" component of the ARCS model focuses on the importance of making the content meaningful and applicable to the learners' lives, work, or personal goals. It involves demonstrating the practical value of learning the information.

TIP

Tips for increasing relevance of the instruction for learners include:

» Conduct needs analyses and learner analyses (see Chapter 3) to better understand the needs and priorities of your learners.

» Early on in the instruction, present how and why the instruction can be useful to learners' goals, jobs, or lives.

» Ask learners to generate what they want to learn from the instruction to prompt them to identify their own needs to know more information.

Take for instance you are designing a training program on time management. To support "relevance," you incorporate scenarios and examples specific to the learners' job roles. Likewise, you can ask learners to list on a whiteboard the most challenging time management situations they face. This type of activity may increase the relevance of the instruction by tying it to their daily work tasks.

Confidence

The "C" component of the ARCS model focuses on increasing learners' confidence that they can achieve success during the instructional experience. This model involves building learners' confidence about their ability to master the material.

TIP

Tips for building learners' confidence during the instruction include:

>> Present the requirements and standards for success. This way, learners know what to expect and gain confidence that the instruction can help them achieve these goals.

>> Give many opportunities for success through using a variety of activities, opportunities for practice, and formative feedback.

>> Sequence difficult activities from simple to complex, keeping an achievable level of challenge for learners. Making the instruction too easy, or too difficult, decreases engagement.

>> If practical, allow learners to have some control over the pace of their learning experience.

EXAMPLE

For a software training example, an instructional designer can support learner confidence by creating a series of activities that gradually increases in difficulty level. Each level is designed to challenge learners but in a way that builds their confidence along the way. This method may include breaking down the skills in into smaller modules and starting with basic functionalities before progressing to more advanced features. Providing step-by-step instructions and hands-on exercises enable learners to practice before proceeding to the next skill level.

Satisfaction

The "S" component of the ARCS model focuses on supporting learners' satisfaction in accomplishing the goals of the instruction. Satisfaction includes learners' overall instructional experience as well as their enjoyment of the instruction and perceived value of what was learned. Positive feedback also influences learner satisfaction.

TIP

Tips for increasing learner satisfaction of the instruction include:

>> Use praise or rewards after learners make progress during the instruction.

>> Present informative and motivating feedback.

>> Design activities that support learners' interests and application to their jobs or lives.

>> Ask learners to self-assess if their learning goals were met at the end of the instruction.

EXAMPLE

In a software training example, strategies to increase learner satisfaction may involve incorporating interactive activities such as demonstrations, group problem solving, and individual activities to make the learning experience more enjoyable. Likewise, presenting practice and feedback activities, as well as reward systems, such as badges or certificates for completing the instruction, may also support learner satisfaction.

REMEMBER

This chapter presented three instructional models that you can draw upon when creating your instructional sequences and strategies. Although each has different steps or ways of structuring the experience, you may notice some common elements across the three direct instructional design models:

>> Instruction typically starts with gaining attention and setting up what learners can expect from the experience.

>> Present content information in ways that guide the learners to make sense of the material in ways that are active and engaging.

>> Learners have an opportunity to practice and get feedback.

>> Learning is reinforced or assessed according to the overall goals.

Chapter 7

Open-ended Design Frameworks

I always want to stress that you can choose between a number of different instructional approaches and models to guide how you go about designing your instruction. In Chapters 2 through 6, I set the stage for understanding the different types of instructional designs that you can employ, depending on your specific configuration of goals, learners, and instructional needs. Chapter 2 lays out a framework for understanding how different learning and instructional foundations can lead to different types of instructional designs, while Chapter 6 explores instructional design frameworks that I refer to as "direct instruction" — instruction that focuses on activities that support acquiring and processing content information according to specific learning outcomes. I provide tips for designers to organize their instruction in alignment with such goals and objectives.

In this chapter, you get a chance to explore instructional design frameworks that provide guidelines for designing instruction that are more aligned with goals of understanding and applying knowledge in new situations. As a result, they draw upon instructional strategies that are intended to support learners in ways that enable them to use and apply their knowledge in more open-ended ways.

In this chapter, I present two instructional design frameworks that you can use as models for designing open-ended instructional designs:

» The Teaching for Understanding (TFU) model

» The Problem-based Learning (PBL) model

These two instructional models draw upon constructivist and learner-centered instructional foundations. (If constructivist is a new term for you, check out Chapter 2, where I first talk about constructivist foundations.) In this chapter, I expand upon that initial discussion in the context of presenting these two design models.

Choosing When to Use Open-ended Design Frameworks

Different types of instructional design approaches draw upon different views about learning and teaching. When planning your instructional design project, deciding which instructional design frameworks will work best for you begins with analyzing your learning goals, your instructional and organization context, as well as gaining an awareness of the design frameworks that you want to use. From there, you select instructional strategies and frameworks that are complementary to the instructional situation for which you are designing.

In the sections that follow, I give you detailed tips for selecting and designing instructional strategies that are aligned with open-ended design frameworks. In addition to these tips, the following general guidelines also need to be met for your instructional design project.

TIP

Make sure your instructional design frameworks and strategies are aligned with the following:

» The instruction's learning outcomes, objectives, assessments, and evaluation strategies

» The needs of the organization and potential learners

» The technology or delivery system constraints and opportunities

» The pragmatic constraints, budget, and expertise needed for implementing the instruction

Choosing a design framework is based on a combination of instructional factors, unique aspects the context, and pragmatic factors.

REMEMBER

You can think about instructional design as a process of aligning our Analysis, Design, Development, Implementation, and Evaluation phases (ADDIE). Within the first "D" or design phase of the ADDIE model, you are not limited to only one type of design framework. The ADDIE framework is broad enough to allow for different types of design strategies and models, depending on your analyses and goals. The main rule of the ADDIE model is that your decisions across various phases of the model are *aligned*.

Examining assumptions of open-ended frameworks

I briefly introduce open-ended instructional design frameworks back in Chapter 2, noting there that such frameworks are based on learner-centered principles in contrast to solely content-focused instruction. Open-ended frameworks are based on an assumption that learners need opportunities to construct their own meaning and demonstrate their understanding of the instructional content. Open-ended design approaches center the importance of learners in constructing meaning and they provide guidance to help learners engage in this meaning-making process.

Open-ended instructional design frameworks emerged in response to shifting educational perspectives towards constructivist views of learning (introduced in Chapter 2). These views signaled a change in the way learning and design itself were approached. At the same time, advancements in technology began changing how designers can conceptualize how to integrate technology resources and tools into instruction, expanding the possibilities for creating new learning environments.

Open-ended instructional frameworks are built on key assumptions about learning, the educational strategies used, and the role of the learner. Table 7-1 provides a summary of the assumptions and strategies that are typically associated with using open-ended instructional design frameworks.

As summarized in Table 7-1, the first assumption of open-ended frameworks is that they prioritize the role of learners' prior experiences and knowledge in shaping their learning. This concept is aligned with constructivist views of learning (introduced in Chapter 2). Open-ended frameworks use strategies to support learners to make their initial understanding explicit, because it serves as the foundation upon which deeper understanding is built. For this reason, open-ended frameworks typically begin with strategies designed to elicit learner ideas or solutions that are shared and discussed with others.

TABLE 7-1 **Assumptions and Strategies of Open-Ended Instructional Design Frameworks**

Assumptions	Example Instructional Strategies
Learning and understanding is a product of personally constructed meaning, often during interaction with others.	Support learners to make initial beliefs explicit through prompting and through collaborative learning opportunities.
Learning is best supported when learners are actively engaged in constructing meaning.	Use active learning strategies such as hands-on exploration, constructing artifacts, or trying out ideas to see how they work.
Knowledge is more meaningful and easily applied when it is learned in the context of solving realistic problems.	Use real-world problems, authentic practices, or open-ended questions to drive the instructional activities, rather than present isolated facts.
Understanding requires supporting learners to monitor their own learning.	Help learners develop an awareness of when they are unclear, what they understand, and what they need to know.

Second, open-ended frameworks assume that learning is best supported when learners are actively engaged in the process of constructing personal meaning. This concept means that instructional strategies must support active (not passive) learning, such as with hands-on exploration, constructing ideas or artifacts, and trying out ideas to see how they work in different situations.

Third, open-ended frameworks assume that learning is most meaningful when it is rooted in realistic, applied contexts. Instructional strategies here would emphasize the use of authentic, problem-based, or case-based contexts to guide learning efforts. Problems are often open-ended, implying that there is no single correct solution or approach to solving a problem. Because problems are complex, learners are supported at critical junctures while they are learning.

Fourth, open-ended frameworks assume that understanding is best supported when learners learn how to monitor their own learning. Instructional strategies, then, support learners to engage in reflection, monitoring, and self-assessment of what they already know and what they need to know.

Choosing frameworks based on your goals

Open-ended design frameworks are best suited for instructional goals that fall into the higher levels of Bloom's Taxonomy, such as Application, Analysis, Evaluate, and Create. (For more on Bloom's taxonomy, see Chapter 4.) From a pragmatic perspective, open-ended frameworks also work well in situations where you have sufficient time to support exploration and collaborative problem solving.

Open-ended learning is particularly well-suited for fostering certain types of learning goals and objectives, such as:

EXAMPLE

>> **Problem solving:** Engaging in complex, real-world problems that often lack a single correct answer

>> **Creativity and innovation:** Creating and generating novel ideas, products, or designs

>> **Hypothesizing:** Proposing hypotheses or new ideas and testing them

>> **Self-directed learning:** Empowering learners to take control of their own learning, such as goal setting, planning, and self-assessment

>> **Collaborative sense making:** Working with others to make sense of a problem by sharing and building upon each other's perspectives

>> **Reflective practice:** Recognizing how to improve one's practice or performance through the process of reflection, often collaboratively with others

REMEMBER

In practice, an instructional design project often entails more than one type of learning goal, and in those instances, feel free to use a balanced approach that may draw from both open-ended and directed instructional strategies. What is most important is that the design strategies you use are aligned with the goals you are designing for in that particular element of the instruction, while also considering the needs of the learners and constraints of the instructional context.

Designing for Understanding versus Memorization

Open-ended design frameworks are designed to support goals of understanding versus memorizing. For some kinds of learning, understanding is the primary goal. We all want learners to understand the instruction that we design. But how is understanding different from knowledge that is memorized? We can likely think of situations where we have memorized facts, equations, or procedures but were not able to *use* them when needed to solve a new problem or apply to a new situation.

At the heart of understanding is the ability to flexibly think, act, and use what we have learned. Knowledge that is memorized is often a crucial foundation for understanding, but knowing facts is not the same as understanding or applying what was learned to new situations.

It is important to acknowledge that sometimes our instructional goals are more about helping learners commit knowledge to memory or apply a specific set of well-practiced procedures rather than understanding. So, it is important to distinguish between understanding goals and knowledge memorization. Learning goals focused on understanding require learners to be able to expand their knowledge to new situations in flexible or creative ways.

EXAMPLE

Knowing the historical facts around the causes of the U.S. Civil War (memorizing), for instance, does not mean that learners can think about a contemporary situation and make insightful connections to what they learned about the Civil war (understanding). Likewise, knowing how to compute fractions of a whole number is not the same as being able to solve a problem in a cooking situation that requires reducing a recipe by one third.

The next section introduces a specific open-ended design framework called the Teaching for Understanding model that gives us a structure for designing instruction to promote understanding goals.

The Teaching for Understanding (TFU) model

The Teaching for Understanding (TFU) model is an instructional framework developed by the Harvard Graduate School of Education that centers on understanding rather than surface-level memorization of facts. At its core, TFU is built on the premise that designing for understanding involves supporting learners to use and apply knowledge flexibly in a variety of contexts.

The TFU model prioritizes understanding as something that can be performed (as opposed to being a thought in the mind), as evidenced by one's ability to use knowledge "in action" in new situations. This model aligns with open-ended instructional frameworks by emphasizing that learners are more likely to understand a topic when they can think and act competently and creatively and by expanding their knowledge by applying it to new situations.

The TFU framework is comprised of four main strategies:

>> Identifying topics that support understanding

>> Generating understanding goals

>> Structuring activities to require that learners demonstrate understanding

>> Providing ongoing assessment

Identifying topics and goals supportive of understanding involves choosing topics that encourage deep understanding. The activities you design lead students to actively apply their knowledge in meaningful ways. Ongoing assessments are about continuously gauging student progress. (I summarize these four strategies along with tips for applying them in the sections that follow.)

Mastering the four key strategies to use for Teaching for Understanding (TFU)

Designing for the TFU model entails four key strategies, each of which I discuss in the following sections.

Identifying topics that support understanding

The first strategy in the TFU model is to choose topics that have enough depth that they can lead to understanding. This concept sounds obvious, but many times the nature of topics we need to teach are inherently about imparting information, such as memorizing content for compliance training, remembering routine procedures, or memorizing commands of a software program. Topics that are potentially effective for understanding goals, on the other hand, support the development of themes, ideas, or concepts that have depth and connectivity and that support analyzing a variety of perspectives. The topics have potential to go beyond imparting information to deeply exploring questions and making meaningful connections among ideas and examples.

TIP

Tips for identifying topics that support understanding include the following:

>> **Look for topics that are central to a subject or practice.** Such topics may include foundational concepts that you can be apply across multiple topics (for instance, structure and function in biology), lasting controversies (such as nature versus nurture in human development), or that are of central importance in a profession or job (such as ethics).

>> **Choose topics that are of interest and are accessible to your target learners.** Topics that support understanding are inherently intriguing to learners and naturally pique their curiosity. This motivates learners to explore and comprehend the topic more deeply. Begin by considering the relevance of the subject matter to the learners' lives and interests.

>> **Identify topics that are of interest to the instructor or subject-matter expert.** Educators' enthusiasm or curiosity about a particular issue can serve as a model for learners who are exploring new understanding. A teacher who genuinely enjoys or finds a topic interesting is inherently more invested in the instruction.

>> **Choose topics that are connectable to other topics.** These topics offer opportunities for learners to make multiple connections to their own prior knowledge, both within and outside of the classroom or workplace. Look for topics that encourage learners to see the relationships and intersections between various concepts. One strategy for identifying topics with many connections is to create a mind map or idea web that lets you brainstorm a topic and visually see its possible connections. Choose topics that have a lot of nodes or possible connections.

Some topics may seem like they are focused on memorization goals but can be designed to support understanding goals. Take for instance the following example:

EXAMPLE

Instruction on the Family Educational Rights and Privacy Act (FERPA) often focuses on memorization of the rules and regulations for privacy of student records. For instance, in a memorization-focused approach, learners may be asked to memorize specific sections of the FERPA law, such as definitions, key clauses, or penalties for violations. They can be required to recite this information and answer questions correctly on an assessment without necessarily understanding its broader context or significance.

In contrast, learners can explore case studies that illustrate FERPA's application to real-life situations commonly encountered by learners. Learners can be given a scenario where a teacher wants to share a student's academic performance data with another teacher who is not directly involved with the student's education. Through guided discussion, learners would explore the reasons why this may or may not be permissible under FERPA, reflecting and discussing foundational concepts of consent, "legitimate educational interest," and the balance between privacy and educational goals.

This example illustrates that a topic and its instructional goals, strategies, and methods work together to promote deeper understanding, not just information about the topic alone.

Generating understanding goals

The second key strategy for designing for the TFU model is to identify the understanding goals for your instruction. *Understanding goals* are statements that identify what learners are expected to understand. This concept is the same process that you use for identifying instructional objectives, a skill that I discuss in greater detail in Chapter 5. The difference here is that instructional objectives more generally follow the type of learning goals and tasks that were identified in the Analysis phase and are inclusive of any type of learning goal, not just those that are focused on understanding.

In the TFU model, the learning goals always focus on understanding or the higher levels of Bloom's Taxonomy. (Again, more on that topic in Chapter 4.) Another difference is that the TFU model encourages designers to use words such as "understand" or "appreciate" in your statements of goals, whereas many other types of objectives would require use of concrete, observable, and actionable behaviors.

In identifying understanding goals, the idea is to identify the outcomes that learners are expected to achieve after completing the instruction. These goals focus on ensuring that learners not only acquire knowledge but also understand the underlying concepts, principles, and relationships within the subject matter. Understanding goals guide instruction in a way that encourages learners to engage with the material at a deep level, promoting critical thinking, problem-solving, and the ability to apply what they learn to various contexts.

EXAMPLE

Understanding goals typically involve strategies that require learners to demonstrate their understanding in tangible ways. This demonstration may include explaining complex concepts, analyzing information, making connections between different ideas, and applying their knowledge to solve real-world problems. For example, in a science class, an understanding goal may be for learners to explain the cause-and-effect relationships in a biological ecosystem. In this case, learners are asked to demonstrate a comprehensive understanding of the interdependencies between different organisms and their environment.

Likewise, another understanding goal in a science classroom may be: "Learners will understand how to use the principles of mechanics to explain how the joints of the body could sustain injury depending on the different forces that are acted upon them."

Similarly, the prior section's example of two different approaches to designing instruction on the topic of FERPA show the distinction between understanding goals and those focused on memorization. In one example, the primary instructional goal was to memorize the specific provisions of the law. In the other, the primary goal was focused on understanding the underlying principles and implications of the law.

TIP

Tips for generating understanding goals include the following:

>> Make your understanding goals explicit and public at the start of the instruction.

>> Ask yourself questions such as, "What understanding do I want learners to develop?" and "Why is teaching this topic important?"

>> Try to find a connecting theme across your goals, especially goals that extend across longer timeframes. Your instruction may have a variety of goals nested within it, but generating themes across all of them can help you come back to what is most important.

>> Leave room for your learners to add ideas for refining or adding to the goals.

I introduce a variety of action verbs associated with different levels of Bloom's Taxonomy of learning goals in Chapter 4. Reviewing the action verbs at the higher levels of the taxonomy may help you with sentence starters for your goals that focus on understanding. Goals that align with the TFU model can go beyond the Understanding level of Bloom's Taxonomy to include higher levels.

Some example verbs to consider in your goals include:

>> Understand

>> Apply

>> Examine

>> Evaluate

>> Generate

>> Construct

>> Integrate

>> Justify

Structuring activities that require demonstrating understanding

The third strategy of the Teaching for Understanding (TFU) model is to design sequences of activities that progressively advance learners' understanding over time. The key characteristic of this strategy is that it emphasizes *demonstrations* — performances of understanding, in other words. Take, for instance, the process of learning how to drive a car. You cannot effectively determine if a learner understood this goal solely through assessments based on text content, videos, or a teacher's classroom instruction alone. It also requires performing the act of driving a car, which is composed of many smaller performances such as braking before a stop sign, merging onto a highway, or parallel parking a car on a busy street in a city. This simple example illustrates that *understanding* something goes beyond *knowing* something. This strategy of the TFU model focuses on performances that demonstrate understanding at various points in the learning process.

A performance view of understanding focuses us on what learners do or demonstrate instead of what content is being taught. Designers can shift their instructional efforts away from mere content and towards examining performances of understanding by considering what types of performances demonstrate extending, applying, or going beyond the content or information provided in the instruction. The TFU model recognizes that demonstrating understanding is the product of various understandings that develop over time.

TIP

Think about how to support learners to progressively build upon their understanding through structured activities that demonstrate learners' understanding at that point in time. This opens up an opportunity for them to receive feedback on their progress.

Table 7-2 illustrates a three-phase sequence for structuring activities that lead to performances of understanding.

TABLE 7-2

Three-phase Sequence for Structuring Activities to Support Teaching for Understanding

Sequence of Activities	Description
Phase 1: Exploration or "messing around"	Early in the instruction, have learners explore the topic in an informal way that piques their curiosity and establish a foundation upon which to build understanding.
	The activities should be accessible to learners who do not yet have knowledge of the topic; typically, such activities occur first before any content has been presented.
	Example: For instruction designed to help learners understand classification systems for identifying trees, an introductory exploration activity may be a scavenger hunt outdoors for finding different examples of tree features and then photographing them. Learners come up with their own classification scheme for what they observe.
Phase 2: Guided inquiry	Provide several phases of activities that lead learners in organized ways to use their knowledge.
	Earlier stages of guided activities set up more complex application of concepts and understanding.
	Example: After finishing the exploratory activity to find different examples of tree features outdoors, provide a series of guided inquiry lessons that are progressively more complex. Early activities can present content on the science topic of tree biodiversity as well as activities to engage in practices of scientific observation outdoors.
	Over time, learners can learn categorization schemes for identifying trees, such as leaves/needles, fruit elements, and branching structures. For example, learners can identify trees outdoors that have different types of tree fruits (acorns, berries, or cones, for example) and explain how they hold seeds and can help them identify the type of tree.
Phase 3: Culminating performance or activity	Create a culminating activity that brings together what learners have learned in ways that demonstrate understanding.
	Examples are often a final project, presentation, or exhibition. For instance, based on the previous example of activities, learners can be asked to create their own classification scheme for the biodiversity of trees that can be used by younger learners or by generating a new classification scheme for identifying different flowers.

Providing ongoing assessment

The fourth strategy of the Teaching for Understanding (TFU) model is to provide ongoing assessment and feedback throughout the instruction. By the time learners tackle the culminating activity, they should have received feedback multiple times during earlier phases of the guided inquiry process. Feedback is a fundamental aspect of learning, and it is most useful when it leads learners to frequently monitor and evaluate their progress.

Practically speaking, frequent assessment and feedback may require too much attention from a teacher to serve as the sole source of feedback. Unlike traditional assessments that are often limited to evaluations by an instructor at the end of instruction, ongoing assessments are integrated into the instructional approach itself, providing regular feedback through multiple methods throughout the process. For instance, ongoing assessment can also be provided by peers through collaboration or peer evaluations or by learners themselves through self-assessment or reflection questions. These additional opportunities for informal assessment work in conjunction with instructor feedback. Providing ongoing feedback requires thinking about feedback more frequently and informally.

TIP

Tips for designing ongoing assessments to support understanding goals may include:

>> **Checking in frequently.** Assessments should be conducted regularly. They are designed to be informal, which means their primary purpose is to provide feedback.

>> **Varying your assessment methods.** You should explore a wide range of assessment methods, such as quizzes, observations, discussions, self-assessments, or peer assessments.

>> **Incorporating self-assessments.** Ongoing assessment can be driven by the learners themselves, by actively participating in self-assessment and monitoring their own progress. Checklists or rubrics are common methods for supporting learners in their own self-assessment.

EXAMPLE

Examples of ongoing assessments can include:

>> Classroom discussions where students exchange points of view, reflect on their understanding, and ask questions if something is unclear.

>> Weekly quizzes to gauge the mastery of key concepts.

>> Daily *exit tickets* — daily informal assessments, in other words. These activities are brief, focused questions that are presented at the end of a lesson to quickly assess learning.

>> Peer review sessions for projects or written assignments as a means of providing constructive feedback.

>> Self-assessment checklists or reflection journals where students evaluate their progress and set goals.

Designing for Problem Solving

Open-ended design frameworks use instructional strategies that support learning that focuses on applying and using the knowledge gained. The last section presented one instructional model that focuses on supporting understanding and the flexible use of knowledge-in-action — the Teaching for Understanding model. This section covers Problem-based Learning, a different open-ended instructional framework that is designed to support applying knowledge to solve real-world problems.

Working with problem-based instructional approaches

Problem-based Learning (PBL) is an open-ended instructional model that places problem-solving and practical experiences at the forefront of the learning process. The model was originally developed for use in medical school contexts but has gained popularity in a variety of educational settings, from elementary and secondary schools to colleges and universities to professional training.

PBL aims to support learners in critical thinking, collaboration, and problem-solving skills necessary for real-world applications. A key element of PBL is that learners engage in self-directed learning while solving complex problems that have more than one answer or way to solve them. They learn new knowledge at the same time they are trying to solve the problem.

PBL uses realistic problems such as selecting the best location for a new city library, diagnosing a medical condition, or solving an environmental problem. PBL is often interdisciplinary and crosses subject boundaries such as science and urban planning. For these reasons, PBL typically involves collaborative teams who work together to tackle the different facets of the problem. The instructor's role in PBL is more of a facilitator or a guide — someone who offers support, provides resources, and helps learners stay on track in productive ways, in other words.

Five characteristics for designing problem-based learning

Common characteristics of PBL vary, depending on the context and target learners. However, at least five main characteristics comprise most PBL models:

>> A challenge or problem is presented.

>> Learners propose their initial ideas, solutions, or hypotheses.

>> Learners identify knowledge gaps and what they need to learn.

>> Learners engage in self-directed learning.

>> Learners apply their knowledge to solve the problem and present a solution.

These five characteristics are typically presented as five different parts of a cycle that proceeds in a specific sequence (sometimes called the tutorial process). Figure 7-1 presents an illustration of a typical cycle followed during PBL.

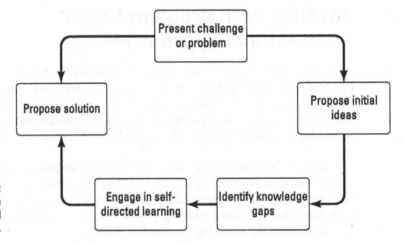

FIGURE 7-1:
An illustration
of a typical
PBL cycle.

I discuss each of the five characteristics of the PBL cycle in the following sections.

Presenting the challenge or problem

PBL begins with the presentation of a real-world problem, scenario, or case. This problem is often complex and open-ended, reflecting the kinds of challenges learners may encounter in their daily lives, jobs, or future careers. Learners initially spend time analyzing the problem, identifying the facts that were presented and/or asking an instructor questions. Learners begin the learning process with a challenging problem or task, and they learn the concepts and information needed to solve it during the PBL instruction.

You find several different types of problems in PBL. The following list presents a few:

TIP

>> **Diagnostic problems:** These types of problems involve learners determining the cause of a problem, such as a medical diagnosis.

>> **Design problems:** These types of problem involve designing a plan, presentation, or an artifact (such as a model), often based on constraints and specifications.

>> **Decision-making problems:** These types of problems involve making complex decisions in response to a scenario that asks learners to make a decision about what to do next, for instance, emergency care, safety protocols, or conflict resolution. Depending on their decision, the scenario changes to reflect what might happen as a result.

Problems can vary in terms of their scope and complexity, depending on the learners being targeted, the length of time available for the instruction, and the extent of prior knowledge. You can write problems as open-ended questions or as scenarios. You can also present problems as a series of progressively more complex challenges, rather than as only one problem.

EXAMPLE

Here's an example of a diagnostic problem for an elementary school science class:

We have learned that pollinators (bees and butterflies) are in danger in our region and are not finding the food, shelter, and nectar that they need to survive. You are part of a team who is being asked to come up with a plan for how to help them at our school by using what you learn about pollinator behaviors and habitats. Your plan will be shared with the school principal and teachers, and based on your ideas, the school will try out some of your plans in a garden plot outside of school.

Here's an example of design challenge for instructors:

How do you create engaging instructional designs for different types of instructional goals that are important in your work setting, such as technical instruction, innovation and teamwork, or interpersonal skills. Based on what you learn about effective instructional strategies, generate design principles for at least three different types of instructional goals you identify that you can teach to others in your workplace context. Present your principles in an instructional graphic or slide show. Back up your design decisions with evidence.

PBL assumes that learning is more meaningful when it's presented within real-world contexts, often while collaborating with others. For this reason, PBL uses authentic scenarios or challenges to support learners to apply concepts to practice.

Proposing initial ideas, solutions, or hypotheses

After the problem is presented, learners are then given a chance to propose an initial idea, solution, or thoughts about the problem even before they have been taught about it. Explicitly giving learners the opportunity to articulate what they think early on gives them a starting point for learning and the opportunity to recognize what they may need to learn to solve the problem. In this stage of the PBL process, learners make their first attempts to generate ideas and solutions that may be relevant to solve the problem.

TIP
A common method for supporting learners to think about initial ideas is to use question prompts for them to discuss the problem and come up with a possible solution, explanation, or hypothesis. You can accomplish this by using a whiteboard, where learners brainstorm and highlight their initial solutions, ideas, or hypotheses. By using a whiteboard or some other form of recording ideas, learners can return to their initial ideas and revise them as well as document what resources or facts they need to examine further. It also makes their initial ideas visible to an instructor who can ask questions or provide guidance.

EXAMPLE
Look at an example of how a designer may support learners to propose initial ideas or solutions to a problem. Take as an example a PBL activity where learners are asked to investigate trees and analyze why they are important within their local community. You can show them photos or videos of woodland settings (or if available, they could go outside and experience the wilderness directly) along with a problem scenario related to a decline in forested regions in the community.

To elicit their initial ideas, the problem may be investigated across multiple phases, with the first phase focused on the following driving question:

> *Look closely at the trees around this forest. How do you think these trees got here? How do you think trees grow in the forest? Discuss with your group and come up with reasons for your ideas.*

REMEMBER
PBL is aligned with constructivist views of learning (see Chapter 2), which emphasize the importance of learners' making their own meaning of the material during learning, starting with what they already know. For this reason, PBL uses design strategies to engage learners' initial experiences, ideas, or beliefs. Prompting learners early on in the PBL process to share what they think, even before they have started learning from the instruction, helps them articulate and build upon their initial ideas in an active way.

Identifying knowledge gaps

After learners identify their initial ideas or potential solutions to the problem, the next part of the PBL process is to encourage them to identify gaps in their knowledge or what they need to learn. Identifying initial ideas helps learners to think about what they know, but it also helps them to consider what else they need to know to solve the problem.

Strategies that instructional designers can use to support learners to reflect on gaps in knowledge that they need to solve the problem include the following:

EXAMPLE

>> Working with a facilitator to identify questions that focuses learners' attention on deeper explanations and encourage them to realize questions that they need to research and find answers to.

>> Generating question prompt cards or guiding questions for facilitators to use when they talk with each group about their initial solutions. These questions provide informal assessment and coaching.

>> Encouraging discussion and sharing with other learners, because it enables them to hear and learn from others' points of view that they may not have initially considered.

>> Providing access to expert opinions or resources to help learners explore the problem and build on their initial thinking. You can introduce expert perspectives via written scenarios or videos that illustrate how an expert may look at the situation. Seeing the contrast between learners' initial ideas and experts' ways of thinking can help them see more nuances and distinctions that they may have overlooked.

Engaging in self-directed learning

After learners have articulated their ideas or solutions to the problem and identified gaps in their knowledge, they are ready to start learning from the instructional materials and resources that you designed. During this phase, learners apply this new knowledge and skills to inform and expand upon their initial ideas or solutions to the problem.

In PBL, learners take an active role in their learning. They oversee the process of determining what they need to know to address the problem, with help from a facilitator. This process involves conducting research, asking questions, and seeking out relevant information. When working as part of a team, learners regroup to share what they learned and discuss how it may alter or extend their initial ideas or solutions. (Chapter 2 presents various collaborative learning strategies that learners can draw upon during PBL.)

EXAMPLE

The self-directed learning phase of the PBL process can include a variety of instructional activities and resources, including:

>> Lectures

>> Readings

>> Example projects, plans, or designs

>> Skill-building lessons

>> Educational simulations or games

>> Case studies (video or text)

>> Data, charts, or spreadsheets

Presenting the solution

The last phase of the PBL process is for learners to present their ideas, plans, or designs that represent their solution to the problem. In PBL, the culminating solution often takes on a project-like quality, but it can also take the form of any of the following:

>> Presentations

>> Videos

>> Plans or designs

>> Models

>> Reports

Ideally, the culminating activity is presented to others, to increase the authenticity of the problem-solving process.

4

Developing, Implementing, and Evaluating Instruction and Technology

Analyze when to use different instructional delivery modes by considering configurations of time and place as well as specific characteristics of technologies to support your instructional strategies.

Explore emerging technologies and their impact on instructional design.

Get to know principles for developing effective instructional materials using different types of technology.

See how to best support accessibility of instruction through universal design guidelines and practices.

Create a foundation for successful implementation of instruction.

Discover how to create four different levels of evaluation to measure success of the instructional design solution.

Chapter **8**

Using Technology to Deliver Instruction

echnology has changed the way we live our daily lives from the tools we use to communicate with family and friends to the ways we use our phones to find our way around a new city to the software we use to enhance our productivity at work.

Instructional design is no different — technology has also changed the ways we design and deliver instruction. Take, for instance, the standard classroom learning experience: A group of students is seated together in a classroom with a teacher who delivers instruction at the same time, in the same place, at the same pace, with tools such as a whiteboard and computer. Consider a different example of visitors to a museum where they can scan a QR code on their phones to learn about the background of the artwork in front of them and learn from the comments of experts. Both examples use different technologies to deliver instruction in different ways. Importantly, they also differ in their instructional purpose and have different constraints and opportunities for learning.

In this chapter, you discover how to analyze the most important factors for selecting the best methods and technologies to deliver your instruction. In practice, selecting technologies for delivering instruction usually begins early in the design process and is often based on the constraints of your situation — cost, infrastructure, time, technology availability, and learner characteristics, for example. In this chapter, I give some recommendations for how to identify what different technologies afford (or offer) for instruction, as well as the pros and cons of different technology selections. You also discover different examples of how technology can be used to deliver instruction as well as the impact of emerging technologies on instructional design.

Categorizing Delivery Modes

You determined that you have a need for the instruction and have a general outline of the instructional tasks, goals, objectives, and strategies. Now it is time to think about how you plan to deliver the instruction and what your best options are, given your goals and the constraints of the context in which the instruction will be used.

A good first place to start is to think about the delivery mode for your instruction. A *delivery mode* is the format that the course is delivered in. Delivery mode typically involves time and place of the instruction. These factors taken together define the access possibilities — that is, where, when, and to whom the instruction is available.

You have several possible delivery modes based on these combined dimensions of time and place. First is time. Time defines whether the instruction is being offered at the same time for all the learners (synchronously) or at different times (asynchronously). Second is place. Place defines the general location of the instruction — is it in the same place for everyone (a classroom, for example?) or are learners participating in the instruction from different locations? Table 8-1 shows the possible delivery modes when considering both time and place.

REMEMBER

Each delivery mode has its pros and cons — what you gain in one dimension of time or place, you limit in another.

In the following sections, you discover more details about each of these delivery modes, including tips on when each mode is suitable for a particular situation.

TABLE 8-1 Categorizing Delivery Modes

Time when the instruction is offered	Place where learners do the instruction	Example(s)
Same time (synchronous) Learners participate in the instruction at the same time.	**Same place** Learners are in the same location together during instruction.	• Face-to-face classroom instruction Best when learners live in the same geographic region or when you have a budget for learners in different locations to travel to a central location.
Same time (synchronous) Learners participate in the instruction at the same time.	**Different place** Learners are in different locations during the instruction.	• Synchronous virtual webinars or classes Best when learners are in different locations for the instruction but within a few time zones of each other and when learning together at the same time with an instructor is desirable.
Different time (asynchronous) Learners participate in the instruction at different times.	**Same place** Learners are in the same location during instruction.	• Place-based instruction but at different times Best when place is an important part of the learning experience, but learners do not need to participate together at the same times.
Different time (asynchronous) Learners participate in the instruction at different times.	**Different place** Learners are in different locations during the instruction.	• Online instruction that is delivered by an instructor via a learning management system to a class asynchronously. • Self-paced individual instruction delivered through printed workbooks, online websites, podcasts, or mobile apps. Best when learners do not live in the same geographic location and they need to participate in the instruction at their own time and their own pace (working adults, for example).
Blended times (synchronous and asynchronous) Learners participate in the instruction with a blend of time — some parts together at the same time and some parts at different times.	**Blended places** Learners are sometimes together in the same place and sometimes in different places during the instruction.	• Blended learning (a hybrid delivery mode that has both face-to-face classroom instruction and online learning activities). • Flipped classroom (a blended mode where lectures are presented outside of class through pre-recorded videos and class time is reserved for discussions, project work, problem solving activities). • HyFlex (hybrid-flexible) instruction (learners choose between attending class in person, online in real time, or online asynchronously) Best when learners are in different locations for part of the instruction for example, viewing online video lectures asynchronously before a class, but are together in the same location at the same time for other parts of the instruction (for example, class discussions, role plays, project work).

Same time, same place delivery mode (face-to-face learning)

You can determine pretty easily if the same-time/same-place delivery mode is the best choice for your instruction. Same time instruction is commonly seen with classroom or face-to-face instruction that is offered to all learners at the same time. The most common situation for same time-same place delivery is when your goals and constraints support face-to-face classroom instruction. This delivery mode is best suited for instruction where the learners live in the same geographic region, work at the same office, or are all enrolled in a single course.

TIP

Use same-time/same-place (face-to-face) instruction when:

>> Your learners live in the same general geographic location.

>> Your budget and facilities support offering the instruction onsite.

>> Learners can be away from their daily jobs at the same time during instruction.

>> Real-time, individual feedback by a qualified instructor is important.

>> Collaboration among learners on a common task in the same location at the same time is an essential instructional strategy.

>> Time and budget are limited when it comes to developing and delivering instruction.

>> Travel to the instructional site is not costly.

>> Your learners prefer traditional delivery modes with an instructor present.

>> The content changes rapidly, making the development of other modalities of instruction quickly obsolete, thereby affecting cost.

EXAMPLE

Suppose you work at an organization, and they are transitioning to a new budget software for 50 financial personnel. The change is significant and affects all financial operations. Assume the learners are located in the same office or nearby region, the software is new, and few individuals have the needed expertise. Because the instruction requires learning new technical skills that are consequential to the financial operations of the organization, you believe it is important that the finance personnel learn from an experienced instructor who can give real-time feedback. The space has an existing training room with laptops for 25 people at a time, along with projection capability sufficient for the target audience. The organization is committed to providing the needed time away from daily work tasks for this training and only half of the staff would be in training at a time. Given that the instruction is needed right away and the learners could benefit from learning alongside each other, you determine that a face-to-face delivery mode (same time and same place for everyone) is your best option. Although other options are possible, such as screen recording the important software steps and procedures that could be viewed asynchronously, you decide that the pros outweigh the cons for selecting this delivery mode.

Same time, different place delivery mode (distance learning)

In this delivery mode, learners participate in the instruction at the same time, but they are at different locations from one another. Same-time/different-place instruction may be very familiar to you. Most of us experienced it when much of the world pivoted to remote instruction with the onset of the COVID-19 pandemic. Zoom became a household name as teachers and students used video conferencing software to hold class virtually during their normal class time.

Same time-different place instruction is typically delivered through the Internet with video conferencing software (such as Zoom) that enables synchronous virtual webinars or classrooms. This delivery mode is best suited for instruction where the learners are in different locations but live within a few time zones of each other, making it practical to offer instruction at the same time. It may also be desirable if your instructional strategies require synchronous collaboration with other learners or instructors who are not at the same location.

TIP

Use same-time/different-place instruction (virtual synchronous) when:

>> Learners are in different locations during the instruction but can be available at the same time.

>> Large numbers of learners need to be taught.

>> Budget and time are limited to support travel for learners or instructors.

>> Budget and time do not support developing self-study instructional materials.

>> Facilities have limited training space or exist fully remotely.

>> Interacting with an instructor in real-time to ask questions and receive feedback is important.

>> Interacting with other learners at the same time is important.

>> The content changes rapidly, making the development of other modalities of instruction quickly obsolete, thereby affecting cost effectiveness.

>> Social, cultural, or personal factors (such as the COVID-19 pandemic) emerge that require a pivot to remote instruction.

>> Supporting equitable access to instruction where location is not a barrier is a priority.

EXAMPLE

Suppose you work at an organization that is prioritizing employee wellness as part of its strategic plan. You have one employee who is an expert in mindful leadership as a strategy to increase presence, creativity, and stress management. You have many employees who are both geographically dispersed and working remotely who need training in this area. Important to this instruction is expert guidance through various mindfulness experiences, recognizing implicit beliefs, role playing difficult situations, and engaging in self-reflection and reflection with others. You assume that the organization has the budget to support video conferencing with large numbers of geographically-dispersed learners. The instructor is a renowned expert and is the best person to train large numbers of employees. Given the need for real-time instruction and learner collaborations, you determine that a virtual, synchronous delivery mode (at the same time and different place for everyone) is your best option. Although other options are possible, such as in-person instruction, it excludes remote workers, and inclusive access to instruction is essential. Given this, you decide that pros outweigh the cons for selecting this virtual-synchronous delivery mode.

Different time, same place delivery mode (mobile learning)

Different-time, same-place instruction is marked by learners participating in the instruction at different times from each other but in the same place. One situation where different-time, same-place delivery occurs is when instruction is located at a specific place (a museum, for example), but learners can participate on their own time at their own pace, such as with a self-directed tour.

TIP

Use different-time, same-place instruction (place-based-asynchronous) when:

>> Learners are in the same geographic location.

>> Budget, time, and facilities support offering the instruction onsite asynchronously via print, audio, video, or mobile devices.

>> The place itself contains essential content for the instruction that cannot be realized offsite (art museum collections or specialized machinery at a particular factory, for example).

>> Expertise is available onsite to develop and oversee the instruction.

>> Collaboration among learners on a common task in the same location at the same time is not an essential instructional strategy.

>> Instructional strategies include interactions within and movements across place (walking tours or learning about a famous monument, for example).

EXAMPLE

Our research team at Penn State University has developed place-based asynchronous instruction for families visiting a community arboretum. The goal of the project is to infuse science learning into families' recreational time by helping them see the science that is around them in the arboretum. Using mobile devices and an app or QR codes, we created walking tours through a bird and pollinator garden to learn how to observe pollinators and understand what they need to survive in meadows, farms, and forests. We had a project team and a budget to create mobile apps that could be delivered on phones or tablets. We could have selected a different delivery mode, such as delivering instruction by arboretum staff who would lead groups of families on educational tours of the garden as a group (same-time/same-place); however, availability of time, staff, and budget to conduct multiple tours daily was limited. It was determined that more people could benefit if an asynchronous, mobile delivery mode was used. This would better support access to the instruction by visitors on their own time frame. This type of delivery mode is common at education-focused tourist destinations (for example, Smithsonian Museums), or in organizations where instruction about specialized equipment onsite is needed (for example, QR codes next to new machinery at a factory to deploy safety videos).

Different time, different place delivery mode (distance learning)

In this delivery mode, learners participate in the instruction at different times and different locations (virtual asynchronous). Different time-different place instruction is common at universities or other institutions that support distance learning, where the size of the audience is large and instruction is typically provided online for working adults or remote learners across distant time zones.

The delivery mode is typically taught by an instructor using a *learning management system* (LMS) — a comprehensive online system that manages enrollment and class rosters, instructional content and assessments, and tools for fostering interactions among students (discussion boards, chat, e-mail, and so on). Examples of LMS's include Blackboard Inc., Canvas LMS, or Moodle. Virtual asynchronous instruction could also be delivered as self-paced, individual instruction using printed workbooks, websites, podcasts, or mobile apps. In the former case of an online asynchronous delivery with an LMS, collaboration with other learners is typically important; remote-asynchronous delivery mode is best used when learners do not live in the same geographic location and they need to participate in the instruction at their own time and pace.

TIP

Use different-time, different-place instruction (virtual asynchronous) when:

>> Learners are in different locations during the instruction.

>> Large numbers of learners need to be trained.

- Budget and infrastructure for the technologies support delivering instruction asynchronously.

- Travel for learners or instructors to participate in the instruction is not possible or cost effective.

- Facilities have limited dedicated training space or exist fully remotely.

- Interacting with an instructor to ask questions and receive feedback may be important but does not need to occur in real time.

- Consistent delivery of the content is important.

- Self-pacing by learners is important.

- Learners have different or unpredictable schedules

- Time away from daily work is not possible.

- Supporting equitable access to instruction where location is not a barrier is a priority.

EXAMPLE

A common example of a virtual-asynchronous delivery mode is an online course that is offered through an LMS or through other media such as video, audio, or website. Suppose you are tasked with delivering an online class on instructional design that both accompanies this book and explores deeper treatments and models of design. Instructional modules can be designed to follow each phase of the ADDIE process (I initially introduce ADDIE, which stands for Analysis, Design, Development, Implementation, and Evaluation in Chapter 1), and text or video instruction can be available and designed by an expert within the course website. The course is able to accommodate large numbers of learners who are geographically dispersed and who are working adults, so the course runs asynchronously. Instructional strategies such as collaboration are supported asynchronously by using discussion boards, and self-assessment of key concepts are supported with online quizzes. Time and budget are available to make the instruction accessible and inclusive to all learners and abilities. For all these reasons, choosing a virtual-asynchronous delivery mode is justified.

Blended time and blended place delivery mode (blended learning)

Not all instruction falls cleanly into distinct time-place dimensions. In blended delivery modes, for instance, learners may participate in the instruction through a blend of time and place. Sometimes they learn together at the same time and sometimes at different times; sometimes they learn together in the same place and other times apart from each other at different locations.

Blended modes are unique in that they provide some of the best advantages that come from synchronous, place-based, and asynchronous delivery. For instance, students in a college classroom can watch videos and lectures before class, having time to take notes and process the material before class. Then, during class, the time could be spent engaging in class discussions with real-time feedback, role plays, or collaborative project work. Often referred to as "flipped" classrooms, blended learning modes are well suited for instructional strategies where some of the content delivery can occur remotely, saving classroom time for more collaborative activities. By flipping the activities and having learners view an instructor's lecture material first when they are out of class, you ensure that learners are more prepared for in-class collaborative projects activities that can be guided by an instructor.

"HyFlex" delivery modes (hybrid flexible) rose in popularity during the COVID-19 pandemic. HyFlex modalities involve setting up an infrastructure that can support learners to choose which modality they want to use and when. For instance, learners can choose to come to the classroom for lectures or to attend via videoconferencing. If a learner has a conflict with the class time, a recorded video with asynchronous discussion board can be made available. HyFlex modalities offer more flexibility and a combination of delivery approaches.

TIP

Use hybrid instructional delivery modes when:

>> Learners are either in the same geographic location or, if not, can be supported to participate remotely.

>> Some of your learners are remote and some are onsite.

>> Budget, personnel, and technology infrastructure are available to deliver instruction both asynchronously and synchronously.

>> Facilities have dedicated instructional spaces with an instructor present for those learners who can attend in person.

>> Learners can dedicate some time to take the instruction in a specific place at a specific time, but also need flexibility for other times.

>> You want to use some of your in-person classroom time for learners to engage in collaborative activities instead of content presentation.

>> Expertise is available to develop and deliver the instruction in varying modalities (synchronous and asynchronous).

The term "flipped classroom" has emerged to describe a way of organizing instruction to support instruction that occurs outside of the classroom location, but also has lessons that occur together in a classroom. Typical lessons include reading, viewing, or listening to background material outside of the classroom and then using the in-class time either for more collaborative projects or for discussion-focused sessions. Blending modalities opens up opportunities to support the best of both worlds. However, this can be difficult for a designer and instructor to design differentially for different combinations of time and place.

Aligning Technology with Instructional Goals

Delivery modes (see the preceding section) serve to constrain the options you have available for your instruction, based on time-place dimensions. In this section, I want to explore the idea that different attributes of technologies lend themselves better to certain types of instructional goals and strategies. *Technology affordances* is a term that describes what a specific technology offers you for your instructional design purposes. Ideally, you align your instructional strategies and technology choices in complementary ways to support your learning outcomes in the most optimal way.

Be careful about focusing too much on finding "the" best technology for delivering instruction or getting caught up in the latest new technology. Assuming instruction is designed effectively, the choice of a delivery mode on its own predominantly impacts the cost, access, and efficiency of the instruction, not necessarily how much better it will be in comparison to another technology. Different technologies have specific features that offer unique learning opportunities, depending on one's needs. Just keep in mind that you need to focus more on aligning your technology choices to your instructional designs than on finding a magic bullet technology!

Technology or media choices are tied to our design — that means focusing on your course objectives and learning outcomes and making the best choices when it comes to using technology to support learning. Given that focus, think of affordances as characteristics of specific technologies that lend themselves better to supporting certain types of instructional strategies, as shown in Table 8-2.

TABLE 8-2   Technology characteristics and how they support learning

Technology Characteristics	Supports learning in these ways
Accessibility	Access to the instruction anytime, anywhere
	Recording or play-back of instruction
Visualization	Visualizing concepts, demonstrations, places, and so on that are difficult or impossible to see otherwise
	Resizing, zooming in, or highlighting attention visually
	Seeing motions, movements, or demonstrations
Collaboration	Communicating to other learners and instructors
	Working in small teams
Construction	Creating products that show what has been learned (presentations or infographics, for example)
	Content creation or curation
Adaptive/Personalized	Real-time adaptation of instruction based on learners' needs or interests
	Personalization of instruction

EXAMPLE

Certain technologies have characteristics that better support different delivery modes and instructional goals. For example, suppose your goal is to teach learners how to properly perform five specific yoga poses. What technologies may best suit your learning goals and context? If your delivery mode requires a different time/different place (asynchronous remote), you may conclude that a visually based technology-like video is your best choice because video can be paused, replayed, and highlighted with arrows, slow motion, and audio. If your delivery mode allows for same-time/same-place, you may instead choose live classroom-or studio-instruction to meet your goals because you can more immediately provide feedback. Likewise, if it is important that your instructional strategies support visualization of difficult concepts, you may want to prioritize selecting technologies that support that goal, such as video or animations; if collaboration is important, you may want to focus on technologies that support communication and working in teams, such as an LMS, video conferencing, or attending in person synchronously.

In short, there are many different possibilities for selecting technologies to deliver your instruction, depending on varying configurations of instructional goals and strategies, pragmatics, learner characteristics, and delivery mode. Selecting the best technology for delivering your instruction entails looking at a number of different factors. Guidelines on selecting media for instruction can be very detailed. The section that follows highlights some of the most common options and tips for choosing an instructional delivery system.

Selecting Media and Technology Delivery Systems

In practice, you often can combine multiple technologies to deliver your instruction, but this section presents technologies individually for simplicity's sake and to highlight the main pros and cons. Check out these different types of technology delivery systems and analyze what they have to offer for meeting your instructional design goals and objectives.

Instructor-led

TIP

While a human instructor is not a type of technology for delivering your instruction, many instructional programs are delivered by a face-to-face instructor. Therefore, when considering the various technology options available to you, it is important to start with an analysis of the pros of cons of instructor-led instruction. Instructor-led instruction is often good for strategies such as role playing, learning from peers, scenario-based instruction, and technical training for inexperienced learners.

Instructor-led delivery of your instruction has the following pros and cons:

Pros

- A live instructor is present to answer questions, give feedback, and adjust pace.

- Most learners are familiar with this delivery mode.

- Does not require specialized hardware and software to participate in the instruction.

- Supports real-time collaboration with peers.

- Can be done with limited development time and cost, assuming learners do not need to travel.

- Learners can focus on the instruction versus fitting it in during their own time or workday.

Cons

- Learners must be available to be at the same time and place (unless blended delivery modes are used such as live video conferencing).

- Learners do not control the pace of the instruction.

- If learners require travel to the training location, costs are high.

- Limited access for learners who do not live within a commutable distance.
- Limited numbers of learners can be taught at one time, depending on the size of available facilities.

Print

TIP

Print is often effective for instruction on specific information or skills such as step-by-step instructions on how to set up and print a spreadsheet for specific types of budget reports. It is also a good choice if your time and expertise to develop instruction is limited because most designers are confident they can use a word processing program. Print is also a good choice if your learners return to the instruction repeatedly to help them complete their job.

Instruction delivered via print or electronic print has the following pros and cons:

Pros

- Content is self-paced and can be taken anywhere and anytime.
- Most learners have access to the needed technologies to view the instruction.
- The instruction is simple to develop and update.
- Costs to develop and distribute the instruction are generally low, especially for electronic PDFs.
- Instruction is consistent for all learners.
- Travel is not necessary for the instruction.
- Training facilities are not needed.
- Large numbers of learners can be supported.
- Instruction can easily be reviewed multiple times by learners.

Cons

- Does not support live interaction, questions, or feedback with an instructor.
- Does not support real-time collaboration with peers.
- Learners have to find time in their schedule to take the instruction.
- Can be expensive if instruction is printed on paper and mailed to large numbers of learners.
- Limited modalities for learning (only text or graphics).

Video

TIP

Video is often a good choice if you want to present narratives, vignettes, or role-playing instructional strategies (instruction on how to manage conflict, for example). Video is also a good choice for instruction focusing on physical movements, such as how to operate machinery or perform a specific exercise. Finally, video is also effective when a learner cannot be present at the event being taught directly, such as learning about the topography of a location in a different country.

Instruction delivered by video has the following pros and cons:

Pros

- Can present stories or narratives from multiple points of view.
- Learners can view the instruction multiple times.
- Can demonstrate motion.
- Can demonstrate physical skills.
- Content is self-paced and can be taken anywhere at any time.
- Most learners have access to the needed technologies to view the instruction.
- Travel is not necessary to take or provide the instruction.
- Training facilities are not needed.
- Can support large numbers of learners.
- Tools for creating and editing video are becoming more powerful and less expensive.
- Can show places or situations that are unsafe or impractical for learners to experience directly.

Cons

- Professional-quality video has high costs and takes time to develop.
- Video-based instruction requires specialized expertise and technology to develop.
- Does not support live interaction, questions, or feedback with an instructor.
- Does not support real-time collaboration with peers.
- Learners must find time in their schedule to take the instruction.
- Is linear and complicated to search for the specific information learners need for their job task.
- May not be accessible for learners with a visual impairment.

Audio

TIP

Audio is often a good choice of media when your instruction can be compartmentalized into short segments. Audio may be an effective media to select when the audience is listening during their own time outside of work. (Podcasts are a good example here.) Audio is a good choice when verbal explanations or story telling is sufficient for learning, in contrast to visual or interactive content. Audio is also a good choice if your time and expertise to develop instruction is limited and you have an expert available who can quickly and easily create the audio.

Podcasts are a popular audio-streaming technology for listening to educational content or entertainment. Podcasts are used instructionally to deliver content as a blended or "flipped classroom" approach, to bring in guest speakers, or to have learners create their own podcasts as assignments or assessments. Examples range from prerecorded lectures to read-along stories to vocabulary and pronunciation of a foreign language. Podcasts are easy to listen to on-the-go on a personal device and can be listened to anytime or anywhere.

Instruction delivered by audio has the following pros and cons:

Pros

- Content is self-paced and can be listened to anywhere at any time.
- Most learners have access to the needed technologies to listen to the instruction.
- Travel is not necessary to take or provide the instruction.
- Training facilities are not needed.
- Can support large numbers of learners.
- Can listen to in small segments while commuting, walking, or driving.
- Reduces screen time.
- Tools and costs for development are inexpensive and widely available.

Cons

- Does not support learning from visuals.
- Has limited opportunities for interaction with material.
- Does not support live interaction, questions, or feedback with an instructor.
- Does not support real-time collaboration with peers.
- Learners must find time in their schedule to listen to the instruction.
- Is complicated to search for specific information.
- May not be accessible for learners with hearing impairments.

Social media

TIP

Social media refers to a broad set of technologies that learners can use to engage in content sharing and conversations with each other or an instructor. You can use social media to supplement static print or video instruction in order to make the instruction more socially interactive. Social media may be a good choice when your goals are to support communication informally by using free and widely available applications (photo sharing sites, Twitter, Instagram, or YouTube, for example).

Instruction delivered by social media has the following pros and cons:

Pros

- Most learners have access to (and are familiar with) social media.
- Can support large numbers of learners.
- Can serve informal community-building goals.
- Tools and costs for development are inexpensive and widely available.
- Works best for asynchronous conversation and content sharing with others.
- Multiple types of media can be shared such as text, photos, or video.

Cons

- Limited opportunities for interaction with instructional materials.
- Live interactions with instructors or other learners are possible but may not be practical and would require scheduling.
- Learners must find time in their schedule to engage the instruction.
- Not easy to find information for later study or to organize or present lengthy content.
- Some learners may not be comfortable sharing on social media with co-workers, employers, or instructors.

Video conferencing

TIP

Instruction delivered via video conferencing is a good choice when your learners are geographically dispersed or when you have large numbers of learners and you do not have the physical facilities to accommodate them. It's also a good choice when instructional content rapidly changes and you need the most current information taught quickly and inexpensively. Finally, when questions and/or feedback by an instructor in real time is needed, video conferencing is the way to go. In-person instruction that does not have specialized equipment can easily be converted to online video conferencing if cost savings for travel is needed.

Even though video conferencing technology has the capability to expand access to learning opportunities for many learners, that is not the case for all. The *digital divide* refers to socio-economic disparities that exist for some individuals (typically people from economically disadvantaged communities) when it comes to having access to technology such as computers or internet connection. This gap in access could create even more educational disparities if you assume that all your learners have equal access to technologies for instruction. This is why it is important to know as much as possible about your target learners so you can choose an instructional delivery system that provides equitable access for all learners.

Video conferencing delivery of your instruction has the following pros and cons:

Pros

- Not limited by geographical location as large numbers of learners can be widely dispersed.

- A live instructor is present to answer questions and give feedback.

- Most learners are familiar with this delivery mode after the onset of the global pandemic.

- Video conferencing technology tools are often free, widely available, and simple to use.

- Supports real-time collaboration with peers in break-out rooms or in large-groups.

- Can be done with limited development time and cost.

Cons

- Learners must be available at the same time, but recording options are possible.

- Learners do not control the pace of the instruction.

- Learners may not have access to computers or high-speed Internet.

- Limited access for learners who do not live within nearby time zones or who are not available for the instruction at a specific time.

Learning management systems

Learning management systems (or LMSes for short) are a good choice when you are designing instruction across multiple weeks asynchronously, such as for a course that has 10 weeks of instruction. LMSes are very common for distance education at colleges and universities for this reason. LMSes are also a good choice if you have large numbers of learners and need a built-in record keeping system, such as rosters and gradebooks. LMSes are a good choice if your instruction requires the integration of multiple strategies, such as information presentation (text or video), quizzes and quiz feedback, asynchronous discussion boards with other learners or instructors, synchronous chat, or links to resources. For this reason, a learning management system provides the most flexibility and integration of multiple instructional strategies and is often a good delivery choice for instruction being converted from in-person to online.

Learning management systems have the following pros and cons:

Pros

- Integrates multiple forms of media (text, video, and discussion boards, for example).
- Not limited to one primary way of delivering information.
- Not limited by geographical location as large numbers of learners can be widely dispersed.
- Supports asynchronous collaboration with peers through discussion boards but some synchronous chat options are available.
- Provides support for organizing complex, multi-week courses with multiple modules or lessons.
- Pacing can either be structured with deadlines set by an instructor or it can be left open to learners to set their own pace.
- Supports built-in grading and grade recording.

Cons

- An instructor may not be present in real-time when a learner needs a question answered.
- Real-time interaction with peers is limited.
- Learners may not have access to computers or high-speed Internet.
- LMSes can be impersonal and isolating for some learners.
- Instruction using an asynchronous LMS requires more self-direction from students to keep up with deadlines.

- LMSes cannot easily detect if there is cheating or academic misconduct by learners.

- LMSes can be costly and/or require some technical knowledge to create and host the course.

REMEMBER

Be sure to think about how you may need to use multiple formats in order to make your instruction accessible to learners with diverse needs (closed captioning or transcriptions of videos, for example). Sometimes this means delivering instruction using multiple technologies for different accessibility needs.

Linking Instructional Strategies with Technologies

Technologies are not instructional methods on their own — they're there to help you deliver your instruction to your learner audience. Yet, taken together with your instructional strategies, technology can influence how effective your instruction will be. Here, I illustrate three examples of how instructional strategies and technologies come together to form best (educational) practices.

Examining drill and practice strategies designed to support factual learning

Factual learning or remembering is a common learning outcome. Assume your instructional goal is to support learners to memorize information and provide an answer both accurately and quickly. This type of instructional goal of factual learning is often best achieved by instructional strategies of learning through repetition. Many of us may remember how we learned to provide the answer to the question of *what is 5 x 5?* Initially, we probably used conceptual instructional strategies to help us visualize and understand multiplication as it is related to addition, such as drawing a matrix with five rows and five columns. Eventually, however, we were likely asked to repeat the multiplication facts over and over until we eventually memorized them correctly every time.

Such instructional strategies are referred to as *drill and practice* strategies. What is known about factual learning is that it is best supported through strategies that provide:

» Repeated practice

» Immediate feedback

>> Progressive increases in speed of recall

>> Record keeping of correct answers

Drill and practice instruction typically draws upon technology. You often see drill and practice strategies used in educational games, software, or apps, as they provide advantages over print-based or instructor-led modalities for factual learning. For instance, quiz programs (Kahoot!, for example) or educational software (IXL math instructional software or Khan Academy) enables you to design for repeated practice and feedback. A computer, unlike a human, does not get tired from repeatedly presenting as many questions as possible to a learner. It also can provide immediate feedback and personalize questions based on whether more practice is needed in a specific area before advancing. Drill and practice also aligns well with gaming strategies to support faster response speeds, such as using a timer to require progressively faster responses or scoreboards that keep track of your time to answer questions in competition with other players. Taken together, the technology and the instructional strategies support a robust approach to supporting factual learning.

Using microlearning to support seamless learning

Microlearning focuses on instruction that is broken down into very small-sized chunks of instruction that can be easily integrated into one's day. Rather than organizing the instruction into lengthy modules that take dedicated time away from work or home life, microlearning sessions typically require no more than 10 minutes of time to complete. Microlearning supports instructional goals that emphasize *seamless learning*, where the boundaries between work, home, or instructional time are more integrated. With microlearning, the goal is to learn and apply new information in a very short period of time without the disruption to everyday work and life tasks that lengthy training sessions can require.

What is known about microlearning is that it is best supported with strategies that encourage:

>> Short learning pathways that can be provided on demand.

>> Maintaining attention, remembering, and applying small chunks of information to the job.

>> Learning anytime, anywhere.

One advantage of a microlearning approach is that it can be integrated into daily performance. For instance, suppose you have designed a series of time management lessons into bite-sized 5-10 minute chunks of instruction. Your learners can listen to a short podcast on the Pomodoro method of time management on the way into work or after they get to their desk. They could then be prompted to apply this method to a two-hour time block of their work time that day.

Microlearning is best supported through mobile technologies. They are simple to use on-the-go or during the workday without the need for specialized equipment. Ease of access and ease of availability of the instructional content is key. Technologies combined with instructional strategies for microlearning may look like:

» Micro-lectures (video or podcast)

» Short paragraphs of text information (daily emails, blogs, or websites)

» Short scenarios with reflection questions (video, podcast, or email)

» Infographics (images with text)

» Self-assessments (websites)

» Reflection questions after micro-lectures or information presentation (text, emails, or websites)

You often see microlearning strategies in training contexts where it is difficult to carve out time away from work to participate in the training. It is also common in everyday contexts with examples such as the Word of the Day, prompts for mindfulness, or short daily podcasts on various aspects of wellness. With microlearning, a "less is more" approach is best for selecting technology — keep it simple, accessible, and short to improve retention and application!

Learning communities: Learning by connecting and collaborating with others

Learning communities support bringing together people with shared goals and interests, which can include people within an organization who work together or individuals who work or live in different locations. Learning communities are interest-driven and collaborative, with participants learning from each other's ideas, practices, and resources. Many of you may be familiar with online communities, as they commonly emerge as virtual groups who come together around an area of shared interest — this could be hobbies, health problems, activism, local community issues, or global interests such as language learning. The key characteristic of such learning communities lies in the fact that they are driven by the interests of the participants, not by an instructor. Learning communities are sometimes established after learning together in a formal instructional setting in order to sustain the community's interests and knowledge sharing after the instruction ends.

Learning communities use instructional strategies and technologies to support the following:

>> Connecting people with similar interests who may not live in the same geographic area

>> Supporting participants to share knowledge, resources, advice, or practices with each other

>> Distributing leadership across multiple individuals who lead discussions, topics, or activities

>> Supporting a sense of connectedness

Learning communities can be in person or virtual. Virtual learning communities work best when combined with technologies that enable the community to communicate, share, and organize resources into a repository and retrieve information when it is needed. Technologies that support online learning communities for collaboration, interaction, and knowledge sharing may include:

>> Online discussion boards or learning management systems

>> Social media groups

>> Video conferencing

In-person learning communities can also be supported to collaborate and develop their interests together with these same technologies that enhance their face-to-face experiences and support members who may not be present.

Looking to the Future

With rapidly advancing technology, you have many exciting new possibilities for using technology to deliver innovative instructional designs. Some new technologies also hold the potential to change how you approach instructional design altogether. With the advent of technologies such as virtual reality, augmented reality, and artificial intelligence, an instructional designer's toolkit has rapidly expanded to consider new ways of design and new ways of learning.

View each new technology with a lens of what it has to offer you in supporting learning in new ways to solve new instructional problems. It's worth repeating that years of research on comparing different media and technology for delivering instruction finds that instructional methods have more of an impact on learning than the specific technology used to deliver it. Although new technologies attract a lot of attention and excitement, in and of themselves they are not a panacea for all instructional needs. As my focus in this chapter has made clear, it is crucial that you look more closely at any new technology that comes down the pike in order to gauge what it may bring in terms of supporting your instructional design goals.

Looking at virtual and augmented reality

Virtual reality (VR) and *augmented reality* (AR) are technologies that enable you to create more immersive experiences for learning that simulate or enhance real-world scenarios. Taken together, they are often referred to XR, or extended reality applications. A common example of the use of VR in education would be a flight-training simulator. VR enables a designer to create different types of scenarios that may be unsafe to learn in an actual airplane. It also enables practice and repetition in both a realistic and safe learning environment. This technology has the potential to open up new learning innovations for complex skills such as aviation or medical procedures.

Augmented reality (AR) enhances our design by adding a virtual layer of information, images, or animations into the actual setting. For example, a printed text can be enhanced with AR to see animations, models, or videos that provide a deeper understanding of the text. In this scenario, a learner can scan an image or a QR code on a textbook page about photosynthesis and then see the image come to life with an animation and narration. Some children's books use AR to make parts of the story seem to pop out of the page. Likewise, a specific place such as a museum can augment a gallery with QR codes that link to a page with more information or for real-time Q&A with an expert.

VR and AR are shaping what is possible for instructional design. As technologies become more widely available and easier to design, these technologies offer a wide range of possibilities for immersive learning.

Exploring generative artificial intelligence (AI)

One emerging technology that has recently attracted a lot of attention is generative AI — Chat GPT is one obvious example. Generative AI has the potential to impact the instructional design process in both positive and negative ways. *Generative AI*, as the name implies, can generate content on its own, with very little intervention from a human, aside from providing the reasoning for the questions to ask the AI to generate. For example, as a designer, I could ask Chat GPT to write a 1,500-word explanation of Plato's Cave allegory, and then to outline five discussion questions and five assessment questions that I could include in my instruction. What does this mean for instructional design and education more broadly? For one, instructional designers can use generative AI to create new learning materials, assessments, syllabi, and course outlines quickly. At the same time, learners can also use generative AI to create their written assignments. This outcome is not necessarily negative; it simply means that educators and designers need to think more deeply about the kinds of activities and assessments that best support and demonstrate their learning goals. New technologies are also being developed that can detect when or if an assignment was produced by generative AI, but this also can create problems if the technology is not yet reliable.

Although the future of generative AI for instructional design is still emerging, promising possibilities can be imagined. One potential example is more personalized learning experiences. For instance, a course delivered by an LMS could integrate generative AI with a chatbot that interacts with learners in real-time, providing feedback and answering questions. This could be particularly useful for asynchronous or print-based instruction where real-time interactions with instructors or classmates are limited. Generative AI has its limits as to what it can answer for learners, but it nonetheless opens up potential pathways for our designs to be more responsive to learner-initiated questions that are hard to anticipate in advance.

In summary, the future of emerging technologies for instructional design is promising and exciting! As technologies continue to evolve, instructional designers have more tools at their fingertips than ever before to create new engaging, and innovative learning experiences.

Chapter **9**

Developing Effective Instructional Materials

nstructional designers swear by the ADDIE model — a great way to remember that *A*nalyzing, *D*esigning, *D*eveloping, *I*mplementing, and *E*valuating are the steps you follow in doing any kind of instructional design. By the time you get to the third phase (and second "D") of the ADDIE model process, you'll have completed your analyses, chosen the delivery system you'll use, and have a solid design plan in hand. The development stage focuses on the actual creation or production of the learning materials according to your design specifications and chosen delivery mode. The end product is a training package that can basically stand alone and is ready to be delivered by an instructor or as a stand-alone technology lesson. There is no single approach to development; it depends on many factors such as time, expertise, budget, and delivery mode.

For instance, instructional development can look like any of the following:

» A classroom instructor or corporate trainer producing a lesson plan, handouts, and resources within a learning management system (LMS) for flipped classroom activities

» An accountant in a firm developing a half-day workshop along with print-based instruction for other accountants about newly changed tax laws

>> An instructional designer working in a large company with a dedicated training and development staff of instructional designers, graphic artists, programmers, and multimedia specialists

In this chapter, you find out what's involved with developing instructional materials for different types of instruction and delivery systems. I give tips, guidelines, and recommendations for managing the process of developing your instructional products that will also help you identify common elements for any development project.

Analyzing the Instructional Development Process

A metaphor that is often used to describe the instructional development process is that of building a house. You start with a detailed blueprint of the house design, and then transform that blueprint into a house by constructing it! Likewise, the instructional development process transforms an instructional blueprint into a developed product by using tools and technologies such as LMS's, multimedia tools (videos, audio, text, and graphics, for example), or print-based manuals for participants or instructors. It is a creative process that ends with the bringing your design to life!

The development phase requires attention to detail, timeline management, and technical expertise. Throughout the development phase, an instructional designer may need to coordinate the process of seeking feedback from stakeholders such as subject-matter experts (SMEs) and supervisors and use that feedback to refine and improve the instruction before it is fully developed.

REMEMBER

Making sure everyone is on the same page before investing significant time, energy, and expense into the development of the instructional plan is always a good idea.

Instructional programs are always going to be developed differently, depending on your design and delivery mode (classroom based versus online, for example) and whether you are a team of one or are part of a larger team of developers with specialized expertise in programming, graphic design, video production, or LMS development. No single, ready-to-use framework for developing instruction is there for this reason. However, general best practices that work for almost every development effort are there. I highlight these common best practices, along with specific variations based on different delivery systems, throughout this chapter.

Although each development effort is different, some common development deliverables include:

>> **Materials for the instructor:** Instructor guides, lesson plans, and syllabi

>> **Manuals or guides for the learners:** Print or electronic packets of content materials, activities, case studies, readings

>> **Media or digital materials:** Presentation slides for the instructor, copies of slides for learners, online discussion boards, videos, flip charts

>> **Scripts, storyboards, or flowcharts for stand-alone technology-based instruction**

>> **Forms for feedback or assessment:** Feedback forms, quizzes, on-the-job performance checklists or *job aids* — quick resource guides like checklists, flowcharts, and diagrams

REMEMBER

No matter what deliverables you end up developing, keeping a good record of your electronic files; managing the development timeline is of the utmost importance.

Time to see what the development process actually looks like, whether you are the only designer and developer on the team or if you are part of a bigger team with specialized development expertise. The next sections show you the way.

Developing instruction by yourself

There are many kinds of instructional designers, including some whose job titles don't actually reflect the term "instructional designer" but whose job responsibilities definitely include instructional design roles. For example, this may include teachers or instructors who are responsible for designing, developing, and delivering instruction each day. This may also include an employee within an organization with specialized expertise (an IT security officer, for example) who's been tasked with developing training for new employees or existing staff.

Also you find individuals who I refer to as "everyday designers" who do not hold an official job title of instructional designer but who are committed to advancing education in their area of expertise in the everyday world. An example of this may be YouTube educators who create instructional videos on how to perform specific exercises properly or step-by-step instructions for anything from home maintenance to technology skills.

What is common about the solitary designer is that they are typically both the subject matter expert and the instructional designer. Although they have the benefit of being subject-matter experts in the area they are designing instruction, they may be limited in their media or technology production expertise. For these reasons, the solitary designer needs to either work within their skillsets and keep the instructional delivery technology simple, learn new technologies to develop training on their own (course authoring software, in other words), or hire the expertise externally.

Due to competing job demands, the solitary instructional designer may need to rely more on in-person workshops (which are faster to design and develop), print-based materials, or LMSes, all of which simplify the development process through standardized templates and functionalities that require little to no programming expertise. Many teachers and professors, for instance, use LMS systems such as Google Classroom or Canvas to supplement their in-person instruction or to deliver courses fully online. As instructional development technologies continue to advance (for example, LMSes), the time requirements and expertise needed to create robust and professional instructional products is decreasing.

Developing instruction with a production team

Instructional designers often work as part of a larger design and development team. This arrangement is often the case in larger organizations where there is a dedicated unit that is charged with developing training and instruction for all employees. For instance, universities often have units made up of large teams of instructional designers, multimedia specialists, programmers, and videographers who work with faculty experts to develop instruction for online courses or who develop university-wide compliance training.

Instructional design consulting firms also may work as a diverse team of specialists to design and develop training for their clients. Usually, when an instructional designer is working as part of a development team, they are not the one with the subject matter expertise; they also may not be the one developing the instruction either, instead handing it off to a technical development team.

Design and development teams within organizations may have individuals working together to perform the following types of roles:

>> **Instructional designers** who work with subject matter experts and production specialists

>> **Multimedia production specialists** who have expertise in specific course development authoring tools (sometimes this is the same role of an instructional designer)

- » **Graphic artists** who develop the artwork assets for the instructional screens, presentation slides, or print-based manuals

- » **Computer programmers** who program code for technology-based instruction (mobile apps, online website training, virtual reality, for example)

- » **Project managers** who coordinate the timeline for deliverables and keep the project moving forward

- » **Quality assurance experts** who check for Internet compliance, make sure that all web links work, and that consistent use of templates and directions have been followed

- » **Copy editors** who proofread the text for grammar, punctuation, and spelling

A key difference between working as a solitary designer and as part of a team is the need for team-based designers to be able to communicate clearly and in sufficient detail with both the subject-matter experts (SMEs) and the technical team. This collaboration often includes frequent check-ins with both sets of experts, sharing prototypes along the way before fully developing them, and providing the technical team with storyboards, scripts, or flowcharts of how the technology should flow and what content and activities should appear on each screen.

EXAMPLE

Consider one example of an instructional design and development team that I participated in. At my university, we have a unit that is responsible for all the instructional design and development efforts for the university's online courses and degree programs. The team consists of a faculty SME, an instructional designer, multimedia developers, quality assurance experts, and copy editors.

The team works together to develop the instruction following a definite pattern. First, a faculty expert is assigned to work with an instructional designer to outline the entire course and develop the instructional content, activities, discussions, quizzes, and grading system for the entire 15-week class. The faculty SME typically first produces a syllabus with the objectives for the course. The SME then works on creating each week's objectives and lessons in a text document that they share with the instructional designer according to a specified timeline that the instructional designer manages.

The designer's role in this example is to serve as project manager — that means keeping track of deadlines while overseeing the work of the instructional designer, and the LMS course developer. (At my university, we use Canvas.) The designer typically meets with the faculty SME weekly and goes over the lesson plan and content that they created. The designer provides suggestions for creating more engaging learner-centered activities, shows examples of objectives or assessment rubrics, or asks questions about content that is unclear in the design document. The faculty SME then makes any needed changes and the designer moves forward to produce the content and activities in the LMS, which is then shared with the faculty SME for accuracy.

Sometimes, an instructional designer may suggest that more media elements would be useful for learning — animations, for example, or perhaps video case studies and interactive graphics. The instructional designer then communicates the design to a multimedia specialist who develops the multimedia elements of the course. The designer creates storyboards to show how the animations and graphics should be displayed. These elements are shared with both the designer and the SME and revisions are incorporated.

After the course content is developed and created in the LMS, the course goes to the quality assurance team who starts checking that all links work, that consistent language and templates have been used, and so on. Finally, a copy editor checks the entire course for spelling, grammar, and punctuation. While the course is being checked for quality, the designer might finalize the gradebook point assignments and any assessment rubrics with the faculty SME. The course is then listed with the registrar's office in the online bulletin and made available for student enrollment. The LMS has built-in rosters that are generated from the registrar's system directly as well as a gradebook that is automatically set up with the names for each student. The course is then ready for the faculty SME to step in and start teaching it.

Developing Instruction for Different Types of Delivery Modes

In Chapter 8, I talk a lot about the different types of delivery modes. I present them there as variations on the standard notions of place and time. For instance, instruction that occurs at the same time and in the same place is often delivered as classroom instruction, where all learners are in the room at the same time with a facilitator or instructor. Instruction that occurs at the same time but in different locations is often delivered via video teleconferencing (a Zoom class, for example).

Here, I'm going to group development practices according to three common patterns of delivery modes. As I point out earlier in the chapter, development processes may be very different for different purposes and contexts. This section details some of the typical development processes and deliverables associated with each broad type of instructional delivery.

Classroom (face-to-face) instruction

Classroom-based instruction is typically delivered to a group of learners at the same time and the same place. This format of instruction may be designed as workshops, all-day or multiple-day training sessions, or short training sessions. This type of delivery mode typically requires developing materials and handouts for both instructors and learners.

Table 9-1 shows the types of materials commonly developed for classroom-based instruction prior to implementing the instructional program.

TABLE 9-1 **Typical materials to develop for classroom-based (face-to-face) instruction**

Type of material to develop	End products
Facilitator/Instructor Guide	Printed document or PDF of an instructor guide that outlines each major instructional activity along with transitions and time requirements for each.
	Directions for how to introduce the instruction, present the content, facilitate learner activities, and facilitate discussions via prepared discussion questions (can sometimes be embedded as "notes" into presentation slides).
	Directions about when instructors should prompt use of classroom materials or media such as flip charts, videos, refer to participant guides, and so on.
	A summary of the steps to follow for any demonstrations.
	Supplies or materials needed for the instruction.
	Prompts to summarize and transition to the next topic.
Participant manuals or packets with essential instructional resources	A printed document or PDF of the materials learners need before, during, or after the instruction
	Pre-assignments such as readings, surveys, pretests, or reflections
	Reading materials, including case studies that are read during class or as pre-work or homework
	Instruments, surveys, exams, feedback forms
	Copies of presentation slides
	Discussion questions
	On-the-job checklists, graphic organizers, or job aids
	Post-assignments such as reflections, fillable worksheets, or action plans

(continued)

TABLE 9-1 *(continued)*

Type of material to develop	End products
Media or materials used during the instruction	Flip charts
	Videos
	Presentation slides
	Games
	Pens, pencils, and paper for notetaking
Feedback forms/surveys for instructors and learners	Instructor feedback survey on how the instruction went and was implemented (see Chapter 10)
	Feedback surveys for learners on perceived effectiveness of the instruction
	Instruments, surveys, or other assessments for learners

TIP

The most comprehensive deliverables required for classroom-based instruction are the facilitator guide and all associated presentation materials.

REMEMBER

Many different types of instructor guides exist, and how detailed it needs to be depends on whether you are the instructor of the program or whether others are facilitating the course. A brief example of an instructor guide is provided at the end of this chapter in Table 9-6.

Instructor-led instruction with a LMS or video conferencing system

In Chapter 8, I talk a lot about the pluses and minuses of the different delivery systems for your instruction, including virtual delivery modes such as an LMS or video conferencing software (such as Zoom). Instruction created to be delivered with an LMS is often asynchronous, but it can be blended and include synchronous experiences with either video conferencing or chat systems. In creating tips for this section, I make the assumption that both asynchronous LMS and synchronous virtual delivery modes make use of an instructor. (Development practices for stand-alone instruction without an instructor are discussed in the next section.)

With asynchronous LMS or synchronous video conferencing, instruction may be delivered at the same time or a different time; but in both cases, learners are located at different places at a distance. This scenario can be inclusive of offsite remote workers, or it might be students enrolled in a distance learning course.

The main development components of an instructor-led LMS or video conferencing instruction are the following:

» Instructor guide

» Technical specifications

» Communication information

» Instruction on how to use the LMS or related technologies

» Templates for each major part of the instruction

» Content, assignments, and discussions for each module

» Syllabus and/or schedule of deadlines and assignments

For a more detailed treatment of each of these elements, check out Table 9-2, which lists recommended end products for virtual asynchronous instruction (LMS, for example) as well as for virtual synchronous instruction (video conferencing, for example).

TABLE 9-2   **Development tips for virtual asynchronous and synchronous instruction**

Instructional component to develop	Example end products
Instructor guide	Printed document or PDF that outlines each major instructional lesson along with time requirements and/or dates for each lesson
	Grading rubrics or answer keys for exams
	Lesson plans for each lesson
	Tips for establishing social presence and community in a virtual space (using video to introduce self to the class or to introduce assignments and/or using break-out rooms for smaller group conversations, for example)
	Sample welcome e-mail for the course

(continued)

TABLE 9-2 *(continued)*

Instructional component to develop	Example end products
Technical specifications	A resource that lists all hardware and software requirements that learners need to participate in the instruction Technical requirements can include: - Operating systems supported - Hardware needed - Internet speed specifications - Browsers that are supported by the LMS - Configuration of cookies or pop-up blockers - Additional software needed - Sound card, microphones, and speakers - Monitor resolution requirements - Viewability on mobile device - Link to affiliated vendors or mobile apps
Communication information	A guide that spells out how to communicate with the instructor and with other students Instructor contact information Instructor office hours and communication preferences (for example, e-mail preferred) Expected engagement from students (such as guidelines for how frequently students are expected to check into the course or how frequently they should contribute to discussions, in other words) Published ground rules for communicating via synchronous and asynchronous discussions (interrupting, raising hand, background distractions)
Instruction on how to use the technology (LMS or video conferencing)	A PDF and/or video or screen cast of how to use the LMS and any technologies needed for the instruction. This segment is needed for both instructors and learners. Instructions on how to use each major feature of the LMS or video conferencing software, such as how to use the discussion boards, assignment submissions, gradebook, or breakout rooms. Instructions on how to navigate the course materials and/or LMS and where and how to access the syllabus, lesson schedule, readings, and instructional modules. Contact information on where to get technical assistance or support for the LMS or video conferencing technology. Instructions on what to do if a connection is lost during a live video conference or chat.

Instructional component to develop	Example end products
Templates for each major part of the instruction	Templates for consistent presentation of content pages such as: title page, overview and learning objectives page, content page, summary page, discussion page, and any activity pages.
	Details of a consistent navigation scheme, such as numbering each page in a lesson (for example, page 1 of 6) and including forward, back, and main menu links on each page.
Module content, assignments, discussions	Developing instructional content pages by using consistent templates and sequences (see Table 9-7 at the end of this chapter for an example). Learning objectives should be stated on the first page along with a short overview of the lesson.
	Creating discussion questions as well as discussion methods (synchronous videoconferencing break-out rooms and asynchronous discussion boards, for example). (See Table 9-7 at the end of this chapter for an example of a discussion assignment.)
	Guidelines and expectations for participating in discussions
	Activities and assessments
	Pre- or post-assignments for the instruction
	Participant manuals (readings, case studies, activities)
Syllabus and lesson timeline	A clear schedule of start and end dates for asynchronous discussions and deadlines for completion of assignments
	A schedule of start and end times for virtual synchronous discussions, considering multiple time zones
	A syllabus with assignments, readings, and deadlines for each lesson

Stand-alone technology-based instruction

Sometimes instruction is developed to stand-alone on its own without an instructor. Typically, you'd see this type of instruction developed as print-based instructional packets or instruction delivered through technology such as a website, mobile app, digital video or audio, LMS, DVD, or downloadable computer application. Because no instructor is there, and the instruction must stand on its own without real-time support from an expert, this type of instructional delivery takes the most time to develop and usually requires a bigger team of developers with technical expertise.

Imagine a situation where all employees at a university must be trained in federal laws regarding the privacy of student records. With over 20,000 employees, the university is required to ensure that the Family Educational Rights and Privacy Act (FERPA) is followed by all employees who have access to student educational records at the university. Given the large number of people who must be trained, the university decides to develop instruction that is accessible to all employees and delivered through a university training website. The online instruction can be taken anytime and anywhere but must be completed within a specified time frame. The training website delivers the content, gives practice questions, and keeps track of faculty/staff compliance in taking the training as well as their assessment scores, with a passing score indicating the objectives were achieved. No instructor is assigned to deliver any part of the instruction.

The previous example has several elements that need to be considered during development of stand-alone instruction:

>> Stand-alone, technology-based instruction is asynchronously delivered (anytime-anyplace). This makes it important to ensure that the instruction follows a well-designed flow and that the content, tasks, and objectives are properly sequenced.

>> Each page or screen of the instruction requires the development of a storyboard that illustrates what content should appear on the page along with any graphics and navigation cues (Forward or Back buttons, for example). (See Figures 9-1 and 9-2 in the next section for examples.)

>> Videos with human speakers or voice-overs require a text script to be developed along with alternative accessibility options.

>> Navigation flowcharts may need to be developed for programmers to show how the navigation options flow from each screen. (See Figures 9-3 and 9-4 in the next section for examples.)

>> If interactive activities are developed (practice questions that provide corrective feedback depending on answers selected, for example), storyboards and flowcharts need to be developed that show what content will be displayed based on each response. (See Figure 9-4 in the next section.)

>> A working prototype should be tested for usability and accessibility before it is rolled out on a full level.

>> Participant manuals, assessments, or supporting media need to be developed, similarly to any other delivery mode.

The next section provides more details and tips for developing storyboards and flowcharts for technology-based instructional designs.

Prototyping Instructional Products

Prototyping in instructional design is widely used in practice. In a nutshell, prototyping creates an early sketch of what the instruction will look like, what will be on the screen, and what interactions will occur. An important reason for prototyping is that it allows stakeholders, including clients who are hiring you to create the instruction, to visualize the end product before investing significant time and resources into the full development. It encourages an iterative design process of gathering early feedback and making changes to the overall usability or look of the instruction. Prototypes are typically done as paper sketches or digital mockups.

When developing stand-alone, self-instructional materials such as the ones I describe in the previous section, the instructional designer and the production team work together to develop a working prototype. The instructional designer typically works with a SME or a client to design the learning objectives and develop the content for each screen of the instruction.

Instructional designers who work with a production or programming team need to develop two important prototype deliverables, which are storyboards and flowcharts. Storyboards provide a visual sketch of the screens to be developed and include an overview of the content. Flowcharts are images that help programmers understand how the navigation system works for learners as they are taking the instruction. I discuss both later in this chapter.

Using storyboards to prototype the content and page design

A designer works closely with a SME or a client on the content that needs to be developed for any technology-based instructional project. When the content is set to be delivered via a computer or mobile device, the content must be broken down for each screen that needs to be developed. Storyboards can take many forms, but they generally serve the purpose of providing a visual blueprint of the instructional content.

REMEMBER

Storyboards enable instructional designers and the development team to outline the sequence of screens, navigation, interactions, and media elements that will be included in the final deliverable. Storyboards serve as communication tools, facilitating communication between the instructional designer, SMEs, clients, multimedia specialists, graphic artists, and/or programmers.

You have a few different, practical formats for creating storyboards. Some designers like to use blank frames with borders and then sketch out the content, images, and navigation. You can create a storyboard by hand or by using a simple-to-use presentation software. Other options include creating tables that organize the content, instructions, and images or filenames in separate columns. See examples in Figure 9-1, Figure 9-2, and in Table 9-3.

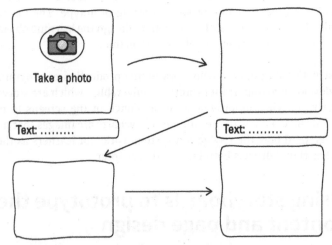

FIGURE 9-1:
Hand-sketched storyboard.

Source: Image by Nick Rossi. Used with permission by Susan Land. This material is based upon work supported by the National Science Foundation under Grant no. 1811424. Any opinions, findings, and conclusions or recommendations expressed in this material are those of the author and do not necessarily reflect the views of the National Science Foundation.

FIGURE 9-2:
Example storyboard made using presentation software.

How does water make a cave?

- Rain combines with carbon dioxide from the air. This makes the water acidic.

- The acidic water goes underground. The acid **water** dissolves the **limestone** over many, many years.

Image by Nick Rossi. Used with permission by Susan Land. This material is based upon work supported by the National Science Foundation under Grant no. 1811424. Any opinions, findings, and conclusions or recommendations expressed in this material are those of the author and do not necessarily reflect the views of the National Science Foundation.

Another common way to create storyboards is by creating a table that lists the screen number, the content, and any visuals or filenames that should be included. Table 9-3 shows an example of a sample storyboard in table format.

TABLE 9-3 **Example storyboard using a table display format**

Screen	Content	Image/Media
1.0 Welcome screen	Today you will learn about how limestone caves are formed in Pennsylvania!	Filename: cave1.png
2.0 Content presentation	Title: How do caves form? Rain water mixes with carbon dioxide from the air. This makes the water acidic. The acid water goes underground. The acid water dissolves the limestone over many, many years. ← "Back" and → "Next" button	 Animation video 1.0

In sum, storyboards are important communication tools between an instructional designer, stakeholders, clients, and the media development team. The storyboards can be very detailed or they can simply be sketches early on in the development process that you use to share and brainstorm ideas with the team about possible lesson activities or screen design layouts.

Creating flowcharts to show the lesson flow

Technology-based instruction can be executed in different ways, depending on the sequence that is to be followed and whether learners may see different content, depending on how they perform or what option they select. If they missed a test item, for instance, they may be branched backwards to repeat the lesson or parts of the lesson again. Others who answered correctly may be branched forward to start the next lesson or to exit the lesson.

Given this structure, you need to communicate to the development team how the overall flow of a technology-based lesson will proceed. Even in design situations where all learners proceed through the instruction linearly in the same sequence, it is still helpful to create flowcharts to show the structure of the navigation. Flowcharts are effective tools for displaying patterns of flow, sequence, and navigation in concrete and visual ways.

The simplest navigation and lesson sequence is the linear instructional design. Figure 9-3 illustrates a flowchart for a linear design. With linear designs, all learners proceed through the instruction in the same sequence. This style may be used in cases where the instruction needs to advance in a specific order of a specific step-by-step procedure or when assessment of learning outcomes happens only at the very end of the instruction and without differential feedback.

Linear Flowchart

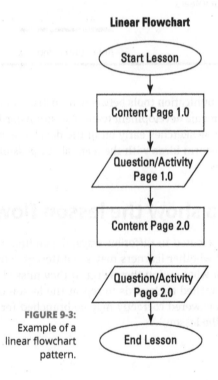

FIGURE 9-3:
Example of a linear flowchart pattern.

The linear flowchart in Figure 9-3 illustrates that a learner begins the instruction and then proceeds to Content 1.0. After finishing the Content 1.0 page, the learner proceeds to an activity or a question page. After they answer the question or complete the activity, they proceed directly to the Content 2.0 page, even if they did not answer the question correctly. Sometimes designers insert a generic feedback page before moving to Content 2.0 that is the same for all learners and explains which answer is correct and why.

Another type of design — the branching design — is more complex. It differentially branches learners to different pages in the instruction based on a specific response. This type of design helps to make instruction more personalized and individualized. It is more commonly seen either in compliance training designs (where mastery of all learning objectives is an essential learning outcome) or in situations where later content builds on previous content and you want learners to be adequately prepared for later lessons. In some instances, a designer may choose to branch the learner back to the initial content page if an incorrect response is given.

Figure 9-4 shows an example of a branching pattern. In this branching design, a learner starts the lesson and proceeds to Content Page 1.0 and then onto the Question Page 1.0. Then, a decision point is made — if a learner answers the question correctly, they continue to Content Page 2.0. If a learner does not answer the question correctly, they will then be given corrective feedback on a separate page and then proceed to Content Page 2.0.

In sum, storyboards and flowcharts are important deliverables that an instructional designer creates in order to communicate with the stakeholders and development team tasked with creating the instructional materials.

The next section provides some tips and best practices for instructional design that entails multiple forms of media, such as audio, video, animations, and/or graphics.

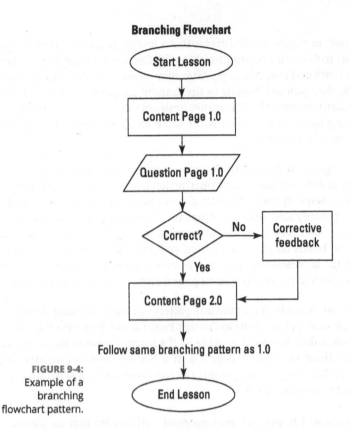

Branching Flowchart

Start Lesson

Content Page 1.0

Question Page 1.0

Correct? — No → Corrective feedback

Yes

Content Page 2.0

Follow same branching pattern as 1.0

End Lesson

FIGURE 9-4:
Example of a
branching
flowchart pattern.

Principles for Developing Effective Multimedia Instruction

The use of multiple forms of media in instruction is often beneficial for learning. Multimedia technologies integrate text, graphics, sound, and video into a cohesive instructional unit, taking advantage of learners' visual and auditory processing. Multimedia can range from media such as text with diagrams, graphic organizers, or videos to more complex simulations and immersive environments.

Researchers have identified core principles and best practices for creating effective multimedia instruction. One leading scholar in the development of research-based principles for multimedia instruction is Richard Mayer. By understanding and applying Mayer's best practices, instructional designers can enhance learners' ability to learn and remember information.

Table 9-4 presents best practices for designing multimedia instruction according to Richard Mayer's principles of multimedia learning.

TABLE 9-4   ## Principles and best practices for developing multimedia instruction

Principle	Best practices for multimedia instruction
Present coherent and essential information	Keep content and media focused on only what is essential for learning.
	Limit extraneous background music, audio, or flashy transitions if they are distracting.
Provide visual cues to direct learners' focus	Channel the learners' attention to where you want them to look.
	Highlight important material by using visual cues such as bold and highlight for text.
	Draw attention by using arrows or animations to point to important words or images on the screen.
Present multiple forms of media	Learning is better when information is presented by using a combination of words and pictures rather than words alone.
	When using audio narration, learning is better and easier with a combination of graphics and narration, rather than graphics, narration, and printed text all presented simultaneously.
	One important caveat to the previous tip — always add optional closed captioning for those learners who prefer subtitles or have other accessibility requirements.
Keep media elements close together in placement and timing	When using narration, present your graphics or animations at the same time that they are being narrated.
	Keep any written text in close proximity to the image it is associated with or is labeling.

(continued)

TABLE 9-4 *(continued)*

Principle	Best practices for multimedia instruction
Segment information into smaller chunks	Learning is better when a multimedia message is presented in smaller, user-paced segments rather than as a continuous, long page.
	Where possible, break down information into smaller, manageable chunks to enable learners to process the content at their own speed.
Use personalization	Learning in a multimedia context is better when the words used are in a conversational style rather than a formal style.
	Learning is better when the message is spoken by a friendly human voice rather than a machine voice.

Creating Accessible Instructional Design Materials

Universal Design for Learning (UDL) is an educational framework that aims to provide all students with equal opportunities to learn, regardless of their individual strengths, abilities, or learning preferences. UDL teaches us to design for variability in our instruction with flexible instructional materials and strategies that a wide range of students can use and access.

REMEMBER

The core principle of UDL is to provide multiple means of representation, expression, and engagement for learners.

In the last section, you had to chance to read more about how multimedia-based instruction provides designers with multiple ways to represent content — visually through animations or videos, text-based such as subtitles, or audio narration. These uses of multimedia are not just sound instructional practices for learning; they also provide a variety of options for meeting UDL goals.

Guidelines for universal design: Ensuring accessibility for all learners

UDL guidelines have been developed that align with the overall values and principles of UDL. The guidelines focus on three main recommendations:

>> Provide multiple means of engagement

>> Provide multiple means of representation

>> Provide multiple means of action and expression

Promoting multiple means of *engagement* means designing your instruction to be engaging, relevant, and motivating for learners. Foster engagement by designing instruction with instructional strategies that encourage active learning instead of passive learning, as well as making the instruction relevant and appropriately challenging.

Promoting multiple forms of *representation* means that instructional designers present information by using various media formats, such as text, images, videos, and/or audio. This format ensures that students can access the content in a way that best suits their needs and purposes.

Promoting multiple means of *action and expression* means providing students with different options to show their understanding or express their ideas. This can include supporting expression through writing, speaking, visual representation, or by constructing or building creative products (artwork, multimedia presentations, and so on). Using multiple modalities, such as asynchronous discussions where learners have more time to think of a response as well as synchronous discussions that occur in real time, support different means of expression.

Summarizing the key principles and guidelines of UDL

Overall, UDL aims to remove barriers to learning and create inclusive instruction that empowers all learners to succeed. By incorporating flexibility, choice, and accessibility into instructional designs, UDL enables you to meet the diverse needs of your students, promote engagement and participation, and achieve overall learning outcomes. Table 9-5 summarizes the main principles for effective UDL.

TABLE 9-5   **Summary of UDL principles and guidelines**

Guideline	Examples
Provide multiple means of engagement	Design engaging and motivating instruction
	Establish relevance and importance
	Support active learning strategies instead of only passive strategies such as lectures
	Include appropriate levels of challenge, self-assessment, and reflection
Provide multiple means of representation	Present information by using a variety of formats, such as text, images, videos, and/or audio
	Offer alternative formats for audio and video instruction
	Use accessibility features for text, PDFs, videos/audio, LMS pages
	Provide captions or "alt text" for images
	Channel attention to important ideas, information, or images
	Consider differing language needs of learners
Provide multiple means of action and expression	Design different ways for learners to show their understanding and express their ideas (for example, writing, speaking, visually, or by physically constructing products)
	Use multiple modalities where possible (asynchronous and synchronous discussions; written assignments and oral presentations)
	Design to support assistive technologies such as screen readers

Examples of Deliverables for the Development Phase

To give you a better idea of the development tasks that an instructional designer performs, I end the chapter with some real-world examples for two types of development tasks. The first example is a sample instructor guide that an instructor would use to lead a workshop. The second example shows a content page and discussion board activity that a designer might create for an online course delivered through an LMS.

Sample instructor guide

Table 9-6 provides a brief example of an instructor guide for a workshop on identifying tree life cycles at a nature center/forest trail.

Title of Module: Identifying five phases of tree life cycles in the forest

Goals/objectives:

1.1 Learners can state the criteria for identifying each phase of the tree life cycle with 100 percent accuracy.

1.2 Learners can accurately identify examples of the five different phases of the tree life cycle on forest trails and provide criteria for their decision.

Time: 2 hours

TABLE 9-6

Sample instructor guide for a workshop on identifying tree life cycles

Time	Instructional content/Media	Notes
5 min	Gain attention and establish relevance	Ask question while on forest trail: Look around at all these trees in this forest. *How do you think these trees grew here?*
		Solicit initial ideas
5 min	Overview screen and graphic organizer of the tree life cycle	Refer learners to graphic organizer of tree life cycles
		Present content on characteristics of each tree life cycle phase
10 min	Introduce the role of seeds as part of the tree life cycle	Refer learners to image of different types of tree seeds, including pinecones or acorns
	Content Screen 2: The seeds of a pine tree are found inside a pinecone. The seed are small and fall out of the cone when the scales open.	Show example of a real pinecone on the ground and where the seeds are located within it

Time	Instructional content/Media	Notes
20 min	Recognizing seedlings and saplings Content on Screens 3 and 4 	Refer learners to content on Screens 3 and 4 Point out examples of seedings and saplings on the trail
10 min	Recognizing mature trees and snags (dead trees). Content on Screens 5 and 6 [refer to images on app]	Point out examples of mature trees and snags on the trail
10 min	Break	
5 min	Transition to observation activity 	Pass out observation checklists and refer learners to Screen 7 Give directions for activity Go over ground rules for trail boundaries and device sharing
20 min	Facilitate small groups of 2-3 to observe and document evidence of tree life cycles in the forest	Walk around and ask learners questions about what they are finding and what their evidence is for their identification

(continued)

TABLE 9-6 *(continued)*

Time	Instructional content/Media	Notes
5 min	Transition to education building to create photo collages of tree life cycles	Walk as a group to the nature center's classroom Seat learners in their small groups around tables
15 min	Facilitate hands-on activity of creating tree life cycle collages from photographs of trees	Hands-on activity: Facilitate learners to create photo collages of the tree life cycles they identified and to provide criteria for their decision
15 min	Hand out 5 question assessment After assessment, wrap up and summarize	Hand out assessment and pencils for each learner Assessment is timed at 10 minutes End with a summary of the 5 phases of the tree life cycle Re-introduce the initial question asked at beginning of session: How did all these trees grow in the forest?

Acknowledgement and permissions: Artwork and design in this Instructor Guide are by Michael Mohney, Brian J. Seely, Heather Zimmerman, and Susan Land, Penn State University. Images used with permission by Susan Land.

Sample LMS Pages

Table 9-7 presents examples of an outline of sample LMS lesson on "Developing Effective Multimedia Instruction." It also provides an example of a sample discussion board activity for a lesson on technology integration.

TABLE 9-7   **Examples of LMS Development Deliverables**

Example of lesson overview, content pages, discussions, and hands-on activities (for Canvas LMS)	⋮ ▾ Lesson 5: Developing Effective Multimedia Instruction
	
	 ⋮ ⧉ Lesson 5 Overview
	
	 ⋮ ⧉ Theory of Multimedia Learning
	
	 ⋮ ⧉ Multimedia Principles
	
	 ⋮ ⧉ Universal Design for Learning
	
	 ⋮ Lesson 5 Activities
	
	 ⋮ 🗩 Evaluating Multimedia Discussion
	       Jun 13 I 15 pts
	
	 ⋮ 📝 Hands-On Activity: Creating Interactive Videos
	       Jun 13 I 20 pts

Sample discussion board assignment	*Lesson 1: Reflecting on Theory and Practice of Technology Integration* Based on the readings from this lesson and your personal experience, complete the following online discussion questions. Answer both following discussion questions (part 1 and part 2) in one post to the discussion forum. (Part 1) What do you think are the most important barriers to the effective and powerful use of computer-based technologies in schools/higher education/organizations right now? Why do you think this? (Part 2) Identify at least one possible example of how technology may be used to help students learn more effectively in a setting in which you work or are interested in working. Connect your example to at least one concept from the readings that stood out to you (learning theories, technology integration models, emerging technologies, and so on). You can also include a link to an example technology if available. Submit your posts to this discussion by Sunday at 11:59 p.m. (ET). You should respond to at least two of your classmates by Tuesday at 11:59 p.m. (ET).

Chapter **10**

Show Time! Implementing Your Instruction Successfully

All your design work eventually leads you to this point: You stop designing and start putting your instruction into effect! This chapter is about the "I" phase of the ADDIE process: Implementing your instruction. (For more on the ADDIE process, see Chapter 1.) At this point, you did your analyses, completed your design, and developed your instruction. Now it's time for you to try it out! While it's true that you already thought long and hard by thinking about the factors related to implementation early in the analysis phase and throughout the design process, now is the time for learners to actually use it. At this point, you need to focus on the final details needed to support your learners and/or instructors for the day they begin the instruction.

In this chapter, you read about a model that you can use when planning the effective implementation of your instruction, taking into account the different factors that can hurt the success of your implementation if they are not considered in advance. These can include organizational factors such as having appropriate leadership support but also logistical factors such as having the necessary equipment and materials set up for the launch of the instruction.

REMEMBER

By considering in advance possible factors that can limit your instruction's success during implementation, you increase the likelihood of an organized deployment of your instruction in the way you intended. In this chapter, I first outline a framework for successful implementation of your instruction and then end the chapter with tips and best practices for managing the logistics of your implementation for different instructional delivery modes.

The Best Laid Plans versus Actual Use

The implementation phase of the instructional design process often gets the least attention. One reason for this is that most of the effort and creative work in designing instruction happens before the learners actually use the instruction — that is, during the analysis, design, and development phases. Also, instructional designers in many cases are not the instructor or trainer of the instruction, so the instruction is often "handed off" and transitioned to others at this phase. Even if an instructional designer is not involved in the actual implementation process, important analytical and logistical considerations can be done in advance to help make the transition more successful.

After all, it would be a huge disappointment to invest so much time in creating well-designed instructional modules and then leave it to chance as to whether they are used as intended! Any new instructional design involves change and because of that you need a plan for organizing how that change is introduced, managed, and sustained.

EXAMPLE

For instance, imagine you have worked with a team of subject matter experts (SMEs) to design and develop an online workshop to teach employees how to use a specific type of software — one that promises to help you develop interactive e-learning modules to be delivered asynchronously through a learning management system (LMS). Your instructional model included well-designed step-by-step instructions, video tutorials, and hands-on-activities with practice and feedback. However, you did not plan for the difficulties learners may have in setting up the software on their computers at home or making sure they met the appropriate hardware/software specifications. Nor did you plan for any technical support for learners, resulting in a frustrating experience that took away several hours of instructional time, putting several learners behind schedule, and ensuring (quite unintentionally) that others cannot participate at all.

Despite the instructional design being well thought-out, the implementation nonetheless fell short because you did not make sure that the necessary resources to participate in the instruction were established at the onset. Also, no plan was in place for how to support learners if they ran into technical problems they could not resolve on their own. This example and its outcomes do not necessarily reflect a failure of the effectiveness of the instructional design itself; rather, they reflect a lack of foresight during the analysis phase and a lack of planning for the implementation phase that led to the unsuccessful outcome.

The RIPPLES Model for Implementation Planning

Typically, you invest in designing instruction with the assumption that it will be implemented multiple times. Designers do not usually go through the time and expense of designing instruction for it only to be used once. Given this, you need to think about fostering the success of your instruction over time and consider whether it will continue to be implemented in a reliable way to achieve similar goals across implementations and over time. This does not mean that your instruction cannot change over time based on issues that are discovered during implementation and that are revised based on sound evidence. But it is important to note that factors that typically impact the success of the implementation of your instruction are issues that can be considered before the implementation begins.

REMEMBER

You need to be mindful of the decisions that you make along the way in your design process and how (or if) these decisions may have a later impact on how the instruction is used and sustained over time.

Certain conditions help you implement your instruction more successfully after the initial decision has been made to design the instruction. Dan Surry, a long-time leader in the instructional design field, and specifically in the area of implementation research, developed a planning model that uses the acronym RIPPLES. The model is comprehensive and covers a wide array of planning support, such as organizational infrastructure, resources, learner support, and technology support. Not all the seven areas may be of relevance to every instructional design project or setting, but the framework nonetheless provides a good starting point for planning.

The seven components of the RIPPLES model use the first letter of each of the following words and are described further with examples in the remaining subsections.

The RIPPLES framework for implementation planning stands for:

>> Resources

>> Infrastructure

- » People
- » Policies
- » Learning
- » Evaluation
- » Support

Resources

You're going to need many types of resources if you want your instruction to be designed, developed, and implemented effectively. In most training or educational organizations, *resources* refer to the financial costs associated to fund the instructional analysis, design, development, implementation, and evaluation phases. In order for your instruction to be implemented and sustained over time, you first must ensure you have considered all the relevant financial costs that are needed to implement it.

REMEMBER

Costs for implementing instruction can be one-time only costs to run the instruction as well as continuing costs over time.

Instructional time and instructional materials cost

Instructional costs are the actual costs to run the instructional implementation. Example costs to plan for include the following:

- » Salaries of instructors or trainers to deliver the training sessions
- » Salaries of support personnel, such as employees who provide facilities, enrollment, or tech support during the instruction
- » Paid time for employees to take the instruction
- » Travel costs for employees to take the instruction or instructors to provide the instruction
- » Facilities' costs to provide the instruction (space rental and food or snacks for learners, for example)
- » Hardware or software purchases for technology-delivered instruction (presentation software, for example)

>> Printing or mailing expenses for print-based instruction

>> Licensing fees for software, such as an LMS or server space

Ongoing costs to maintain offering the instruction

You're also going to have instructional costs that extend beyond the initial expenditures made to run the instructional program. These include costs such as:

>> Upgrades to technology hardware and software systems

>> Maintenance or repair expenses of technologies and facilities (projector bulbs, displays, audio systems)

>> Annual fees for LMS use

>> Ongoing payments made to instructional designers, SMEs, or technical developers for their time to regularly monitor, update, revise, and improve the instruction

Infrastructure

Having an infrastructure for instructional implementation means having the necessary elements within an organization to ensure you can deliver the instruction reliably and, where needed, delivered at scale. It means having the infrastructure in place to support the end-to-end process of designing, delivering, and managing instructional programs. Infrastructure concerns ask the question, "Will it work in our current system?"

EXAMPLE

If, for instance, you have developed an instructional model using the latest augmented reality technology, do you have the organizational infrastructure to update the instruction as technology changes and the resources needed to scale up the instruction to larger numbers of users? These are learning infrastructure considerations that are particularly important to think about when designing for technology-based instruction with new technologies you may need to scale up.

Table 10-1 outlines Dan Surry's five infrastructure components for effective implementation.

TABLE 10-1   Five Types of Infrastructure Needed for Implementing Instruction

Type of Infrastructure	Description
Teaching	The resources needed to deliver the instruction for the lifecycle of the instruction. Teaching resources include requirements such as the technology used to deliver instruction (software, hardware, devices, peripherals, LMS licenses), internet bandwidth, and other materials (flipcharts, projectors). Teaching resources may also include availability of teaching expertise and facilities use.
Production	The resources needed to develop the instruction (video production, design and development expertise, or podcasting software, for example) and to revise and update the instruction are available and budgeted.
Communication	The resources needed to communicate with learners. These include the communication technologies needed during the instruction (LMS discussion boards, or e-mail and office hours with instructors, for example) as well as prior to the instruction (e-mail lists to recruit, register, and follow up with learners, for example). This information can also include the necessary personnel and expertise for registration and tech support.
Student	Students are provided the resources needed to access and use the instruction. This facet is most commonly seen as time resources (for example, time off from regularly daily work to participate in the instruction) and technology resources (for instance, students have the needed hardware, software, and bandwidth requirements to participate in the instruction).
Administrative	The resources needed to manage educational functions, such as staff for recruitment, enrollment, book orders, and collecting end-of-instruction assessment data. Administrative infrastructure may also require project management, scheduling support, and monitoring of instructional quality.

People

Education is a human endeavor and requires many levels of human resources to support implementation. For instance, instructional programs require access to human expertise. You need the expertise of SMEs to define the content requirements and objectives for the instruction as well as to facilitate or teach the instruction. You also need access to instructional design expertise and in some instances technology production expertise as well. (See Chapter 9 for more on that topic.) Determining that your organization has the level of expertise it needs to design, develop, and sustain the instruction over time is important.

REMEMBER

The analysis phase of instructional design (see Chapter 3) is based on the assumption that the development of instruction is based on an identified need and, as such, is typically requested by administrators or managers as a solution to a performance problem or to meet a new instructional need. So, it is important that management is on board with strong support for the instructional program, including a willingness to create time and space for employees to take the instruction.

Similarly, it is also important to account for the attitudes and perceptions of the learners. Are they on board with the instruction and the time required of them? Are they dissatisfied with the current status quo in their job performance and likely to be motivated to engage in the instruction? Or are they satisfied with the way conditions are? How do your learners feel about the format of instruction you are offering? Are they familiar with it?

REMEMBER

Learner attitudes toward the instruction are important factors to explore during the early phases of analysis and design. Doing so helps to ensure that, during implementation, your participants are more present, more engaged, and more active in their learning.

Shared decision making and stakeholder communication is an important element of the instructional design process that may impact the success of your instructional intervention. By involving learners, instructors, and managers in the communication process at all prior stages of design, you increase the likelihood of creating a shared vision for the change that is needed; in sum, better communication with all stakeholders leads to better implementation.

Policies

It is important that your instructional programs do not interfere with existing organizational policies — technology use policies or by requiring use of technologies that are blocked or unsupported by the organization, for example. This type of situation may be the case for instruction that is intended to be delivered to military organizations, schools, or for young children. It can also be the case in higher education or corporations if they have existing software contracts with specific vendors that must be used.

New instructional programs need to align with existing employment, training, or other related policies. Examples of questions to consider in terms of policy implications for implementation may include the following:

>> Is the training required for onboarding? How is completion of it communicated to HR?

>> Are employees allocated a specific budget amount and leave time for training, and does the required training fit within these requirements?

>> What are the stated policy expectations for employee professional development and are there incentives for participating?

>> Is this instruction required for compliance training, and if so, what are the consequences for employees not taking the training within an expected time frame?

>> Are there eligibility requirements for training (number of months in the position, for example)?

>> What are the travel policies for the instructional program? Who makes the travel arrangements?

>> Is proof of participating in the training required to be sent to participants' managers?

>> Are there enrollment or course drop deadlines to participate or receive a refund?

>> Are there incentives for instructors to teach the instruction in the way designed?

>> If the course requires an examination, are employees required to submit their results to management?

These questions are just a few examples of training-related policies that may require advanced planning prior to implementation.

Learning

Throughout the design process, you have been working to answer the question of *how will your design improve learning and performance?* During implementation, you get to try out your assumptions!

If you are using a new delivery system such as a new LMS (see Chapter 8 for more on this), it is important to plan for how its various features should be used by learners in order to meet your learning goals. For instance, if you have planned for online asynchronous discussions of case studies, plan for how you can logistically support learners during implementation when it comes to them posting to the discussion and replying to others. One simple strategy is to provide guidelines and a schedule for when learners should post and reply. Likewise, for synchronous discussions, prepare the start and end times for different time zones. (I provide some additional examples for different types of delivery systems in the next section.)

Evaluation

I discuss evaluating instruction more in the next chapter (Chapter 11), but you want to be prepared during your implementation to give any assessments you have planned. This can include handouts or online documents such as the following:

>> Knowledge assessments to determine what was learned (pre and/or post-tests)

>> Survey of perceptions — how did learners like the instruction?

>> Sign-up sheets or questions for post-instructional debrief interviews

Before running your instruction for the first time, it is also a good idea to conduct a pilot test to try out the instruction (or at a minimum, try out parts of the instruction). The audience for your formative evaluation can consist of a few sample learners and an SME to give you their opinions on the material. Others to possibly include for feedback are fellow instructional designers and the learners' supervisors.

TIP

Ask debrief questions to your audience about what they liked and did not like about the instruction. Keep track of any questions that are asked while SMEs or instructors go through the instruction. If the instruction is planned to be stand-alone, it is important to determine if learners can indeed complete it independently! Ask if the directions are clear, the pace is good, and if the material is effectively broken down into manageable chunks of information.

If using technology to deliver your instruction, make sure to ask if all the links and features worked without errors. Be sure to ask if there were any areas in the instruction that were confusing and what they would like to change (see more or less of, for example).

Support

The last component of the RIPPLES model is to plan for how to logistically support learners and instructors during your implementation. Strategies and tips for providing implementation support for instructors include:

TIP

>> Creating an instructor guide that walks an instructor through each lesson, including discussion prompts

>> Providing training on how to use any technology in advance of the implementation

>> Providing training on how to create and upload any media elements into the course (instructor videos, for example)

>> Providing class rosters, name tags, and other supplies and materials for the instruction

Support for students include:

TIP

>> Planning for enrollment support and questions from learners

>> Creating a short introductory module on how to access course elements, contact an instructor, and tips for keeping up

>> Providing links on where to download software needed for the instruction along with directions on how to use it

>> Providing a clear summary of all hardware and software requirements to participate in the instruction

After you have gone through the process of planning for all components of the RIPPLES model, you are ready to begin your implementation! This stage is usually an exciting (but sometimes nerve wracking) time for an instructional designer. The next section provides a summary of tips and strategies for making your implementation process easier and smoother. By helping you identify common patterns of instructional implementations, including different delivery systems, you are in a better position to navigate obstacles and challenges more smoothly.

Accounting for Potential Barriers to Successful Implementation

Every implementation is unique. Each instructional design has different types of learners, situations, instructional strategies, settings, and ways of delivering instruction. Although you can't possibly account for every type of possible problem or need during implementation, you can use effective planning approaches and best practices to help increase the chances that your instruction is used and implemented as designed. This section summarizes sound implementation practices for common types of instructional implementations.

Knowing what challenges you may face

The challenges instructional designers experience during implementation show up in different ways, but mostly due to mismatched assumptions about your design, learners, or setting. Challenges are also likely if you did not try out your instruction with a few learners and experts in advance, or if you did not provide all the materials and support for learners and instructors to effectively execute the instruction. These areas you can anticipate and plan for in advance.

Anticipating every challenge in advance is impossible, and you are sure to make many assumptions during the design process that don't always turn out as planned. This misstep is to be expected when trying out instruction for the first time and is not something that can be completely avoided. However, some common challenges faced during implementation of instruction that you can anticipate include some of the following:

>> Not planning for adequate time for presenting the instruction, class discussions, or addressing questions from learners

>> Failing to effectively support the transition from handing off the instruction to an instructor who must teach it

>> Making the instruction too complex to either understand or too hard to navigate online

>> Presenting too much material at too fast of a pace

>> Presenting instruction in a confusing sequence, making it hard for learners to build on what they know

>> Learners don't want to be in the training and don't see the value for them to justify the time commitment

>> Learners don't engage in discussions, especially if they do not know each other

>> An instructor changes the instruction on the fly without covering all the objectives

>> More or fewer learners show up for the instruction than initially planned

>> The facilities are not set up with the materials needed (and no one anticipated that extra materials may be needed)

Navigating obstacles when they arise

By thinking about possible obstacles in advance, you are better prepared with back-up plans to navigate obstacles when they arise. If you can observe the instruction while it runs for the first time, you'll get important information about how the instruction is proceeding and can be in a position to make minor adjustments in consultation with the instructor as it progresses.

Remember, the best way to be prepared is to expect the unexpected! Here are some tips on how to do that:

>> Monitor the instructional implementation if possible.

>> Have a back-up plan for common potential challenges.

>> Be flexible! Adjust timelines and scope as needed.

>> Have extra materials, discussion questions, flipcharts, and supplies such as pens and paper.

>> Support the instructor to teach the instruction as intended through either a train-the-trainer class or a provided instructor guide.

>> Make sure you have a plan for who provides tech support if you or your learners are using it.

Tips for Successful Implementation of Common Types of Instruction

Although the instructional programs you end up designing are sure to be unique in terms of the specific strategies, audiences, and goals that you are setting out to achieve, it is still possible to identify general patterns for planning purposes. This section introduces common types of instructional approaches and delivery systems and identifies specific tips for successful implementation.

In-person classroom instruction

A common type of instructional design and delivery system is in-person instruction. This type of instruction utilizes a same-time, same place delivery mode (see Chapter 8 for more about this) and is typical of classroom instruction or training of groups of learners at the same time. When planning for implementing your instruction, consider the following tips for best practices, as outlined in Table 10-2.

TABLE 10-2   Implementation Tips for In-Person Classroom Instruction

Implementation Challenge	Best Practices
Preparing the instructor	Create a train-the-trainer class
	Create an instructor or facilitator guide that outlines the flow of the instruction
	Provide syllabus and lesson plans
	Provide a roster of participants
Materials and room set up	Arrive early at the facility to set up materials
	Set up flip charts for brainstorming or posting records of discussions or decisions in the classroom
	Set up presentation slides and test projector
	Bring pens, pencils, paper for notetaking
	Make copies of handouts and presentation slides
	Bring name tags
	Prepare spare materials and equipment
Logistics support	Schedule use of the facilities
	Schedule breaks and communicate when they will occur and where food is located
	Order snacks, drinks, or meals for learners (if applicable)
	Have on hand a sample set of implementation preparation questions that can be prepared in advance (Table 10-3 has some examples)
Discussion support	Provide a facilitator's guide with probing questions for the instructor to lead discussions, along with follow-up questions in case participation is low.
	Provide handouts for participants with discussion questions or post them where they can be seen
	Provide guidelines for discussions, such as guiding questions, ground rules, or time allocations.

(continued)

TABLE 10-2 *(continued)*

Implementation Challenge	Best Practices
Instructor or observation debrief of how the implementation went	Create a checklist of debriefing questions for instructors and/or learners.
	Allocate sufficient time for the instruction
	Ask if directions were clear
	Ask if instructor guides were clear and helpful
	Ask if sufficient practice for learners was provided
	Determine whether technology worked as planned
	Ask if discussions were facilitated effectively
	Determine whether learners were active and engaged in discussions and activities
	Determine whether content was covered as planned
	Note whether changes were made by the instructor during the instruction
	A sample Implementation Debrief Checklist worksheet is provided in this book's Appendix.

As promised, here's Table 10-3, with sample set of implementation preparation questions.

TABLE 10-3 **Sample Implementation Preparation Checklist for *Tree Investigators*, an Outdoor Educational Workshop and App on Tree Life Cycles**

Instructor Preparations Check Y or N	Have you . . .?
Y N ☒☐	Tried out the instruction with a few learners, experts, instructional designers, or supervisors? *Response: The design team went to the nature center to test the mobile app on the provided iPads. Two families with children over eight tried out the mobile app.*
Y N ☒☐	Developed training programs or instruction manuals for the instructor? *Response: An instructor guide was created to introduce the instruction, guide the directed activities, and facilitate the learner-centered explorations to identify evidence of tree life cycles on their own.*

Instructor Preparations	
Check Y or N	**Have you . . .?**
Y N	Provided the instructor with syllabi, lesson plans, course rosters?
☒☐	*Instructor guide was created along with suggested time frames for each phase of the instruction. (See the example instructor guide in Chapter 9.)*
Y N	Trained the instructor on how to use any technology required for teaching?
☒☐	*The development team met with the instructor to teach him how to proceed through the mobile app, along with a list of FAQs. He was trained a week in advance of the instruction to give him time to revisit it multiple times.*
Y N	Provided the instructor with a guide for facilitating discussions, along with follow-up questions?
☒☐	*Instructor was provided with laminated cards to pass out to participants that reminded them of the criteria for tree life cycle identification.*
Y N	Given the Implementation Debrief Checklist (see Appendix) to instructors to give feedback on the instruction?
☒☐	*Instructor was asked the questions on the debrief checklists verbally in an interview immediately following the first instructional implementation. Notes on areas for improvement were taken.*
Y N	Clarified communication expectations from the instructor? (Office hours or when to reach out for help, for example.)
☐☒	*Not applicable*
Y N	Scheduled use of the facilities for the instruction (if applicable)?
☒☐	*Yes, the Director of Educational programming was contacted via e-mail and the schedule was confirmed. See e-mail confirmation from June 15.*
Y N	Ordered snacks, drinks, or meals for participants (if applicable)?
☐☒	*N/A*
Y N	Arrived early at the facility to set up materials? (flip charts; name tags; pens, pencils, paper for notetaking; copies of all handouts and presentation slides; test presentation slides and projection equipment)
☒☐	*The team arrived early with several plastic Tupperware boxes, each of which included: an iPad, name tags, 50 copies of assessments, script for instructor, laminated index cards with checklist criteria for tree identification, cleaning wipes, video recorders, wireless microphones. The route for the outdoor education program was walked to make sure diversity of trees were found.*
Y N	Scheduled breaks for participants and provided information on where restrooms, vending machines, and so on are located.
☒☐	*Yes, a break was scheduled in the instructor guide. Locations for bathrooms were pointed out at the beginning of the instruction.*

(continued)

TABLE 10-3 *(continued)*

Instructor Preparations Check Y or N	Have you . . .?
Y N ☒ ☐	Tried out technology materials in advance with participants and/or instructors? ***Yes, see previous***
Y N ☐ ☒	Sent electronic PDFs to participants in advance (if applicable)? ***N/A***
Y N ☐ ☒	Provided a recommended timeline and schedule for completing asynchronous discussions or assignments? ***N/A***
Y N ☒ ☐	Provided contact information for tech support? ***Tech support was provided by instructor and a member of the design team onsite.***
Y N ☒ ☐	Provided a list of all hardware or software requirements learners and instructors need to participate in the instruction? ***iPad devices with the required technical specifications were provided onsite.***
Y N ☒ ☐	Trained students and instructors on how to use the LMS or other technologies for instruction? ***Learners were instructed on how to use the technology during the instruction by the instructor. A member of the design team was onsite if questions were raised.***
Y N ☒ ☐	Given instructions for where learners are to submit assignments and what to do if they have a technical problem during the instruction or an assignment submission? ***Yes, at the beginning of the instruction (raise hands).***
Y N ☐ ☒	Clearly communicated start and end times for any synchronous learning sessions to all learners, instructors, and guest speakers? ***N/A***
Y N ☒ ☐	Arranged to meet any speakers or instructors in advance to test out the system and presentation slides? ***Met instructor in advance to try out the app.***
Y N ☒ ☐	Established ground rules for communicating, interrupting, raising hands, background noise (if applicable)? ***Guidelines for sharing iPad devices were provided.***

Self-instructional print materials

Instruction that is designed to be delivered in a self-study format follows a different-time, different-place delivery mode. (See Chapter 8.) A common technology used to deliver self-instructional materials is print — either via printed handouts or electronic PDFs. When planning for implementing effective print-based instruction, consider the following tips:

TIP

- » Try out the materials with some target learners in advance to determine if the instruction is appropriately sequenced and time estimates are accurate.

- » Send electronic PDFs to participants via email in advance.

- » Provide a recommended timeline and schedule for completion of each module.

- » List contact information and office hours for instructors and tech support if learners have questions.

- » Provide printouts of electronic materials upon request.

- » Have participants complete a debrief questionnaire about how the implementation went for learners (see Appendix).

Virtual asynchronous

A common way of delivering instruction is via an LMS such as Canvas, Blackboard, or Moodle. Typically, an LMS has support for asynchronous online instruction that takes place anytime and anywhere. Tips for implementing virtual, asynchronous instruction include making sure you do the following:

TIP

- » List all hardware and software requirements learners need to participate in the instruction.

- » Clarify communication expectations from the instructor.

- » Provide learners with training on how to use the LMS and any technologies needed for the instruction.

- » Facilitate community building with the instructor and other learners through introductions, ice breakers, or video-based announcements.

- » Provide guidelines for instructors to facilitate asynchronous discussions.

- » Outline a schedule of start and end dates for asynchronous discussions along with guidelines for discussions.

- » List contact information and office hours for instructors or tech support if learners have questions.

>> Train the instructor on how to use the LMS for announcements, e-mails, grading, and navigation.

>> Provide lesson plans or instructor guides.

>> Give instructions on where learners are to submit assignments and what to do if they have a technical problem during an assignment submission.

Virtual synchronous

Instruction that is delivered at the same time but with learners in different locations uses virtual-synchronous delivery modes. This type of instruction commonly uses a video conferencing platform such as Zoom or other synchronous communication tools embedded into an LMS. In order to implement a successful virtual-synchronous instruction model, you need to do the following:

TIP

>> Clearly communicate the start and end time of the synchronous learning sessions to all learners, instructors, and guest speakers.

>> Consider whether start and end times need to be scheduled across multiple time zones, and if so, try to choose a time that can work for learners across various time zones.

>> Give clear instructions on what to do if a connection is lost during the session.

>> Create a written tutorial in advance (for instructors and learners) on how to use synchronous tools for raising a hand to speak, muting, turning video on and off, whiteboard use, breakout rooms, and so on.

>> Arrange to meet the instructor and any guest speakers in advance for them to try out the system, test their slides, and so on.

>> Establish ground rules for communicating, interrupting, raising hand, background distractions and noise, and so on.

>> List all technical requirements for participating in the video conference.

Blended

Blended delivery systems use a blend of synchronous and asynchronous delivery modes. Tips for effective implementation of blended instruction can be selected from the previous sections, depending on your situation.

The one unique implementation consideration for blended instructional programs is to create a master schedule for when sessions are synchronous and when to complete any asynchronous discussions or activities.

Place- or field-based

Some instruction takes place at specific sites, either outdoors or indoors. Examples are field-based instruction such as learning about horticulture by making observations and soil testing within a local garden.

Tips for effective place-based or field-based implementations include:

TIP

>> Planning for a rain date if the instruction is held outdoors

>> Considering weather-related factors that can interfere with instruction such as temperature (too hot or cold) or weather (too sunny or rainy)

>> If utilizing mobile devices, making sure that devices are charged before arriving at the site

>> Providing recommendations for electronic notetaking, because writing on paper can be difficult outdoors or when doing field work

REMEMBER

You will not be able to plan for every possible contingency or miscalculation! You are sure to learn a lot from your first implementation, and those lessons will be a strong foundation for your future implementation planning. The key is to stay flexible, plan ahead, bring extra materials, and work closely with your experts!

Chapter **11**

Evaluating Instructional Materials

I n the ADDIE model (see Chapter 1), the final phase is the evaluation phase — the "E" in ADDIE. At this point in the design process, you have likely completed the first four phases of the ADDIE model — the analysis, design, development, and implementation of your instruction. The evaluation phase occurs after implementation, as it focuses on evaluating the impact and success of the instructional program or intervention.

When it comes to instructional design, any evaluation seeks to answer important questions such as:

» Did the instruction effectively address the identified problems?

» Did the instruction achieve its intended goals?

» Is it justifiable to continue offering the instructional program in its current form?

These questions are closely related to the ones you may have asked during the analysis and design phases, where you identified problems and established your goals and assessments. An evaluation revisits these problems, needs, and goals to measure their attainment.

REMEMBER

Remembering that evaluation is an ongoing process throughout instructional design, not just a one-time event at the end, is important. However, during the final evaluation phase, you are tasked with conducting a comprehensive assessment of the instructional program by building on the insights gained during implementation.

In this chapter, I describe the principles and practices of evaluation that instructional designers use to determine the success of an instructional design. This determination helps you navigate what to evaluate and how to go about it.

Determining the Success of the Instruction

It is important to start any discussion of the evaluation phase of ADDIE by returning to what you set out to accomplish during the Analysis phase. (Chapter 3 covers this topic.) During the Analysis phase, you determine the purpose of the instruction or the performance gap — that is, the gap between ideal and actual performance. Now, during the Evaluation phase of the ADDIE model, you're going to see if the instruction you created was successful in closing the gap. The Evaluation phase is all about seeking answers to the questions asked during the analysis phase.

You evaluate an instructional program to determine if it accomplished what it set out to do. This evaluation can involve solving a performance problem identified by management in the analysis phase, such as a low rate of adherence to compliance regulations. Or it can involve fulfilling a need to train employees on a new technology or process that is being introduced into an organization. A lot of time and money may be invested in the instructional design, so finding out whether it is effective and should continue is important.

EXAMPLE

What is considered "effective" varies depending on the setting and goals. Take for example, the following situations:

>> A university program offered a three-course certificate in instructional design that was delivered online via an LMS. In this situation, "success" means that the certificate program led to an increase in applications to the master's degree program from those earning the certificate.

>> A school of nursing developed an eight-hour, online course to help their graduates achieve passing scores on mandatory state examinations. Here, "success" means that the instruction resulted in an increase in the percentage of students with passing scores on the exam when compared to prior years.

>> A corporation converted its in-person instruction to virtual. Any evaluation here focuses on the costs and benefits of transitioning from in-person to virtual training.

Different evaluation questions require gathering different types of information to answer them. Some questions may be answered with student performance data while others may be answered with financial data or on-the-job performance indicators. This chapter helps you to identify which type of evaluation information is best for you.

Distinguishing between formative and summative evaluation

Clarifying the distinction between ongoing evaluations that occur throughout the instructional design process and the final evaluation of the instruction's impact is helpful. In instructional design, evaluations are categorized into two types: formative and summative. These two different types of evaluation have different goals and processes.

Formative evaluations

The main goal of a formative evaluation is to seek feedback during the analysis, design, development, and implementation phases so that you can make adjustments to the instruction as you go along. The point is to gather and apply this information while the instruction is still being designed and developed.

On the way to implementation, an instructional designer consults with a) subject matter experts (SMEs) to ensure content accuracy, b) multimedia experts to develop and test prototypes, and c) supervisors, clients, learners, and/or instructors to gather early input. A good instructional designer collects feedback from these stakeholders at different stages of the design process, which (hopefully) yields some valuable insights and also makes it possible to make necessary adjustments before the instruction is finalized.

The feedback you're able to gather during a formative evaluation ensures that the instructional product you developed is not only of better quality but that it also effectively addresses the identified problems and needs of the intended learners. This ongoing evaluation process helps to create a more successful and impactful instructional design.

Summative evaluation

Summative evaluation has a different purpose; rather than gauging your progress as the design is developed — the formative approach — it evaluates the impact or success of the instructional design as implemented. Summative evaluation, the focus of this chapter, happens after instruction has occurred.

REMEMBER

A designer conducts a summative evaluation to determine if the instruction has led to the outcomes it was designed to achieve. The questions being asked during a summative evaluation differ, depending on the problems and goals that stake-holders set out to accomplish. The answers to the evaluation questions provide information for decision makers and shed light on whether the instruction should be revised or continued to be offered in its current form.

The information used to answer questions on effectiveness may look like any of the following:

>> Comparisons on measures taken before and after the instruction, such as job performance or learning assessments

>> Cost-benefit analyses of offering the instruction

>> Reports of learner satisfaction with the instruction

>> Learner use of the skills learned in the instruction (such as the workplace or everyday life)

>> Contributions to the strategic mission or values of the organization

>> Productivity measures, such as increases or decreases in errors, customer complaints, completion time, workplace satisfaction

The steps and procedures of a summative evaluation are tied to what the stake-holders want to know, solve, or enhance. In the next section, I provide some general tips that are useful for starting any summative evaluation.

Steps in the evaluation process

Although every evaluation is different, three main steps that most evaluations cover are:

1. **Clarify the purpose and audience for the evaluation.**

   As I spell out in earlier chapters of this book, one goal of the analysis phase is to generate a clear vision of the problem at hand as well as the desired outcome. By confirming goals and problems early in the process, you better ensure that your efforts throughout the design process are aligned with those goals. Having a clear sense of the problem being addressed is essential for identifying the kinds of information you will need for the evaluation. For instance, gathering baseline data on performance indicators (complaints from customers, for example) can be helpful if you intend to make pre- and post-instruction comparisons.

EXAMPLE

It is equally important to determine the primary audience for whom the evaluation is intended, whether it's upper management, supervisors, instructors, or the designer themselves. This answer goes hand-in-hand with clarifying what you are going to evaluate and the level of evaluation needed (discussed further in the next section). For example, if employees completed training on how to successfully use new accounting software, your main question may be whether these learners are now able to successfully use the new software in their job roles.

It is important to note that a summative evaluation takes place within a broader cultural, political, and organizational context. The data you are collecting take on meaning within that context and could ultimately have a negative impact on some people. For instance, stakeholders reading an evaluation report are typically in positions of power. The data you include in the report might be highly sensitive and utilized as justification for layoffs, mergers, or negative performance evaluations.

2. **Collect the data needed to answer the evaluation questions.**

After you have clarified your evaluation focus, it is time to collect any data that can help answer your questions. You can use several different techniques for gathering data, including the following:

- Surveys or questionnaires of learners

- Surveys of supervisors

- Interviews with stakeholders, supervisors, or learners

- Knowledge assessments (tests, in other words)

- On-the-job performance assessments or observations

- Organizational metrics (cost and retention rates, for example)

The specific data collection methods you use depend on your evaluation questions and the level of impact you want to report. Some data may be more difficult to gain access to than others, especially those that may have privacy implications such as the financial or human resources information within organizations. You then further focus your evaluation questions based on what kinds of data are available to you.

3. **Report the findings and recommend next steps**

After you gather and analyze the evaluation data, your next step is to report the findings. After you analyze the data, you summarize them in a report. Your analyses may include average test scores, summaries of learner feedback, or percentages of responses from surveys or questionnaires. You can present your findings in a written report or through a presentation to stakeholders.

Based on the gathered data and findings, you have valuable insights to make informed recommendations on the next steps. Recommendations can include revisions to the existing instruction to improve its effectiveness or suggestions for implementing future iterations of the instructional program. The evaluation plays a role in shaping continuous improvement of the instructional design as well as establishing accountability to stakeholders who are involved in the decision-making process.

Counting Down the Four Different Levels of Evaluation

As I (hopefully) have established so far, evaluation can focus on a variety of purposes and measures of success. One well-known framework for evaluating instruction is Donald Kirkpatrick's levels of evaluation. Kirkpatrick, a distinguished professor who was long associated with the Management Institute of the University of Wisconsin, developed a model that categorized four distinct levels of evaluation: reaction, learning, behavior, and results.

The four levels of evaluation are hierarchical and progress in complexity and scope. In a nutshell, Level 1 focuses on the participants' reactions and satisfaction with the instruction. Level 2 evaluates what participants learned. Level 3 evaluates whether learners applied their knowledge through behavior changes in the workplace, in school, or in life. Finally, Level 4 evaluates if the instruction impacted broader organizational goals, such as productivity, cost savings, or institutional values.

Although evaluating all four levels gives a comprehensive approach to measuring success, it is not always necessary nor practical to evaluate all four levels. The levels you choose are tightly aligned to your goals and desired outcomes as well as the amount of time and budget you have available. As the levels progress, the evaluation's complexity as well as the resources, time, and expenses associated with it increase as well. Table 11-1 provides a summary of the four levels of evaluation for easy reference.

The sections that follow go into more detail for each of Kirkpatrick's four levels of evaluation.

TABLE 11-1 **Kirkpatrick's Four Levels of Evaluation**

Evaluation Level	Description and Evaluation Focus
Level 1: Reaction	Evaluates learners' satisfaction with, or reaction to, the instruction
	One of the most commonly-used evaluation categories
	Focuses on perceived effectiveness, interest, engagement, and enjoyment of the instruction
	Typical instruments here include questionnaires, surveys, or course evaluations
Level 2: Learning	Evaluates if learners achieved the goals and objectives of the instruction
	Typical assessment methods here include paper-and-pencil tests or online quizzes
	Occurs at the end of the instruction or as a pre- and post-test comparison
Level 3: Behavior	Evaluates if learners are now using what they learned on the job or in their lives
	Focuses on whether learners are applying what they learned and whether there are potential barriers in the setting interfering with their performance
	Typical ways of assessment here include observations of on-the-job performance or reports from supervisors, customers, and so on
Level 4: Results	Evaluates whether the improved learner performance resulting from the instruction had an impact on organizational goals or needs
	Results here may include cost-benefit analyses, workplace productivity, job satisfaction, retention, improved health and safety, and so on
	Evaluation data may be difficult to obtain due to access, cost, or time limitations

Level 1: Did learners like the instruction? (reaction)

The primary focus of a Level 1 evaluation is to find out if the learners had a positive experience with the instruction and whether they find it useful. This type of evaluation is commonly used by instructional designers, because it provides valuable information from the learners' perspective and it is relatively quick and easy conduct.

REMEMBER

All instructional designs should seek to answer Level 1 questions (at a minimum) as part of the formative and summative evaluation process. Two reasons to collect this information include:

>> **Level 1 evaluation provides you with information about revisions that may be needed.** For example, despite your best design efforts, learners may report that some content was covered too quickly or that they need more

practice and time to learn the skills being taught. This feedback is important for simple changes that can make the next iteration of the instruction better.

>> **If an instructor is used (or if you were the instructor), it is important to find out what learners thought about the instruction and any activities that are used.** Examples of such activities include case studies, role playing, discussions, and/or lectures. Likewise, this provides important feedback for revision.

TIP

Following is a list of possible questions that you can use to gather data for a Level 1 evaluation:

>> Did you like the instruction?

>> Was the instruction relevant to you?

>> Were you engaged and interested during the instruction?

>> Will you be able to use what you learned outside of the instructional environment?

>> How did you like the following activities:

- Lectures

- Case studies

- Demonstrations

- Discussions

- Collaboration with peers

- Practice

>> Did you have any problems using the technology delivery system (LMS, video conferencing, and so on)?

>> What did you like best about the instruction?

>> What did you like least and would like to see improved?

Using surveys and questionnaires

The most common way for collecting data for a Level 1 evaluation is through a survey or questionnaire. You have multiple ways to format a survey for a Level 1 evaluation, depending on how much information you want to receive and how much time is available to learners to give this feedback.

Some surveys can be designed to be short with open-ended questions such as:

Please answer the following questions about your experience with the instruction.

> What did you like best about the instruction?

> What part(s) of the instruction need the most improvement?

You can also use different combinations of question formats such as "yes-no" questions (see the following) or rating scales. (See "Instructional rating scales" in the next section.)

Please circle Yes or No to the following questions:

> I feel I learned new knowledge that will help me in my job. *Yes or No*

> Overall, did the instructor promote a meaningful learning experience for you? *Yes or No*

> Do you think you will use what you learned in your job? *Yes or No*

Instructional rating scales

Another way to collect data for a Level 1 evaluation using a questionnaire or survey is with a rating scale. Rating scales can capture more nuance than yes-no questions but still can be answered fairly quickly. One type of rating scale, called a Likert scale, provides statements and asks learners to indicate their level of agreement or disagreement. Such scales often use five response options, ranging on a continuum from "strongly disagree" to "strongly agree" or "lowest rating" to "highest rating." Each response option is assigned a value that is listed as a number or words.

Here's an example:

Please rate your level of agreement with the following statements about the instruction. Select the response that most represents your experience.

1. The instructional content was relevant and applicable to my job.

   - Strongly Disagree
   - Disagree
   - Neither Agree nor Disagree
   - Agree
   - Strongly Agree

2. The instructional materials were clear and easy to understand.

- Strongly Disagree
- Disagree
- Neither Agree nor Disagree
- Agree
- Strongly Agree

3. The instructor was knowledgeable and presented the material effectively.

- Strongly Disagree
- Disagree
- Neither Agree nor Disagree
- Agree
- Strongly Agree

4. The case study activities helped me grasp the concepts better.

- Strongly Disagree
- Disagree
- Neither Agree nor Disagree
- Agree
- Strongly Agree

Another example using numerical ratings is the following:

Please rate the following statements on a scale from 1 to 5:

1. Rate how well this instruction increased your understanding of the topic:

Low		Average		High
1	2	3	4	5

2. Rate how well the instructor promoted a meaningful learning experience for you.

Low	Average			High
1	2	3	4	5

After participants complete the survey, you gathered feedback on their perceptions of the instruction. Their responses can then be reported as tabulations of frequencies, averages, or bar charts. Where possible, keep all data anonymous. This gives learners more security to speak freely about their feedback.

Level 2: Did they learn? (learning)

Level 2 evaluation focuses on assessing what participants learned after they completed the instruction. Unlike Level 1, which evaluates learners' reactions to (and satisfaction with) the instruction, Level 2 measures what was learned. This level of evaluation measures if learners achieved competence in the goals and objectives of the instruction. (This process of defining objectives and measuring them by using assessments is something I discuss in detail in Chapter 5, but I briefly summarize it in the following.)

REMEMBER

The foundation for evaluating the extent to which learning has occurred starts with your objectives!

A brief recap of aligning objectives and assessments

To measure any kind of learning, aligning your instructional goals and objectives with your assessment items is essential. Your goals and objectives define clear and measurable outcomes that learners need to achieve after completing the instruction. With those in hand, you can then create assessment items that match these objectives and measure whether learners have achieved success. Your assessments form the foundation for the Level 2 evaluation because they demonstrate whether learning of the objectives has occurred.

As I discuss in Chapters 4 and 5, your objectives tell you what type of assessment you need. As a quick recap, objectives target different types of learning outcomes. Some learning outcomes are considered "lower level," such as remembering facts and information. Other objectives address "higher level" outcomes, such as applying, evaluating, or creating.

REMEMBER

The key to Level 2 evaluation is that your assessment items match the overall level of learning objective you created. A common illustration of this principle is to think about the assessment process required for getting a driver's license. The best way to assess whether someone can drive a car is by observing them driving and evaluating whether they showed competence in all required skills. In contrast, you wouldn't try to assess someone's driving competency by only given them a factual test of road rules and traffic laws!

Distinguishing different outcomes and assessment types

As I state earlier in this chapter, a key point to remember when dealing with evaluations is that your assessments match your objectives. Take a look at a few examples to see how this looks in practice.

EXAMPLE

The first example illustrates a sample objective and assessment item for a learning outcome at the level of remembering facts.

> **Objective:** Given a blank diagram of the human respiratory system, learners can recall and label the key components of the human respiratory system. The learners need to correctly identify and label each part for successful completion.
>
> **Assessment Item:** Given the diagram of the human respiratory system, label its main components, including the trachea, lungs, bronchi, and diaphragm.

EXAMPLE

The second example shows an objective and corresponding assessment item at a higher level of applying what is learned:

> **Objective:** At the end of the customer service training, learners can demonstrate effective and professional handling of customer complaints by using the concepts learned. They are evaluated based on specific criteria, including active listening, empathy, offering solutions, and maintaining a positive tone throughout the interaction.
>
> **Assessment Item:** Participants are presented with a simulated customer complaint scenario, and they are asked to demonstrate their ability to apply the techniques learned in the instruction to address the issue.

REMEMBER

You can use a variety of methods to carry out Level 2 evaluations, such as pre-tests and post-tests, quizzes, role plays, scenarios, or skill demonstrations. You can conduct assessments before instruction, during, or after (or at all three times to allow for comparisons and evaluation of progress).

Level 3: Did they apply what they learned? (behavior)

Level 3 evaluation focuses on determining whether learners have successfully applied the knowledge and skills gained from the instruction in real-world situations. It examines whether learners have effectively transferred their learning beyond the instructional environment to the workplace or their everyday lives.

EXAMPLE

For instance, in a Level 3 evaluation of a healthy eating workshop, the evaluation may assess if participants have adopted more nutritious eating habits in their daily lives. Similarly, for a communication skills course, the evaluation may measure whether learners are now using those skills during challenging customer interactions. The ability to apply what one has learned to the real-world is the gold standard when it comes to instructional effectiveness.

However, Level 3 evaluation is not frequently conducted due to several challenges. Access to participants in their jobs or everyday lives after the instruction ends may be limited, and the evaluation process can be time-consuming and resource-intensive. In this way, it shares some overlap with Level 4 evaluation, in that access, time, and costs are factors.

Given this, the first task in conducting a Level 3 evaluation is to find out what type of access you have to participants after the instruction ends. The second task is to choose an assessment technique that best suits the questions you want to answer as well as the practical constraints you are facing. By carefully considering these factors, you are in a better position to gather the data you need to evaluate the real-world impact of the instructional program.

Conducting a performance assessment

A Level 3 evaluation typically takes place several weeks to months after the instruction ends. The main goal is to determine if learners are applying what they learned to real-world situations. This evaluation can be at a workplace or other life context (health or fitness, for example). As with the prior levels of evaluation, Level 3 is tied to the overall goals for the instruction.

REMEMBER

Level 3 evaluations typically focus on a performance assessment. Performance can be directly observed, or it can be measured more indirectly. A direct observation may include a supervisor observing if a nurse is correctly performing IV-line placement with patients or an experienced teacher observing a student teacher's classroom lesson. Direct observations are typically done by an expert or a supervisor, and they often use checklists or rating scales to focus their observations.

On the other hand, indirect measures involve gathering feedback from supervisors or learners themselves. Indirect measures may include surveying a supervisor and asking them to rate the changes in employees' performance since the instruction ended. Another example is asking participants to produce action plans that illustrate how they are using the skills learned during the instruction on the job, and then sharing the plans with a supervisor who rates them and gives feedback.

TIP

In sum, performance assessments can involve:

>> Direct observations of performance by an expert

>> Checklists or rating sheets to evaluate performance

>> Action plans from participants

>> Questionnaires or rating sheets of performance from supervisors

When resources are limited

Level 3 evaluations are resource intensive — specifically time and financial resources. For this reason, instructional designers may find themselves needing to gather the best data available to them with limited time, access, and budget. The book, *Rapid Instructional Design* by George Piskurich, gives examples of rapid shortcuts for conducting a Level 3 performance evaluation.

EXAMPLE

One example of such a shortcut highlighted by Piskurich is to use brief surveys that are given to participants after the instruction ends. This approach is like a melding of a Level 1 evaluation and a Level 3. Survey questions may include:

Select the rating that best reflects your experience after the instruction:

1. Before the instruction, my ability to apply the knowledge and skills of using electronic medical records (EMR) to my job was:

    high – average – low – none

2. After the class, my ability to apply the knowledge and skills of using electronic medical records (EMR) to my job was:

    high – average – low – none

3. I feel I am using the knowledge and skills learned during the instruction on the job now.

    Yes or *No*.

    If no, why not?

4. What was the most useful point I learned that I use regularly on my job now?

Surveys of participants can also be supplemented with surveys sent to supervisors. Although shortcuts may produce more limited data for a Level 3 evaluation than direct observations, they nonetheless provide useful insights into the how (or if) the skills from the instruction are being applied to the performance context.

Level 4: Did the instruction impact the results of an organization? (results)

A Level 4 evaluation focuses on measuring longer-term impacts of the instruction on an organization's performance, mission, or results. (In contrast, the prior three levels of evaluation I discuss earlier in this chapter focus on more short-term reactions, learning, or behavior changes.) For this reason, Level 4 evaluations are the most complex and resource intensive; they also typically involve taking benchmark measurements before the instruction and comparing them to data taken after the instruction ends. This requires planning during the early phases of analysis.

Level 4 evaluations use metrics to gauge the instruction's impact on key performance indicators, business outcomes, or organizational goals. Examples may include improvements in productivity, revenue, cost savings, customer satisfaction, diversity, employee wellbeing, or retention. Data routinely captured by organizations that is used in planning a Level 4 evaluation include sales figures, expenses, errors, enrollment numbers, and/or customer complaints.

Additional examples may include increases in the number of visitors to a museum, increases in volunteerism, or increases in social media traffic, advertising revenue, or numbers of downloads. Level 4 evaluation is comprehensive and helps organizations connect learning outcomes with organizational results. This aids stakeholders in making decisions about future instructional efforts.

EXAMPLE

Consider an example of a Level 4 evaluation that a team of designers, students, and researchers at my university conducted several years ago. The evaluation was for a major automobile manufacturer who created an eight-week online course on customer service designed for service advisors and managers, sales managers and sales consultants. The instruction covered the skills needed to maintain and increase customer loyalty, using industry-specific case studies, sharing of best practices, and creating action plans to solve known performance problems.

To evaluate the impact of the instruction on organizational results, we compared car owner loyalty scores for both the period of the third quarter (Q3, before the instruction) and the fourth quarter (Q4, after the instruction). These measures came from customer surveys and contained items that directly tied to concepts covered in the customer service course. If the instruction had an impact on important organizational results related to customer service, we expected to see the survey scores increase from Q3 to Q4. The Level 4 evaluation bore this finding out and showed a significant increase in customer loyalty survey scores for those dealerships who participated in the instruction from Q3 to Q4.

Making Revisions Based on Your Findings

After completing an evaluation, an instructional designer analyzes all the available information and makes recommendations for revision. This evaluation involves identifying strengths and weaknesses of the instruction based on the insights gathered from the evaluation.

Recommended revisions include refining the learning objectives, developing more engaging activities, or clarifying aspects that were confusing or that needed more time and practice for learners. By evaluating and refining instructional materials, a designer can work to constantly improve the learning experience for the next iteration.

Your recommendations may also explain if there are new or unexpected barriers within the organization that are limiting the extent to which learners are effectively applying their knowledge and skills from the instruction to the job. If this is the case, a designer can present an analysis of these barriers and propose ways of minimizing them.

REMEMBER

When preparing a report to make recommendations to stakeholders, remember to address each level of the evaluation that was conducted. Highlight any areas where learners are still not performing effectively and suggest new solutions (instructional or otherwise) for addressing them. Also remember that an evaluation report is interpreted by stakeholders within a broader cultural and political context. Having the report read first by a team of people with different perspectives is a good strategy for ensuring the report is received by all parties in the intended spirit.

5

The Part of Tens

Chapter **12**

Ten Best Practices for Creating Engaging Instruction

The chapters in this book have covered a variety of tips, models, and strategies for creating successful instructional designs. It is important to underscore that there is no single best technique that we can apply as designers to make our instruction optimally engaging. The ultimate effectiveness of our instruction depends on the design decisions that we make during the different phases of the ADDIE process and how well aligned they are. Asking which instructional design strategy is best is like asking what type of tool is best for all home improvement projects! There is no single best instructional technique for all situations.

However, with this in mind, this chapter synthesizes some common best practices for creating instruction that encourages learners to actively engage, participate in, talk about, and process what they are learning. Each of the following best practices assume that they are aligned with the outcomes of your analysis and design phases.

Design Activities for Learner Collaboration, Discussion, and Sharing of Ideas

One strategy for increasing learner engagement is to design activities that promote collaboration with other learners during the instruction. Collaboration encourages learners to work in groups with others to enhance their understanding of the content.

Collaborative learning can be supported with different types of activities:

>> Group discussions about an issue, question, or problem.

>> Brainstorming sessions as a group at the beginning of an activity.

>> Working together in small groups to solve a problem.

>> Sharing individual ideas, best practices, or perspectives over the course of the instruction in order to expand the learning of others.

>> Peer teaching or peer feedback.

>> "Jigsaw method" activities, where learners research a specialized topic and then come together with other groups to share what they learned.

>> "Think-pair-share" activities, where learners think about a question or problem individually, then discuss it with a partner, and then share with the larger group. This strategy works best when teaching a large group.

Collaborative learning activities encourages learners' active engagement in the instruction through sharing different points of view.

Design Activities that Relate to Real-World Applications

Instruction is more motivating and meaningful when learners see both the usefulness and relevance of what they are learning. This instruction works because instructional content is more easily applied to learners' daily life or work when it is learned in a context of a realistic problem or situation. It also supports learners' awareness of why the instruction is relevant to them, which is a condition that facilitates motivation.

Some common strategies for designing activities that connect to real-world applications include:

>> **Creating a complex, realistic problem that learners may encounter in life or on the job and ask them to work together to solve it.** Some problem-based instruction models suggest presenting the problem at the start of the instruction, and then teaching learners the knowledge and skills needed to solve the problem. Other models suggest teaching concepts and skills first, and then presenting a complex problem at the end of the instruction. Either approach has its benefits and drawbacks, depending on the context and goals for the instruction.

>> **Using case studies to illustrate a range of possible situations and solutions that others have applied in the past.** Learners then apply what they learned from these cases to reason through a new case.

>> **Designing a culminating activity at the end of the instruction that asks learners to engage in an activity that is similar to what they may be doing after the instruction ends.** For instance, at the end of instruction on how to create a business plan, learners can work together on an activity to create a future business plan.

Use Technology Wisely Based on Learning Goals and Needs versus Jumping on the Latest Trend

Yes, technology can be used as a tool to create exciting and interactive instruction, but technology choices should be complementary with the pragmatic constraints of the setting where they are implemented, such as budget, facilities, and access constraints. Getting lured into using an exciting new technology is easy without considering the broader constraints such as whether it will be accessible to learners, whether organizations can afford it, or whether human resources are available to provide the needed expertise, maintenance, and technical support.

REMEMBER

There is no "best" technology for delivering engaging instruction. If anything, technology is simply a tool you can use to support better access to your instructional materials, increase efficiency, and possibly reduce the costs of instruction. Technology can also play a unique role in supporting instructional strategies such as visualizating concepts, collaborating at a distance, or providing simulations that would be difficult or dangerous to learn through direct experience.

Include a Variety of Interactive Instructional Activities

Instruction is more engaging if you create a variety of instructional activities that are interactive and that encourage active participation. This element is particularly important for instruction that is lengthy in time. Imagine sitting through a four-hour technology workshop with no other activities aside from the instructor talking! Instead, it is more engaging if you break up the time with different types of interactive activities.

You can make activities more varied and interactive by using strategies such as:

» Role playing exercises

» In-class debates

» Hands-on activities with technology, objects, or models

» Presenting a variety of examples and scenarios

» Games

» Practice activities

Give Learners Feedback on How They're Doing

Getting feedback on one's performance at various times during the instruction supports engagement by helping learners make their understanding visible to themselves, other learners, and instructors. Using quizzes or graded assignments at the end of the instruction is not the only method that you can use to give feedback on learning and performance.

Instead, you can provide formative assessments using other techniques that capture learners' thinking and performance at multiple points during the instructional process:

» Support learner self-assessment through checklists or reflection questions.

» Structure collaborative activities with peers to provide an opportunity for learners to verbalize their thinking and compare it with others.

>> Use ungraded quiz-like games or review sessions.

>> Ask learners a short question as an "exit ticket" at the end of the session to see how well they understood the lesson.

REMEMBER

Feedback stresses the importance of providing informal opportunities to demonstrate learners' thinking at multiple points during the instructional process.

Create Activities with the Right Amount of Complexity for Learners

Instruction is more meaningful when activities are designed to help learners actively process the information delivered without overtaxing them. Here are a few tips for accomplishing this balance:

>> Organize the content and activities to proceed from simple to complex.

>> Eliminate irrelevant information and activities to help learners' focus their attention on the content that is needed to achieve the learning objectives.

>> Break down your instruction into smaller chunks or lessons to support learners processing the instruction without making excessive demands on their memory.

Design Activities that Enhance Transfer of What is Being Learned to Real-World Situations

No matter what type of learning outcomes your instruction supports, it is beneficial to think about how to support learners to use their knowledge after the instruction ends. We have all probably experienced situations where we learned something in a classroom but were not able to call upon that knowledge when we needed it in the real world.

Although transferring knowledge to a new setting is a complex skill that takes time to develop, instructional designers can create activities that can enhance the likelihood that learners are able to use and apply what they have learned after the instruction ends. Here are some guidelines to follow:

>> Design activities or examples that show how the information can be applied across multiple contexts, not just one. Demonstrating a wider application of the content better supports transferring to different possible situations.

>> If the task being learned should only be applied in one way or sequence, then teach the specific sequence and provide multiple practice opportunities.

>> Present a specific problem or case and then give learners a similar case that varies one or two characteristics. Ask "what-if" questions that change different factors of the problem or situation.

Don't Focus Only on "Telling"

Although there are situations where listening to lectures or reading text content can be an effective and efficient method to communicate new information, it is usually not a strategy that, on its own, supports active learning. Learning is an active process of creating meaning, not a passive process of receiving information. Active learning requires learners to pay attention to important information, reflect on that information, and organize their thinking in response to what they learned. You can support more active engagement by designing activities that support learners to organize what they are learning from a lecture or text:

>> Provide frequent opportunities for learners to summarize and explain what they are learning. You can accomplish this through written activities or discussions with others.

>> Build in question prompts during lectures, text, or video information that encourage learners to pause and summarize or explain what they are learning.

Use Activities that Support Learning-By-Doing

Another best practice for creating activities that support active and engaged learning is to encourage learning-by-doing — that is, learning by constructing or creating artifacts, graphical representations, or media that represents what one has learned. Here are some examples:

- » Organizing content into concept maps or graphic organizers

- » Creating models of a phenomenon with materials such as clay, computer graphics, or other supplies

- » Creating interactive presentation slides of a plan, idea, or solution

- » Creating content that represents what has been learned via video, audio, drawings, photographs, or graphical media

Connect with Other Designers to Learn Best Practices and New Ideas

The last best practice is to connect with a network of instructional designers to keep learning new design ideas and technologies. Over time, it's easy to get stagnant and continue to use the same instructional designs and activities that you have honed from prior experience. After you have a repertory of design models and strategies that have proven to work well for you, it is easy and efficient to continue using them. However, being open to learning new approaches and expanding our practices also is important.

One way to continue learning as an instructional designer is to get involved with professional associations or online networks devoted to the topic of instructional design. Through these networks, you connect with other instructional designers and professional development opportunities. For instance, you can find several tutorials on topics and technologies related to instructional design through LinkedIn Learning, as well as professional associations such as Association for Educational Communications and Technology or Association for Talent Development. Also certificate programs are offered through colleges and universities that also can help you to stay current and learn new instructional design practices.

Chapter **13**

Ten Questions to Ask Before Selecting Technologies for Your Instruction

C learly technology has changed the way we live and work today, but in many ways, it has also changed the possibilities for how we can design and deliver our instruction. Technologies are tools that help us expand the possibilities for reaching more learners, designing new ways of interaction, or enabling new ways of representing or visualizing content material.

Technologies for teaching and learning today range from commonly available print-based PDFs to emerging technologies such as virtual reality simulators. With so many options at our fingertips, how do we go about selecting from the range of technology possibilities for delivering our instruction? In this chapter, you find ten questions you can ask yourself that can help you successfully narrow down your selections for using technologies to deliver your instruction.

What Type of Learning and What Kinds of Instructional Goals Need To Be Supported?

Technology choices are tied to your design goals and learning outcomes. Your choice of technology as a delivery tool should align with your objectives as well as characteristics of the learners and the setting in which the instruction is used. Technology can be used to reinforce, illustrate, or provide practice for specific learning objectives, based on specific attributes or functions that it supports for learning.

Pay attention to the features that certain technologies offer and align them with the tasks that learners need to perform. Take, for instance, the features of digital video. Video is a great delivery system choice for your instruction if the tasks you are trying to teach involve instructing physical movements or motion, such as how to perform an exercise or operate equipment correctly. It is also a good choice if you need to present role plays of exemplary (or non-exemplary!) interactions with customers.

You can also think about your instructional goals and strategies, such as whether you want learners to be able to replay the instruction multiple times or refer to it on the job. Similarly, if your instructional goal is to create a learning community that is collaborative, then you will want to select a technology delivery system that supports learning from each other's ideas.

TIP

Thinking about both the tasks that you are trying to teach and the goals and instructional strategies that you want to support can quickly narrow down the best options available to choose from.

Does the Instruction Need to Be Delivered as Self-Paced or Group-Based Instruction?

During your analysis process, you spend time learning about the instructional context and the needs and constraints regarding where and how the instruction needs to take place. Do your learners participate in the instruction onsite together in one place? Or are some or all of them remotely located and dispersed geographically and take the instruction from different locations?

If your instruction needs to be delivered to a group of learners located within the same space, then you may want a technology delivery system that takes advantage of the ability to have an instructor available to deliver the instruction in real time. If your learners are not located in the same place, then virtual technologies such as a learning management system (LMS) or video conferencing technologies (Zoom, for example) are better choices.

What Are Your Budget Constraints?

Budget and costs play an important role in the selection of a technology delivery system. We have upfront costs of the technology itself, with varying price points ranging from free and open-source options to expensive proprietary systems or licensing fees. Some low-cost technologies for instructional delivery include electronic PDFs, audio, and video, depending on whether you have the expertise and the equipment needed to create the instruction. More expensive options are those that involve subscriptions or licensing fees such as LMSs or software to develop multimedia-based instruction.

REMEMBER

Be sure to pay attention to long-term costs, such as maintenance, updates, support, and technology training. Ongoing technical support is essential for the smooth operation of educational technology, especially on a large scale. The cost of support services, whether from a vendor or in-house team, are factors to consider. New technologies are always exciting, but it is essential to strike a balance between the desired technology and your available financial resources over time.

How Rapidly Will the Content Change?

If the content for your instructional materials is going to change rapidly, use a technology delivery system that is flexible, scalable, and capable of accommodating frequent updates. Some technologies (think of LMSs) are easy to update, where new content pages can be quickly created and shared, and the old content removed.

In-person instruction and video conferencing technologies are also good choices when instructional content rapidly changes and you need the most current information taught quickly and inexpensively. When selecting a technology delivery system, always ask yourself if it is easy to update, especially if your content evolves rapidly.

Is Real-Time Feedback from an Instructor Important?

If immediate, real-time feedback from an instructor is central for your instructional needs, then you want to use a synchronous delivery technology, such as in-person instruction or video-conferencing software. It may be important to have real-time instructor feedback when you anticipate the need for an instructor to closely monitor the learning process, observe learners' practice or conversations, adjust the pace, and give immediate feedback.

If your instructional goals can be met through self-paced instruction with an instructor available for questions or feedback asynchronously, then you could consider other technologies such as print or electronic PDF, LMSs, online websites, video, or audio.

Is Collaboration and Interaction with Other Learners Essential?

Another factor in selecting a technology delivery platform for your instruction is whether collaboration with other learners or peers is needed to meet the goals for your instruction. If your goals require collaborating, such as working as a team to solve problems or learning from the perspectives and experiences of others, then you want to select technologies that support collaboration with other students.

Collaboration with other learners can be in person or virtual. Online collaboration tools support communicating and sharing information. Technologies that support collaboration may include:

>> Online discussion boards or LMSs

>> Social media groups

>> Video conferencing software

>> In-person instruction

Alternatively, if learning individually is a goal, then technologies such as print or electronic PDFs, video, audio, or online websites can be effective for learning specific information or following step-by-step instructions.

REMEMBER

Instruction that is self-paced also has the feature of being consistent for all learners. Self-paced instruction delivered with technology can often accommodate large numbers of learners and be easily reviewed multiple times by learners. It also can support delivering instruction that can be taken at a time convenient to the learner.

Is Using Technology for Instruction the Most Effective Way to Learn?

Technology can provide you with many opportunities as an instructional designer when it comes to delivering your instruction, and technology can support learning in powerful ways. However, it cannot solve all instructional challenges on its own and should not be viewed as a magic bullet or panacea for all learning. Instead, think about it as a tool that can enhance and support your instructional strategies and methods.

REMEMBER

Technology can help us to make our instruction more accessible or cost beneficial, and it sometimes has unique features that work well for teaching certain types of content, but solid instructional practices are the most important factor in learning.

TIP

New technologies attract a lot of attention, but they may not make your instruction any more effective than other technologies (or not using technology at all). Look more deeply at what the technology has to offer for learning and keep your focus on your instructional strategies and goals.

Is Your Instruction Going to Be Delivered Over the Course of Many Weeks or Months?

One factor to consider is whether your instruction is delivered over many weeks or months. Instruction delivered over multiple weeks (such as a course with 10 weeks of instruction) can be delivered using synchronous or asynchronous technologies. An LMS supports asynchronous instruction that has several lengthy instructional parts offered over time. LMSs enable you to organize several weeks or months of instruction into lessons or modules that have drop boxes for assignments, timelines, content information, and discussion boards. For synchronous instructional sessions, video conferencing or in-person sessions may be a good choice.

Another related consideration is whether the instructional segments are lengthy (several hours per week) versus short (several minutes per week). Delivering small segments of instruction asynchronously (referred to as *microlearning*) over several weeks or months may be best delivered by using audio (such as a podcast) or video. These technologies can be used in short increments of time when it is most convenient to your learners, thus supporting anytime-anywhere learning.

Is the Technology Delivery Selection Accessible and Inclusive?

Selecting technologies to deliver instruction requires attention to accessibility and inclusivity, in addition to being aligned with your instructional goals. Asking questions about your learners' accessibility needs ensures that all learners can fully participate and benefit from the instruction. Technology can exacerbate educational inequalities if not implemented with consideration for access and equity. Not all students may have equal access to electronic devices, Internet bandwidth, and so on. The Universal Design for Learning (UDL) framework recommends using technologies that can be accessed by a wide range of learners.

TIP

When it comes to choosing accessible and inclusive instructional technologies, do the following:

>> Choose accessibility features that support screen readers, different languages, and the differently abled — individuals with visual or hearing impairments, for example. Choose technologies that enable you to use closed captions for video or audio and alternative text for images.

>> Choose technologies that support multiple content delivery methods, such as text, audio, and video. Offer alternatives to accommodate different accessibility needs.

Is There Adequate Tech Support?

A well-informed selection of technology for your instruction also takes into account whether you have the appropriate support needed for learners and instructors to succeed. This support includes having the technical expertise needed to develop the instruction as well as the technical support that is needed by learners and instructors after it is implemented.

Your needs for technology support also increase as the scale of the instruction increases — the more you expand your reach to a broader audience, the more support that is required. Likewise, before selecting a technology to use for your instruction, make sure you have the expertise needed to design, develop, and update the instruction using that technology. If you want to use virtual reality technology for your instruction but you don't have the expertise on your team to develop it, then VR may not be the best selection of technology for your instruction.

TIP

A few tips for supporting learners' and instructors' use of technology:

>> Train instructors in advance on how to use the technologies being used to deliver the instruction. This includes training on how to create and upload any content or material into an LMS or presentation software, or how to use grading or communication systems.

>> Create instruction for learners on what software or hardware is required, how to download the software needed, how to submit assignments, and what to do in case of a technical problem.

Chapter **14**

Ten Ways to Put Your Instructional Design Knowledge to Work

Instructional design as a field is not limited to one type of career path. In fact, instructional design is found anywhere that you find people, materials, or technologies for the purpose of helping people learn. Instructional design facilitates learning in workplaces, homes, schools, summer camps, clubs, libraries, and even on your phone. In fact, no matter what field you are passionate about, you can likely find ways to apply your instructional design skills as a professional. Remember, you don't have to have a job title as an instructional designer to do instructional design!

Yet, some of you may be wondering: What types of careers do instructional designers have? Where are they working? How do they get started in the field? At the time of this writing, the employment website *Indeed* lists over 9,000 jobs for the search term "Instructional Design." This chapter provides you with some answers to these questions about how instructional design is applied as a profession.

Instructional Design in Business and Industry

One of the primary settings for instructional design professionals to find work is in the private sector, broadly labeled here as business and industry. The corporate world is one of the largest employers of instructional designers. Example industries hiring instructional designers include the hospitality industry, banking and finance, insurance, technology companies, automobile manufacturing companies, aviation, and many more examples. Instructional designers are found in just about any industry!

The most common application of instructional design in organizations is employee or workforce training. No matter what size company you may be working for, there is always a need for the employees to be knowledgeable and current in their skillset, and the organization has a vested interest in supporting employees' development.

For example, many organizations design instruction for:

» Onboarding new employees after they are initially hired to learn about their new position as well as human resource policies

» Compliance training related to mandatory government regulations or safety protocols

» On-the-job instruction to get up to speed quickly on new products, skills, or technologies needed for effective performance

» Professional development opportunities for future job advancement

Instructional designers typically hold one of two roles in industry: a solo instructional designer or a designer who is part of a bigger team. In larger companies, an instructional designer may work as part of a team with many instructional designers and other professionals. The designer is typically responsible for designing or revising several instructional projects, working together with a team of subject-matter experts (SMEs), technology developers, and other stakeholders.

In smaller companies, only one instructional designer may be responsible for designing the training for the organization; sometimes, that individual has a different role in the company, such as financial analyst, but takes on the role of instructional designer for their area of expertise. In these contexts, the employee is often both a SME and instructional designer.

Instructional Design in Higher Education

A growing sector in recent years for instructional design is post-secondary, higher education systems, such as colleges or universities. This growth is largely because higher education has been progressively expanding access to their course offerings to students beyond the physical location of the university to include online students. These online course offerings range from:

>> A specific online or hybrid course that is available to students attending the physical (or "brick and mortar") university

>> Online certificates (typically three to five courses) on emerging topics or skillsets, all of which a student can take virtually

>> Bachelor's, master's, or even doctoral degrees that are accessible to students to complete fully online and at a distance

Instructional designers who work in distance education for a college or university typically collaborate with faculty to help them translate their face-to-face classes into a fully online educational experience. The designer collaborates with the faculty member to create engaging strategies for online activities, instructional media, and online discussions. The instructional designer in distance education positions is typically responsible for setting up the content, syllabus, videos, media, gradebook, and/or activities into a learning management system (LMS), such as Canvas or Blackboard Learn and so on. The LMS houses the course and all its lessons and administrative activities (gradebook, roster).

Instructional designers also work with faculty in higher education to design innovative classroom-based experiences for students on campus. This design work might include collaborating on hybrid instructional modules or incorporating new ways of teaching such as educational games, simulations, or virtual reality. Instructional designers might also work with faculty who teach large lecture classes to help them incorporate active learning strategies.

It is common in higher education to have entire units dedicated to instructional design. These units hire experienced instructional designers in high-level management positions, such as directors, associate deans, or associate vice provosts. It is also worth noting that higher education employs researchers and scholars of instructional design. Typically, these instructional designers work as part of a research team or as faculty members who teach and conduct research in an academic program.

Last, higher education systems also use instructional designers for employees' onboarding, compliance training, software training, and so on, similar to what one sees in the private industry sector.

Instructional Design Consulting

Instructional design work also takes place within instructional-design consulting companies. Instructional design consultants may work for a consulting firm that hires many instructional designers and developers to work as employees on large-scale contracts or that is large enough to serve multiple clients simultaneously. Instructional design consultants may also work for their own business as a free-lance consultant. Companies sometimes hire instructional designers as external consultants, rather than hiring full-time instructional designers within the company.

Consultants work externally to the business who is hiring them. They are hired by the client to design instruction in a specific area, usually in response to a defined need that the company has identified. The consultant(s) work collaboratively with SMEs, managers, and employees of the client company and are contracted to design, develop, and/or implement the instructional product.

Instructional Design in the Military

Instructional designers also are found in careers within the military. In fact, the origins of instructional design in the United States are often attributed to the need for military services training during World War II. Instructional designers in military settings design instruction for training military personnel in all aspects of the armed forces.

Simulations and virtual reality are commonly used emerging technologies for training in the military, as they replicate real-world situations in a more risk-free environment. Given the sensitive nature of military services training, instructional designers working in this sector often require security clearances.

Instructional Design for Medical and Health Sciences Education

The medical and health care sector employs instructional designers to design and develop medically focused education for health care practitioners, medical students, and/or patients. The health sciences field encompasses more than hospitals and clinics. It also includes related subspecialties such as pharmaceutical, bio-technology, or medical equipment companies that need to train practitioners on their products. Other medical subspecialities include nonprofit, public, or private organizations that promote public health education.

Well-designed instruction for medical practitioners is important, as making errors can pose significant risk for patients. Therefore, it is common to see medical education use emerging technologies such as simulations, 3D images, or virtual reality to provide instruction with minimal patient risk. Medical education often uses problem- or case-based learning to facilitate real-world problem solving.

Designing Instruction for Schools

Instructional designers can be employed by school districts or government educational units, but they are not usually hired to design instruction and teach in schools (in the United States) unless they also have a teaching certificate. With that said, teachers do instructional design work daily, from designing lessons and engaging activities for their students, integrating educational technologies, and designing assessment items.

More recently, virtual K-12 schools (kindergarten through 12th grade in the United States) have become more common, creating possibilities for instructional designers to work alongside curriculum developers and teachers to deliver online instruction to students remotely. Similar to the trend in higher education with distance learning, virtual schools are also emerging to provide opportunities for younger learners to take classes at the K-12 level.

Instructional Design in Informal Learning Institutions

Another setting where instructional designers work is within informal learning institutions such as non-profit educational organizations, museums, libraries, nature centers, historical sites, summer camps, and botanical gardens. Instructional designers in these settings may collaborate with others to design exhibits, self-guided tours (audio-, video-, or QR- (quick response) based), workshops, play spaces, or demonstrations. A key skill for instructional designers working in informal educational environments is designing activities that stimulate interest, are entertaining, and allow for visitor's free choice of what and how much they want to learn.

Instructional Designers as Educational Content Creators

Instructional designers are commonly hired to create instructional experiences for learners within an organization or for an organization's clients or visitors. Yet, with the prevalence of social media platforms, instructional designers can reach wider audiences of learners outside of a specific organization by designing content that aligns with common interests. We have all likely consulted YouTube for instruction on how to do a home repair when we have lost the manual or don't know how to fix something! You may also routinely follow specific individual's podcasts or social media sites in order to learn from them every day or week. Although instructional designers are not typically hired to be content creators, having a solid knowledge of instructional design can help any content creator provide more robust educational material.

Getting Started in a Career in Instructional Design

You can choose a few different pathways to get started in a career in instructional design. One common pathway is through higher education with either a bachelor's or master's degree, typically offered within a College of Education. These days, many universities offer instructional design degrees online, especially at the master's degree level.

One advantage of a formal educational pathway is the network of alumni and industry partnerships that are connected to an academic program. Others have become an instructional designer more informally, by having either a career change within their existing company or learning the new skills on the job or through other sources of professional development.

TIP

Here are some tips for getting started in instructional design:

>> Seek out a bachelor's or master's degree in instructional design from an accredited university; many programs are offered online.

>> Pursue a certificate offered by a university or other organization on a focused skillset; certificates are usually around three to five courses.

>> Build your instructional-design skills through websites such as LinkedIn Learning and create a portfolio that showcases your skills.

>> Seek instructional-design experience. Many instructional design jobs require or prefer at least three years of experience, so look for as many informal opportunities to create instruction as you can until you get your first instructional design position.

>> Network with other instructional-design professionals through online networks (Instructional Design Groups on LinkedIn, for example) or by joining professional associations such as the Association for Educational Communications and Technology or the Association for Talent Development. These associations offer professional development and career postings. For more information on professional associations in the field of instructional design, visit the following websites:

- Association for Educational Communications and Technology (AECT): `https://aect.org`

- Association for Talent Development (ATD): `https://www.td.org`

>> Follow job postings from websites such as Indeed, LinkedIn, or Learning Guild.

Common Instructional Design Job Competencies

Employers of instructional designers look for a variety of required and desired competencies. The job requirements typically differ based on factors such as the size of the organization, the level of expertise in a specific area, as well as the audience being served. Instructional design jobs in medical education, for instance, often seek an instructional designer with some prior expertise in the health professions. Likewise, a software company may expect some level of expertise in the company's software.

A recent review of instructional design job requirements reveals some common trends in job competencies and skillsets. Not all these competencies are required for all instructional design positions; rather, these are intended to give you a range of competencies and potential specializations:

>> Strong analytical and design skills, such as knowing how to perform task analyses, create instructional objectives and assessments, select an appropriate technology delivery system, and apply learning and instructional-design theories to create engaging instructional strategies and materials

>> Technology production skills for designing instruction, such as a basic knowledge of one or two Learning Management Systems (LMSs), authoring programs such as Adobe Captivate or Articulate 360 (Rise and Storyline), or graphic design or video production software such as Adobe Photoshop or Final Cut Pro

>> Strong communication skills

>> Ability to collaborate with subject-matter experts and multimedia developers to prototype technology-based instruction

>> Experience working on and managing multiple projects at one time

Appendix

Example questions, checklists, and worksheets

Appendix

Example Questions, Checklists, and Worksheets

1: Example Questions for a Needs Analysis (for SMEs)

1. **Background:**
   - What is your area of expertise or specialization?
   - How many years of experience do you have in this field?

2. **Optimal or critical performances:**
   - What are the critical tasks or job responsibilities that employees in this role need to perform effectively?
   - What tasks do you perform exceptionally well?
   - Are there any skills or tasks that you consider essential but may not be obvious to those with less expertise?

3. **Actual performances (performance gaps):**

   - Are there any performance gaps or deficiencies you observe among employees in this role?

   - Can you provide specific examples or data to illustrate these gaps?

   - Are there any specific skills or knowledge areas that are the most important for all employees to do well?

4. **Assessment and evaluation:**

   - How do you know if learners mastered the performance or skill?

   - Are there organizational results that are measured to evaluate effectiveness of the intervention?

5. **Potential barriers to implementing a solution:**

   - Are there any potential challenges or obstacles to consider?

   - Are there any industry regulations, legal issues, safety standards, or compliance requirements that the solution must address?

6. **Currency of existing methods:**

   - Are there any emerging trends, technologies, or best practices in your field that are needed?

   - Are the current resources or instructional materials up-to-date and aligned with industry changes?

7. **Open-ended:**

   - Do you have any additional comments, suggestions, or concerns?

2: Example Questions for a Learner Analysis

1. **Professional Experience:**

   - What is your job title or role within the organization?

   - How many years of experience do you have in your current role?

- Have you received any prior training related to your job and the topic or problem being addressed? If so, please specify.

2. **Self-assessment of Performance:**

   - On a scale of 1 to 5 (1 = not at all knowledgeable, 5 = highly knowledgeable), how would you rate your current knowledge and skills related to the subject matter?

3. **Instructional Delivery and Design:**

   - How do you prefer to learn new information or skills? (For example, through in-person training, online courses, reading materials, hands-on practice, and so forth.)

   - Do you prefer a self-paced learning environment or a structured, instructor-led approach?

4. **Technology Availability and Accessibility:**

   - How comfortable are you with using computers and digital technology on a scale of 1 to 5 (1 = not at all comfortable, 5 = very comfortable)?

   - Do you have access to a reliable Internet connection and necessary devices for online learning?

   - Do you have any accessibility needs to be successful in an instructional program? If so, please describe.

5. **Implementation challenges and barriers:**

   - What challenges or obstacles do you anticipate in completing this training program successfully?

   - Do you have any time constraints or scheduling limitations that we should consider?

   - How much time can you allocate per week to engage in learning activities?

6. **Open-ended feedback:**

   - Do you have any specific topics or areas you believe should be covered in the instruction that have not been mentioned?

   - Do you have any additional comments or suggestions?

3: Example Questions for a Needs Analysis (for Potential Learners)

1. **Actual performances**

   - On a scale from 1 to 5, how would you rate your current level of knowledge and skills related to your job responsibilities:

   1. Not at all knowledgeable

   2. Mostly unknowledgeable

   3. Knowledgeable about some skills

   4. Knowledgeable about most skills

   5. Highly knowledgeable

   - Do you feel that you have all the necessary skills and knowledge to excel in your role? If not, please specify the areas where you feel less confident.

2. **Knowledge and Performance Challenges**

   - What are the biggest challenges, difficulties, or roadblocks you face in performing your job (or specific task) effectively?

   - What specific skills or knowledge areas do you believe would help you perform better in your job?

   - Can you provide examples of situations where instruction would have been beneficial?

3. **Job Tools, Equipment, and Technologies**

   - How comfortable are you with using technology, equipment, or other tools in your work on a scale of 1 to 5 (1 = not at all comfortable, 5 = very comfortable)?

   - Are there specific technologies, equipment, or tools you need instruction on?

4. **Work Environment and Resources**

   - Are there any environmental factors, such as tools, equipment, or workplace conditions, that affect your performance?

   - Are there any workplace policies or procedures that hinder your ability to perform your job effectively?

   - Do you have access to the necessary resources, materials, or support to perform your job optimally?

- What incentives are in place for you to perform your job well?

- Are there any resources or tools you believe are lacking?

5. **Feedback on Performance**

- Have you received feedback from colleagues or supervisors regarding your performance?

- Is there anything your colleagues or supervisors have suggested you improve upon?

6. **Open-ended feedback**

- Are there any additional comments, concerns, or ideas you want to share regarding your job performance?

4. Implementation Preparation Worksheet

Instructor preparations Select Y/N	Have you...
Y N ☐ ☐	Tried out the instruction with a few learners, experts, instructional designers, or supervisors?
Y N ☐ ☐	Developed training programs or instruction manuals for the instructor?
Y N ☐ ☐	Provided the instructor with syllabi, lesson plans, course rosters?
Y N ☐ ☐	Trained the instructor on how to use any technology required for teaching?
Y N ☐ ☐	Provided the instructor with a guide for facilitating discussions, along with follow-up questions?
Y N ☐ ☐	Given the Implementation Debrief Checklist (later in the appendix) to instructors to give feedback on the instruction?
Y N ☐ ☐	Clarified communication expectations from the instructor (for example, office hours; when to reach out for help)?

Instructor preparations	
Select Y/N	**Have you...**
Materials and facilities	**Have you...**
Y N ☐ ☐	Scheduled use of the facilities for the instruction (if applicable)?
Y N ☐ ☐	Ordered snacks, drinks, or meals for participants (if applicable)?
Y N ☐ ☐	Arrived early at the facility to set up materials (flip charts; name tags; pens, pencils, paper for notetaking; copies of all handouts and presentation slides; test presentation slides and projection equipment)?
Y N ☐ ☐	Schedule breaks for participants and provide information on where restrooms, vending machines, and such are located?
Technology support	**Have you...**
Y N ☐ ☐	Tried out technology materials in advance with participants and/or instructors?
Y N ☐ ☐	Sent electronic PDFs to participants in advance (if applicable)?
Y N ☐ ☐	Provided a recommended timeline and schedule for completing asynchronous discussions or assignments?
Y N ☐ ☐	Provided contact information for tech support?
Y N ☐ ☐	Provided a list of all hardware or software requirements learners and instructors need to participate in the instruction?
Y N ☐ ☐	Trained students and instructors on how to use the LMS or other technologies for instruction?
Y N ☐ ☐	Given instructions for where learners are to submit assignments and what to do if they have a technical problem during the instruction or an assignment submission?
Y N ☐ ☐	Clearly communicated start and end times for any synchronous learning sessions to all learners, instructors, and guest speakers?

Instructor preparations	
Select Y/N	Have you...
Y N □ □	Arranged to meet any speakers or instructors in advance to test out the system and presentation slides?
Y N □ □	Established ground rules for communicating, interrupting, raising hands, background noise (if applicable)?

5. Implementation Debrief Checklist

Title of the Instruction: _____

Date and Time: _____

Instructor Name: _____

Check Yes (Y) or No (N); provide comments as needed.

Y N □ □	Sufficient time was allocated for the instruction.
Y N □ □	Directions were clearly presented.
Y N □ □	Instructor guides and materials were clear and helpful.
Y N □ □	Sufficient practice for learners was provided.
Y N □ □	Technology worked as planned.
Y N □ □	Discussions were facilitated effectively.
Y N □ □	Learners were active and engaged in discussions and activities.

Y N	Content was covered as planned.
☐ ☐	
Y N	Changes were made by instructor during the instruction.
☐ ☐	

Index

artificial intelligence (AI), 181–182

Assess Learner Performance step, in Nine Events of Instruction, 122, 127, 129

assessments
  aligning, 241
  distinguishing different types of, 242
  linking objectives and, 111–112
  ongoing, 150–151

assignments, 193

Association for Educational Communications and Technology (AECT), 18, 255, 271

Association for Talent Development (ATD), 18, 255, 271

assumptions, of open-ended frameworks, 141–142

Attention, in ARCS model, 134, 135

attitude development, 76, 77–78

audiences, identifying, 107–108

audio delivery, 173

augmented reality (AR), 181

B

Behavior level, in Kirkpatrick's Four Levels of Evaluation, 237, 242–244

behaviors
  describing, 108–109
  learning as a change in, 30–31

benchmarking, for identifying optimal performance, 58

best practices
  aligning five foundations for, 42–45
  for creating instruction, 249–255

blended instruction
  about, 166–168
  implementing, 228–229

blended-time/blended-place delivery mode, 166–168

Bloom, Benjamin (taxonomist), 79

Bloom's taxonomy
  about, 79–80, 105–106
  Analyzing level, 80, 83, 87, 106
  Applying level, 80, 82–83
  Creating level, 80, 84–85, 88, 106
  Evaluating level, 80, 84, 87, 106
  Remembering level, 80–81, 86, 105
  Understanding level, 80, 81–82, 86, 105

budget constraints, 259

business settings, for instructional designers, 15, 266

C

careers, in instructional design, 17–18, 265–272

ChatGPT, 181–182

Cheat Sheet (website), 5

classifying
  delivery modes, 160–168
  goals and tasks with Bloom's taxonomy, 79–85
  tasks and objectives, 104–106
  types of learning, 76–79

classroom (face-to-face) instruction, 189–190

client data analysis, for identifying actual performance, 60

cognitive learning, 76, 77

cognitive theory, 31–33

collaboration
  about, 36–37, 38
  designing activities for, 250

collaboration *(continued)*
  importance of, 260–261
  open-ended learning for, 143
  as a skill for instructional designers, 16
  of technology, 169
communication
  information on, 192
  as a skill for instructional designers, 16
Communication infrastructure, for implementing instruction, 216
complexity, of activities, 253
compliance-oriented motivations, 66
computer programmers, 187
conditions, stating for behaviors, 109–110
conducting
  context analysis, 52–55
  performance assessment, 243–244
  task analysis, 88–95
Confidence, in ARCS model, 134, 136
connecting, with other designers, 255
consistency, as a benefit of instructional design, 13
construction, of technology, 169
constructivist theories, 33–34
content
  breaking down, 90–92
  instructional-design frameworks and knowledge of, 121
  speed of change for, 259
context analysis, conducting, 52–55
context constraints, 41–42
continuous improvement, as a benefit of instructional design, 13

copy editors, 187
costs
  savings, as a benefit of instructional design, 13
  of technology, 42
creating
  attitude, 76, 77–78
  goals and objectives, 100–104, 106–111
  understanding goals, 146–148
Creating level, of Bloom's taxonomy, 80, 84–85, 88, 106
creativity, open-ended learning for, 143
cultural foundations
  about, 30, 40
  illustration of, 43, 44, 45
  informal compared with formal learning, 41
  rote learning compared with 21st century skills, 40–41
  values and mission of organization, 40
customer data analysis, for identifying actual performance, 60

D

data collection
  for identifying
    actual performance, 59–60
    optimal performance, 58
  methods for, 68–73
debates, as collaborative learning, 38
decision-making problems, 153
degree of accuracy, specifying, 110–111

Example icon, 4
example questions
  for learner analysis, 276–277
  for needs analysis for potential learners, 278–279
  for needs analysis/assessment, 275–276
examples, for identifying actual performance, 60
expertise
  as a benefit of instructional design, 14
  of technology, 42

F

face-to-face (classroom) instruction, 162–163, 189–190
facilitator guide, 189
facilities constraints, 42
Family Educational Rights and Privacy Act (FERPA), 146, 194
feedback
  giving to learners, 252–253
  offering, 31
  speed of, 260
feedback forums, 190
field-based instruction, implementing, 229
financial constraints, 41
finding instructional designers, 14
Five Whys technique, 61
flipped classroom, 168
flowcharts
  for lesson flow, 197–200
  for task analysis, 92, 94–95

focus groups
  for data collection, 69–71
  for identifying optimal performance, 58
formal learning
  about, 41
  institutions for instructional designers, 269
formative evaluation, 233
frameworks
  about, 117–118
  choosing based on goals, 121
  common approaches to ordering activities, 120–121
  determining assumptions behind direct, 119–120
  Gagné's Nine Events of Instruction, 25, 122–129
  Mayer's Selecting-Organizing-Integrating (SOI) Model, 129–137
  open-ended design
    about, 139–140
    assumptions of, 141–142
    characteristics for designing problem-based learning, 152–156
    key strategies to use for TFU model, 145–151
    for problem solving, 151–156
    problem-based approaches, 151
    selecting based on goals, 142–143
    Teaching for Understanding (TFU) model, 144–151
    for understanding compared with memorization, 143–151
    when to use, 140–143
  when to use, 118–121

G

Gagné, Robert, 122–129

Gagne's Nine Events of Instruction, 25, 122–129

Gain Learners' Attention step, in Nine Events of Instruction, 122–123, 128

general information, in learner analysis, 65

generative artificial intelligence (AI), 181–182

goals and objectives
  ABCDs of creating, 106–111
  about, 99–100
  aligning, 241
  benefits of well-written objectives, 101–102
  classifying
    with Bloom's taxonomy, 79–85
    tasks and, 104–106
  creating, 100–104
  for finding organizational information, 52
  in instructional design process, 12
  limitations of instructional objectives, 102–103
  linking assessments and, 111–112
  selecting frameworks based on, 121–122, 142–143
  tips for sequencing, 112–115

graphic artists, 187

group discussions, as collaborative learning, 38

group-based instruction, 258–259

H

hardware, requirements and availability of, 42

higher education setting, for instructional designers, 15, 267

"hindsight is 20-20" questions, for identifying optimal performance, 58

hy-flex delivery modes, 167

hypothesizing, open-ended learning for, 143

I

icons, explained, 4–5

identifying
  actual performance in needs analysis, 56, 58–60
  audiences, 107–108
  essential job tasks and content using SMEs, 88–90
  incentives, 66
  initial solutions in needs analysis, 56, 62–64
  knowledge gaps, 155
  motivations, 66
  optimal performance in needs analysis, 56, 57–58
  possible causes in needs analysis, 56, 60–62
  topics that support understanding, 145–146

implementation
  barriers to successful, 220–222
  planned compared with actual, 212–213
  tips for successful, 222–229

Implementation, RIPPLES model, 213–220

implementation context, 53–54

Implementation phase (ADDIE model)
  about, 22–23, 28–29, 211–212
  debrief checklist for, 281–282
  preparation worksheet for, 279–281

incentives
  identifying, 66
  lack of, 62

about, 26, 139–140

assumptions of, 141–142

characteristics for designing problem-based learning, 152–156

key strategies to use for TFU model, 145–151

for problem solving, 151–156

problem-based approaches, 151

selecting based on goals, 142–143

Teaching for Understanding (TFU) model, 144–151

for understanding compared with memorization, 143–151

when to use, 140–143

open-ended instructional strategies, 35–36

opportunities, for finding organizational information, 52

optimal performance, identifying in needs analysis, 56, 57–58

ordering instructional activities, 120–121

organizational context, 53

Organizing, in Selecting-Organizing-Integrating (SOI) Model, 130, 131

outcomes, selecting action verbs to describe, 85–88

outline format, for task analysis, 92–94

P

participant manuals/packets, 189

PBL (problem-based learning), 151–156

peer review, as collaborative learning, 38

peer teaching, as collaborative learning, 38

People, in RIPPLES Framework, 54, 214, 216–217

people constraints, 41–42

performance

common problems for problems with, 61–62

conducting an assessment of, 243–244

identifying "actual" in needs analysis, 56, 58–60

performance needs in learner analysis, 65

performance gap analysis, 57–58

personalized nature, of technology, 169

personnel expertise constraints, 42

Piskurich, George (author)

Rapid Instructional Design, 244

place-based instruction, implementing, 229

planning considerations, 50–55

Policies, in RIPPLES Framework, 54, 214, 217–218

possible causes, identifying in needs analysis, 56, 60–62

pragmatic foundations

about, 30, 41

illustration of, 43, 44, 45

people and context constraints, 41–42

technology constraints, 42

Present the Content step, in Nine Events of Instruction, 122, 124–125, 129

print delivery, 171

private consulting setting, for instructional designers, 15, 268

problem solving

as collaborative learning, 38

open-ended learning for, 143, 151–156

problem-based learning (PBL), 151–156

procedural order, for instructional objectives, 113

procedural skills, instructional-design frameworks and, 121

Production infrastructure, for implementing instruction, 216

production team, developing instruction with a, 186–188

project management, as a skill for instructional designers, 17

project managers, 187

prototyping instructional products, 195–200

Provide Feedback to Learners step, in Nine Events of Instruction, 122, 126–127, 129

Provide Learning Guidance step, in Nine Events of Instruction, 122, 125–126, 129

psychomotor skill development, 76, 78–79

Q

quality assurance experts, 187

questionnaires
for data collection, 71–72
using in Reaction level of Kirkpatrick's Four Levels of Evaluation, 238–239

R

rapid design methods, 24–25

Rapid Instructional Design (Piskurich), 244

Reaction level, in Kirkpatrick's Four Levels of Evaluation, 237–241

real-world applications, designing activities for, 250–251, 253–254

reason for participating, in learner analysis, 65

reflective practice, open-ended learning for, 143

reinforcing behaviors, 31

Relevance, in ARCS model, 134, 135–136

reliability, as a benefit of instructional design, 13

Remember icon, 5

Remembering level, of Bloom's taxonomy, 80–81, 86, 105

Resources, in RIPPLES Framework, 54, 213, 214–215

resources, limited, 244

Results level, in Kirkpatrick's Four Levels of Evaluation, 237, 245

revisions, making based on findings in Evaluation phase, 246

RIPPLES Framework
about, 54–55
for implementation planning, 213–220

role plays, as collaborative learning, 38

root cause analysis, 60–62

Rosset, Allison (needs analysis expert), 56, 61–62

rote learning, 40–41

S

SAM (Successive Approximation Model), 24–25

same time/different-place delivery mode, 163–164

timeline, for delivery, 261–262

Tip icon, 4

top performer interviews, for identifying optimal performance, 58

Toyoda, Sakichi (founder of Toyota Industries), 61

training, instructional-design frameworks and, 121

travel constraints, 42

U

understanding
activities that require, 148–149
designing for, 143–151
identifying topics that support, 145–146

understanding goals, 146–148

Understanding level, of Bloom's taxonomy, 80, 81–82, 86, 105

Universal Design for Learning (UDL), 202–204, 262

V

values
determining organizational, 51–52
development of, 76, 77–78
of organization, 40

video conferencing delivery
about, 172, 174–175
instructor-led instruction with a, 190–193

virtual asynchronous/synchronous instruction
development tips for, 191–193
implementing, 227–228

virtual reality (VR), 181

visualization, of technology, 169

W

Warning icon, 4

websites
Association for Educational Communications and Technology (AECT), 18, 271
Association for Talent Development (ATD), 18, 271
Cheat Sheet, 5
Indeed, 17

Y

yourself, developing instruction by, 185–186

About the Author

Susan Land, Ph.D. is a Professor of Learning, Design, and Technology at Penn State University, where she is currently Head of the Department of Learning and Performance Systems in the College of Education. She has over 25 years of professional experience doing both instructional design work, teaching, and research. She's co-edited two books with David Jonassen on *Theoretical Foundations of Learning Environments*, one of which sold nearly a record number of copies for an edited book in its field. Susan has published over 95 scholarly articles, and *Google Scholar* has listed her as the most cited author in the category of instructional design and technology. Her current research at Penn State examines the design of mobile, augmented reality to support family science learning in outdoor community spaces. You can find out more about Susan at her website: www.sites.psu.edu/susanland.

Dedication

To Uncle Tom

Author's Acknowledgments

I am grateful to Wiley Publishing for giving me the opportunity to introduce instructional design to a new audience through this book. It's been an exciting project, and I'm thankful for the incredible support from the entire Wiley editorial team. I am also deeply grateful to my family for their enthusiastic encouragement throughout the duration of this project, especially Chloe and Anna.

Writing this book meant combing through stacks of instructional design texts written by scholars with amazing insights that could not be fully cited or captured here. I want to acknowledge a few authors of instructional design texts that informed this work, such as Walt Dick, Charlie Reigeluth, Barbara Seels, Zita Glasgow, Miriam Larson, Barbara Lockee, Bob Reiser, Jack Dempsey, Mike Spector, Abbie Brown, Timothy Green, Marcy Driscoll, Jerrold Kemp, Gary Morrison, Steve Ross, as well as the contributions of the late Mike Hannafin and Dave Jonassen. Thank you to Dan Surry for your invaluable feedback and suggestions on all these chapters. Last, I owe enormous gratitude to my Penn State colleagues and The Augmented and Mobile Learning Research Group who collaborated with me on some of the projects I reference here, especially Heather Zimmerman.

Publisher's Acknowledgments

Acquisitions Editor: Jennifer Yee
Senior Project Editor: Paul Levesque
Copy Editor: Jerelind Charles
Tech Editor: Dan Surry, Ed.D.

Production Editor: Saikarthick Kumarasamy
Cover Image: © DenisZav/Shutterstock

Leverage the power

Dummies is the global leader in the reference category and one of the most trusted and highly regarded brands in the world. No longer just focused on books, customers now have access to the dummies content they need in the format they want. Together we'll craft a solution that engages your customers, stands out from the competition, and helps you meet your goals.

Advertising & Sponsorships

Connect with an engaged audience on a powerful multimedia site, and position your message alongside expert how-to content. Dummies.com is a one-stop shop for free, online information and know-how curated by a team of experts.

- Targeted ads
- Video
- Email Marketing
- Microsites
- Sweepstakes sponsorship

20 MILLION
PAGE VIEWS
EVERY SINGLE MONTH

15 MILLION
UNIQUE
VISITORS PER MONTH

43%
OF ALL VISITORS
ACCESS THE SITE
VIA THEIR MOBILE DEVICES

700,000 NEWSLETTER
SUBSCRIPTIONS
TO THE INBOXES OF
300,000 UNIQUE INDIVIDUALS EVERY WEEK

# of dummies

Custom Publishing

Reach a global audience in any language by creating a solution that will differentiate you from competitors, amplify your message, and encourage customers to make a buying decision.

- Apps
- Books
- eBooks
- Video
- Audio
- Webinars

Brand Licensing & Content

Leverage the strength of the world's most popular reference brand to reach new audiences and channels of distribution.

For more information, visit dummies.com/biz

PERSONAL ENRICHMENT

Staying Sharp
9781119187790
USA $26.00
CAN $31.99
UK £19.99

Facebook
9781119179030
USA $21.99
CAN $25.99
UK £16.99

Guitar
9781119293354
USA $24.99
CAN $29.99
UK £17.99

Investing
9781119293347
USA $22.99
CAN $27.99
UK £16.99

Beekeeping
9781119310068
USA $22.99
CAN $27.99
UK £16.99

Digital Photography
9781119235606
USA $24.99
CAN $29.99
UK £17.99

Meditation
9781119251163
USA $24.99
CAN $29.99
UK £17.99

Pregnancy
9781119235491
USA $26.99
CAN $31.99
UK £19.99

Samsung Galaxy S7
9781119279952
USA $24.99
CAN $29.99
UK £17.99

iPhone
9781119283133
USA $24.99
CAN $29.99
UK £17.99

Crocheting
9781119287117
USA $24.99
CAN $29.99
UK £16.99

Nutrition
9781119130246
USA $22.99
CAN $27.99
UK £16.99

PROFESSIONAL DEVELOPMENT

Windows 10
9781119311041
USA $24.99
CAN $29.99
UK £17.99

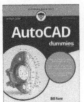
AutoCAD
9781119255796
USA $39.99
CAN $47.99
UK £27.99

Excel 2016
9781119293439
USA $26.99
CAN $31.99
UK £19.99

QuickBooks 2017
9781119281467
USA $26.99
CAN $31.99
UK £19.99

macOS Sierra
9781119280651
USA $29.99
CAN $35.99
UK £21.99

LinkedIn
9781119251132
USA $24.99
CAN $29.99
UK £17.99

Windows 10
9781119310563
USA $34.00
CAN $41.99
UK £24.99

SharePoint 2016
9781119181705
USA $29.99
CAN $35.99
UK £21.99

Fundamental Analysis
9781119263593
USA $26.99
CAN $31.99
UK £19.99

Networking
9781119257769
USA $29.99
CAN $35.99
UK £21.99

Office 2016
9781119293477
USA $26.99
CAN $31.99
UK £19.99

Office 365
9781119265313
USA $24.99
CAN $29.99
UK £17.99

Salesforce.com
9781119239314
USA $29.99
CAN $35.99
UK £21.99

Coding
9781119293323
USA $29.99
CAN $35.99
UK £21.99

dummies.com

dummies
A Wiley Brand